MW01127517

Inclusive Growth and Development Issues in Eastern and Southern Africa

Editor

Herman Musahara

**Organisation for Social Science Research in
Eastern and Southern Africa (OSSREA)**

OSSREA acknowledges the financial support of the Danish Development Agency (DANIDA), without which this book wouldn't have been a reality.

Published 2016
Printed in Ethiopia
ISBN: 978-99944-55-88-1

Copyediting and layout design: *Matebu Tadesse*
Formatting: *Alemu Tesfaye*

Organisation for Social Science Research in Eastern and Southern Africa
P. O. Box 31971, Addis Ababa, Ethiopia
Fax: 251-11-1223921
Tel: 251-11-1239484
E-mail: info@ossrea.net
Website: www.ossrea.net

OSSREA acknowledges the financial spport of DANIDA

Table of Contents

Acronyms

ADF	Augmented Dickey-Fuller
ADF	Augmented Dickey-Fuller, unit-roots tests (statistics)
ADLI	Agricultural Development-led Industrialisation
AGOA	African Growth and Opportunity Act
ASEAN	East Africa Community and the Association of Southeast Asian Nations
BEE	Black Economic Empowerment
CAM	Carte d'Assistance Médicale
CBHI	Community-Based Health Insurance
CGE	Computable-General-Equilibrium
CIA	Central Intelligence Agency
CMPHS	Continuous Multi-Purpose Household Survey
COMESA	Common Market for Eastern and Southern Africa
CSMBS	Civil ServantS' Medical Benefit Scheme
DRG	Diagnosis-related Group
DRG	diagnosis-Related group
EDPRS	Economic Development for Poverty Reduction Strategy
EPA	Economic Partnership Agreement
EPRDF	Ethiopian People's Revolutionary Democratic Front
EPZ	Export Processing Zone
ERHS	Ethiopian Rural Household Survey
EU	European Union
FDI	Foreign Direct Investment
FGD	Focus Group Discussions
FGT	Foster-Greer-Thorbecke
GDP	Gross Domestic Product
GEAR	Growth, Employment and Redistribution
GEE	Generalised Estimating Equations
GII	Gender Inequality Index
GLS RE	Generalised Least Squares RE
GMM	Generalised Method of Moments
GNP	Gross National Product
GPI	Gender Parity Index
GSP	Generalised Scheme of Preferences
GTP	Growth and Transformation Plan
HCI	Head Count Index
HDI	Human Development Index
HDR	Human Development Report
ILO	International Labour Organisation

IORA	Indian Ocean Rim Association
IRA	Insurance Regulatory Authority
IRDP	Integrated Rural Development Program
ISCO	International Standard Classification of Occupations
IUCN	International Union for the Conservation of Nature
LDCs	Least Developed Countries
LODA	Local Administrative Entities and Development Agency
LPM	Linear Probit Model
MDGs	Millennium Development Goals
MEDaC	Ethiopian Ministry of Economic Development and Cooperation
MFP	Mutuelle de la Fonction Publique
MINALOC	Ministry of Local Government
MINECOFIN	Ministry of Finance and Economic Planning
NHI	National Health Insurance
NHIF	National Health Insurance Fund
NISR	National Institute of Statistics Rwanda
NPC	National Planning Commission
OECD	Organisation for Economic Cooperation and Development
OOP	Out-of-pocket Payments
PA	Population-averaged
PASDEP	Plan for Accelerated and Sustained Development to End Poverty
PGI	Poverty Gap Index
PHC	Primary Health Care
PNFPS	Private Not-for-profit Providers
PP	Phillips-Perron, unit-roots tests (statistics)
PQT	Proportion of Qualified Teachers
PSR	Pupil-Section Ratio
PSSOP	Public Sector System of Provision
PTR	Pupil-Teacher Ratio
RMF	Retirement Mutual Fund
RNP	Rural Non-Poor
RP	Rural Poor
RSDP	Road Sector Development Program
SACCO	Umurenge Savings and Credit Cooperative
SADC	Southern African Development Community
SDGs	Sustainable Development Goals
SDPRP	Sustainable Development and Poverty Reduction Program

SHP	Social Health Protection
SNNPR	Southern Nations, Nationalities and Peoples Region
SP	Social Protection
SPGI	Squared Poverty Gap Index
SPSS	Statistical Package for Social Sciences
SSS	Social Security Scheme
THE	Total Health Expenditure
UCS	Universal Coverage Scheme
UHC	Universal Health Coverage
UN	United Nations
UNDP	United Nations Development Programme
UNICEF	United Nationals Children's Fund
UNP	Urban Non-Poor
UP	Urban Poor
VAR	Vector Autoregressive
VCHF	Voluntary Community Health Funds
VECM	Vector Error Correction Model
VECM	Vector Error Correction Model
VUP DS	Vision Umurenge Programme Direct Support
WHO	World Health Organisation
WTO	World Trade Organisation

About Authors

Herman Musahara: Herman Musahara is currently Acting Executive Director of the Organisation for Social Science Research in Eastern and Southern Africa (OSSREA). He holds a Ph.D. in Development Studies from the University of Western Cape in South Africa, and an M.A. in Economics from the University of Dar es Salaam. He has more than 30 years experience as an academic, researcher and consultant. He was formerly Dean of the Faculty of Economics and Management 2005, Director of University Consultancy Bureau 2008, Director of Planning and Development 2010, and Acting Vice-Rector Academics in 2011–2012 at the former National University of Rwanda. He was till April 2014 an Associate Professor in the College of Business and Economics of the University of Rwanda. Besides teaching Development Economics, Poverty Analysis and Research Methodology at post-graduate level, he has researched, consulted and published in several fields of the social sciences, including poverty analysis, human development, environment, land and land use, governance, post-conflict transitions, entrepreneurship, SMEs, value chains and agricultural development. He has recently published papers on inclusive and sustainable development in Sub Saharan Africa.

Sheereen Fauzel: is a lecturer in Banking and Financial services at the University of Mauritius. Having completed a B.Sc. in Economics and Finance and a Master's degree in Banking and Finance, her areas of expertise are related to Banking, Finance and Economics. She has participated in international conferences and has publications in notable international journals of business and economics. She is currently a doctoral student at the University of Mauritius. Email: s.fauzel@uom.ac.mu.

Muluadam Alemu: Muluadam Alemu is a Ph.D. candidate in Public Management and Policy in the Faculty of Business and Economics at Addis Ababa University. He has received his MA degree in Regional and Local Development Studies and BA degree in Accounting and Finance from Addis Ababa University. He has also received BA degree in Geography from Debub University. Muluadam has published a monograph and articles in seminar proceedings and journals. His research interest includes inclusive development, local development, rural development, urban development rural-urban linkage, policy analysis, livelihood, climate change, investment, taxation and finance.

Degye Goshu: Dr. Degye Goshu is Assistant Professor of Agricultural Economics at Haramaya University, Ethiopia. His research experience includes food and nutrition security, multidimensional poverty and inequality, market and price dynamics, efficiency and productivity, agricultural commercialisation and technology adoption, and program impact evaluation. He teaches various postgraduate courses with econometric software applications. He has published about 20 works on reputed journals and books. He has won and coordinated various competitive research and capacity building projects financed by the European Union, Global Development Network (GDN), International Food Policy Research Institute (IFPRI), Ethiopian Development Institute (EDRI), Ethiopian Economics Association (EEA) and other partners. He has successfully supervised more than 45 theses and PhD dissertations.

Claudious Chikozho: Dr. Chikozho is a Social Scientist with more than 16 years of experience in research, development and education sectors in Africa, with special focus on rural and urban development processes. Over the years, he has published more than 20 peer-reviewed papers in refereed journals and books. His areas of research interest include programme monitoring and evaluation, responsible leadership, science and innovation processes, public service delivery, environmental sustainability, and adaptation to climate change.

Jean B. Ndikubwimana: Mr. Ndikubwimana is Assistant Lecturer and the Head of the Department of Political Science and International Relations in the School of Social, Political and administrative Sciences, College of Arts and Social Sciences at the University of Rwanda. He holds Masters in International Law of Human Rights and Peaceful Conflict Resolution and Masters in Development Studies. He conducted research in the areas of entrepreneurship and development, political participation and social protection in Rwanda. In 2015 he won a grant from UR-SIDA to conduct a research on *"One cow per poor family as an instrument of conflict transformation in Rwanda"*. From January 2016, he enrolled in the University of Nairobi, Kenya, for a PhD study focusing on natural resources-related conflict in Rwanda.

Marie P. Dusingize: Dr. Dusingize is Dean of the Faculty of Social Economic Sciences and Management at Institut Catholique de Kabgayi, Rwanda, where she has been Faculty member since 2011. Dusingize completed her Ph.D. in Social Sciences at Pontifical Gregorian University in Rome, Italy. Throughout 5 years of her career, Dr. Dusingize has been engaged in scholastic research. She also teaches sociological theories to undergraduate students in the Department of Sociology She has research interest in the field of population displacements where she is commissioned by Institut Catholique de Kabgayi as co-coordinator of a research project on *"Study of socioeconomic impact of population displacement on local communities in Rwanda: Strategies, educational actions and prevention— Case of Gishwati forest area and Nyabarongo hydropower project"*. Her recent publication is Dusingize M.P (2015), *Institut Catholique de Kabgayi (Ick) entre deux poles : Education et réduction de la pauvreté* in Acuhiam Journal, Vol. 2 no.2.

Rukundo B. Johnson: Mr. Johnson is a Lecturer and researcher in the Department of Economics, School of Economics, College of Business and Economics, University of Rwanda. He is currently a PhD student, Jönköping University, Sweden and holds a Master's degree in Economics (Economic Policy Management from Makerere University (Uganda) as well as a Bachelor's degree in Economics from the former National University of

Rwanda. He has been in the academic area for the last eight years teaching and undertaking research activities. He has research interest in employment and growth, economic development, industrial organisation and gender economic policy. He has research publications in the development and growth thematic area.

INTRODUCTION

Herman Musahara

The concept of 'inclusive growth and development' is complex and current. It is complex because it is used to refer to multiple concepts that have emerged in the search for the true meaning of development. These are concepts like pro-poor growth, inclusive growth, equality, social exclusion, opportunities and vulnerability, employment and non-income inequalities, to mention but a few. While these are invariably used, sometimes interchangeably, in different contexts and under different disciplines, it is important that the meanings and distinctions of these are epistemologically clarified for the purpose of this chapter. The first task of this introduction is to make this conceptual clarification. It is also remarkable that each chapter starts with a similar but not necessarily robust clarification of concepts.

The concepts are meanwhile very crucial to the understanding of development. There has been a time dimension in the discourse on development. Since the Second World War, the search for the real meaning of development has taken an unusually fast pace in almost all major fields. Various schools of thought have emerged. It has been agreed in the realm of development studies that measuring development by GDP and GDP per capita alone is not enough. Economic growth is necessary but not sufficient to explain economic development. The welfare of the people and a rise in standard of living is the expected outcome and the process should include poverty reduction and reduced inequality of all sorts.

Inclusive development is a current concern. In many African countries some considerable economic growth has been attained over the last ten years. Yet, poverty and inequality are still rampant. Understanding the current dynamics and what can be done to make growth in Africa more inclusive is the focus of the book. On the other hand, the world is entering what has been called the Age of Sustainable Development. Indeed, the United Nations has launched new Sustainable Development Goals to replace the Millennium Development Goals. Development has entered a new paradigm. Sustainable development does not involve economic growth and poverty reduction only. It involves social inclusion, care for the environment and the promotion of good governance. Inclusive growth and development is a current agenda. Agenda 2063 is an African Union roadmap to attaining inclusive and sustainable development by the year 2063. The book is a contribution to the knowledge of Inclusive and Sustainable Development in a few countries in Eastern and Southern Africa, under different policy frameworks, focusing on some sectors other than others and using different methodologies under different disciplines. It is not exhaustive but reflects how diverse and broad the concept is and the current challenges countries in particular and the region at large still face.

Chapter 1 also by the Editor gives an overall overview of inclusive development for several countries. Firstly, it provides a conceptual frame of inclusive growth and sustainable development more elaborately and ensures the number of countries in the collection truly reflects a regional agenda. Secondly, it gives salient features of the major challenges of inclusive and sustainable development in the region by using common data sets, especially the World Development Indicators, to show the case of economic growth without proportionate rises in standards of living and human development. Using a selected indicator, poverty, inequality, gender and other challenges are presented and analysed. Finally, gaps in research that would have provided evidence and policy directions are identified and recommendations for global and individual countries made.

Chapter 2 by Fauzel is about trade and inclusive development using the case of Mauritius. The chapter uses a dynamic framework, which is an econometric tool in methodology. It is a bold attempt to show that trade openness has led to transfer of knowledge and technology, entrepreneurship in the private sector, foreign capital and increased employment. It is further argued that trade openness has encouraged production of goods and services and promoted growth and, most notably, social welfare. It is emphasised that trade openness takes time to impact on inclusive development.

Trade openness in Mauritius has shown both short- and long-run effects and has raised the standards of living of the people. While the chapter empirically shows the relationship, more studies will be required to track the process of how the trade openness has raised living standards of the people and the possible intermediate policies that made that possible over time because, besides trade openness, there must be other causal factors as well since, as noted earlier, development is complex and cannot be related to trade regimes and policies alone. Perhaps not said is that Mauritius is among the few better-off countries in the region and sub-Saharan Africa. Drawing lessons from its development experience provides a benchmark for several possible study areas.

A distinction which obviously bears on the inclusive development concept is the rural-urban divide in Africa. Alemu in Chapter 3 analyses the phenomenon using Ethiopia as a case study. The myriad of interactions between the rural and urban areas have an effect on economic growth and development dynamics. Ethiopia is a country and economy where significant economic growth has been realised. Despite the common knowledge that there is a wide gap between the rural and urban Ethiopia, the nature of the challenges resulting from the gaps has to be better understood.

The chapter argues that, despite the rapid economic growth, Ethiopia still has 27 million people under poverty. The millions are subject to economic exclusion, high levels of inequality, undefined mechanisms of social protection, and marginalisation. Using inferential statistics and official data sets, the chapter shows that there is some evidence of prop-poor growth policies in Ethiopia. But there is also evidence of inequality and a wide rural and urban divide. A gap to be filled, which is also the aim of the book, is what can be recommended based on sound analysis for closing the divide in a time-bound strategy.

Using panel data for 2495 farming households, Chapter 4 by Goshu on Ethiopia is used to articulate the dynamics of poverty, vulnerability and welfare. The chapter notes that in the five years, 33 per cent of the households have escaped the poverty trap. However, it finds out that 42 per cent of the non-poor households descended into poverty and some 52 per cent remained in poverty. Using econometric modelling, the chapter shows that the speed with which the poor are escaping from poverty is sluggish. Thus, there is persistence of poverty and a need for further policy interventions. Ethiopia as a case study country is also useful to the collection. Recent figures indicate that the growth of the economy has been on average about 10 per cent on GDP and Ethiopia is by the time of writing the fastest growing economy in Africa. It has a population approaching 100 million people making it the second largest economy in that regard in Africa. Yet despite all evidence of an emerging economy the chapter like the previous one indicates rampant poverty. The imperative lesson is how can the high growth rates on GDP and relatively large number of the poor can be reconciled to lead to more inclusive and sustainable development which the main theme of the collection.

Chapter 5 by Chikozho on South Africa presents an interesting test case for lack of inclusive development. The articles indicate that there has been a significant economic growth since 1994. Yet, poverty, unemployment and inequality are still rampant. Economic growth has, thus, not been inclusive enough to improve access to social services by the majority of South Africans. Using qualitative and quantitative data, the article analyses the reasons for the disjuncture between economic growth, poverty reduction and social inclusion. Institutions and policies that were set were not meant to be pro-poor. More systematic efforts at inclusive growth are required to make the dreams of post-apartheid South Africa come true. South Africa has been interesting as a case study of inclusive and sustainable development in Africa on two grounds. Firstly, as a relatively more industrialised economy in Africa yet with high levels of poverty, inequality and unemployment provides a real time exhibit of how mere economic growth does not guarantee improved livelihoods for the majority despite having policies to the expected effect in place. Secondly South Africa is a good laboratory case for inequality based on non-economic differences and in this case colour. While it is still a challenge to make the economy less unequal in South Africa the big challenge is to ensure the inequalities and gaps in opportunity between the black and whites that defined the apartheid policies are completely obliterated.

Chapter 6 is by Omona on social protection through universal health insurance in Uganda. Although essentially it is a case on Uganda which is in the sub region the article is based on a comparison of two countries. This article is important in that it looks at inclusiveness and sustainable development through a social inclusion lens. It provides evidence on how a health coverage system works and gives you a picture of social exclusion. But, as noted, the most important question answered by the article is why Thailand has recorded a universal health coverage while Uganda has not. Although it looks as if the author answers that it is political will to provide universal health coverage and that it has been lacking in Uganda in fact the author provides other intermediating drivers particularly the financing mechanisms of universal health systems as well as creating the institutions and legal framework to ensure a universal health coverage system. The good lessons from this chapter on Uganda are twofold. A universal health coverage system has direct impact on social inclusion, population and the economy. Secondly in the struggle to ensure inclusive and sustainable development it will be useful for countries to learn from each other in the region and abroad. Thailand's success in universal health coverage could be used in offering lessons in inclusive development at sectoral levels and the challenges to overcome in the process.

Chapter 7 is on the informal sector in Rwanda by Rukundo. Particularly it is on the determinants of informality using an empirical analysis from data collected from 200 food processing units sampled from all over the country. The paper uses an econometric tool to compare productivity in the sector. Determinants to informality include gender, taxes, government initiatives, experience and age. The most significant lesson related to inclusive development is the contribution of the sector to employment. On one hand the informal sector provides employment and income to the poor. Promoting it and removing barriers to its evolution to formalised production and enhancing its productivity is using the empirical evidence better for inclusive and sustainable development than disbanding the sector. Rwanda as a rapidly developing economy in the region provides a good case to look at one dimension of inclusive development in form of productivity and employment growth in the informal sector.

Chapter 8 is on Rwanda on a social protection scheme appropriately called VUP or Vision 2020 Umurenge Programme. The programme includes direct support to poor families by cash transfers The chapter presents the concepts, methodology and findings as a research report. This underscores the original approach of the collection which is knowledge harvests based on ongoing or completed research. But above all it emphasises on the shortcomings of the programme and what is recommended as course of action. But the most important and relevant aspect of the chapter is how the Rwandan social protection has worked from the perspective of the beneficiaries. Despite an analysis of the demographics of the programme from below there are qualitative responses that have implication to the link between social protection and inclusive development. It has shown perhaps very indirectly and unintended the explanation of why Rwanda has managed to challenge poverty but not as quickly as it has promoted economic growth

The book ends with a conclusion by Musahara who emphasises the usefulness of the findings and the collection as a pointer to the need for further research.

CHAPTER ONE

Inclusive and Sustainable Development Challenges in Eastern and Southern Africa: Issues and Social Research Gaps for the Post-2015 Era

Herman Musahara

Abstract

The paper has two major thrusts all nested in the discourse on the meaning of development. First the concept of inclusive and sustainable development is a product of the evolution of the concept of development after the Second World War. It's a current consensus that can be appropriately referred to as a settlement for the age of sustainable development which in itself is a shift of paradigm to development based on a broader meaning than mere economic development. The second thrust is that the concept of inclusive and sustainable development is normative. The reality is that it should be a positive process leading to an ideal position tenable in some decades to come. In specific terms, the first sections of the paper tracks the evolution of the concepts of inclusive development and sustainable development from the times of the economic growth models to the current versions of human development. To clear a confusion surrounding the concept of inclusive development such as using it synonymously with inclusive growth, a clear distinction between growth, pro- poor economic growth, inclusive growth and inclusive development is provided. The rest of the evolution of the concepts is done through assumptions that give content to the current policy implications of inclusive and sustainable development. Nine eastern African countries are used for indicators. These are chosen not only because they constitute the Chapters of Organisation for Social Science Research in Eastern Africa but also because they represent a number of countries which are party to the new concepts of 'emergence of Africa' and 'Africa rising'. We argue in the paper that Africa has indeed performed very well in the last ten years but its growth trajectory has to subscribe to inclusive and sustainable development precepts if current dilemma of emergence with jobless, poverty and inequality, among other limits, has to be addressed. Finally is an analysis of a methodological challenge of how social science research can provide evidence needed to support the inclusive and sustainable development process. The article undertakes an analysis of these emerging issues using secondary data which is available from international databases.

Keywords: Economic development, human development, inclusive and sustainable development, Eastern Africa

1. Introduction

The concepts of inclusive and sustainable development can be located in development studies following up the evolution of the development debate mainly after the Second World War. The main preoccupation of scholars has been to look at the inadequacy of concepts of development basing their arguements on real experiences of countries and coining new ones that seem to be reflecting the type of durable development that is generally and contextually desired.

In this article we trace the evolution of the conceptualisation of development. One approach of analysing challenges facing inclusive and sustainable development efforts is the search for pro poor growth. Although generally accepted as a good basis for inclusive development it is often used tautologically as a buzz word that is used for legitimating an argument. Looking at its content and context gives a better understanding of its dynamics and its possible trajectory in the years after 2015.

The rest of the article looks at current development challenges of a number of countries in Eastern and Southern Africa. The main point is to assess the shortcomings of the rapid economic growth experienced by many African countries in the last decade and in particular to posit the argument that real development needs to be inclusive and sustainable. Two narratives emerge. One that sees Africa as needing after all the economic growth as the initial condition that had never been experienced before; and another narrative that points out critically that the image of "Africa rising" is not real enough to promise sustainable development of Africa given the gravity of the issues analysed. It's the onus of research and its support to policy in the post-2015 era to take up the debate further and deeper into action such as activities planned under Agenda 2063 of Africa and Sustainable Development Goals of 2030. The article has resulted from a synthesis of papers, chapters and presentations made by the author in various parts of Africa and abroad in the last few years.

2. Conceptual Basis

Inclusive and sustainable development is regarded as yet another shift of paradigm in the meaning of development. The earliest interpretation of development of countries was based on a simple analysis of economic indicators particularly Gross Domestic Product (GDP) and GDP per capita differences. Economic growth models grounded on the rigorous demonstrations of Harrod (1939) and Domar (1946) influenced planning for growth and development since the 1960s in large parts of the developing world. According to these models, the engines of growth and development were saving and investment and the best indicator of development was since then economic growth. As with Schumpeter (1961), growth is part of development. To other scholars, development is a process in stages (Rostow 1960). To Kuznets, what is being experienced is what can be generically seen as the U curve of development (Kuznets 1955). To Solow, this is a convergence where in poor countries experience faster rates of economic growth (Solow 1956 and Swan 1959).

Despite a rapid recognition that economic growth alone was not sufficient in explaining development of nations it is interesting to note that even today, seven decades later it is still relied upon to indicate emergence or rising of nations. The emergence of Africa or the now popular 'Africa Rising' is based largely on exemplary economic growth experience in Africa in the last 10 years. Although, between then and now, there has been a lengthy evolution of the concepts of development, it seems to have not provided a definite meaning of development. An overview of that evolution is the focus of the rest of this section.

Development means reduction of poverty through meeting basic needs of life. This assumption is based on what, in the 1980s, was referred to as the Basic Needs Approach (Streeten 1979). It was preferred by the UN organisations especially ILO and UNDP. Defining features of development include how individuals, households and societies had access to food, shelter and clothing as indicators of their development.

The 1990s saw emergence of the most effective and affective concept of development: Human Development. Human development has emphasised that the whole purpose of development should be the human being. It brought in a new conceptual outlook of development, new empirical tools of measurement and the emergence of a broader understanding of development including a global lobby benchmarked on development goals. By 1990 the concept of Human Development had taken root and soon the Human Development Index was launched (UNDP 1990; Sen 1988; UNDP 1990). It embraced a broad meaning of development to include choice, entitlements, capabilities and freedom (Sen 1999).

While the concept of human development was emerging the economic scholarship was further interrogating the limits of economic growth as a means of explaining development. For instance the World Bank had initiated and continued with Redistribution with growth studies (Alesina and Roderick 1994; World Bank 2001; Dollar and Kraay 2001). Poverty, inequality and unemployment had started being real economic concerns to understanding development by mid 1990s. On other fronts Institutional Economics and Poverty reduction studies had developed (North 1990; Amaceoglu and Robinson 2013). Within the World Bank Group for example a Human Development Unit had been established meaning it was no longer an exclusively UN concept only and studies started being interested in looking at the link between economic growth and human development (Stuart 2011).

In a matter of years the Human Development concept became popular. A Human Development Report was compiled every year on a contemporary theme reflecting the world's immediate concern. It has been based on a new measure developed for the purpose, as a Human Development Index, on a common yardstick using life expectancy, literacy rate and rate of economic growth through Gross Domestic Product per capita. What is noteworthy is that the emergence of the concept of Human Development and Human Development Index led also to the emergence of the human security concept and the Gender Development Index among others.

Secondly, in 1990 world leaders endorsed a unified global approach to the promotion of human development through the Millennium Development Goals commonly referred to as MDGs. The MDGs have guided the world, especially the developing ones towards working for human development till 2015. A common justification of the Sustainable Development Goals succeeding the MDGs is to ensure development is both inclusive and sustainable. The next section focuses on inclusive development.

Since it is apparent that it is this wide ranging debate that gives content to the concept of inclusive development we give attention to the components of sustainable development by drawing out the distinction between pro-poor growth, inclusive growth and inclusive development. What has been noted is that pro poor growth has become a buzz word and almost been interchangeably used as meaning inclusive growth and at times inclusive development. The concepts have to be clearly distinguished if inclusive development is to be understood (Kanbur and Raynmar 2010).

When poverty is reduced substantially compared to the rate of growth of say GDP per capita, the phenomenon is called pro-poor growth. But, the problem that arises which is useful to the emergence of Africa is where growth of the economy has led to poverty reduction but has also   resulted in high levels of inequality in income and consumption. This means growth can be pro-poor without being inclusive. In fact, there can be growth with poverty reduction while there are segments of the poor that have become worse in the process. The definition and debates on pro-poor growth occupied scholars for the most part of the 2000s (UN 2000; Kakwani and Pernia 2000; OECD 2001; and Ravallion and Shen 2003). At a more elementary level let us make a clear analysis of which pro poor growth is referred to in this article.

It can be argued that the basis for an inclusive and sustainable development is a pro poor growth. A pro poor economic growth will reduce poverty. But, for the reduction in poverty to be sustained and for it to have a lasting impact on development, the entire pattern of development has to be influenced (OECD 2005). Pro-poor growth is also necessary but not sufficient, as argued earlier. It is not enough to know that economic growth is to the benefit of the poor without information on how to implement the pro-poor policy approach. In emerging economies of Africa it is important to distinguish between growth that benefits the poor and other growth. It is important to see whether the growth of incomes of the poor is disproportionately higher than the growth of income of the non poor (Grosse *et al.* 2005). Examples show how pro-poor growth is not as simple as used by most people. According to OECD (2001) and UN (2000) growth that leads to significant reduction in poverty is pro poor. In this sense reference is to absolute poverty only. After being criticised as being narrow, Kakwani and Pernia (2000) suggested that pro-poor growth should benefit the poor more than it should do to the rich. This simply means that pro-poor growth occurs when other groups that are non poor benefit less from growth compared to the poor. This is what is appropriately called inclusive growth. A good example given to students of pro-poor growth is two situations where income increases by 5 per cent but income of the poor increases by 7 per cent compared to a second scenario where growth of the poor increases by 7 per cent while national income grows by 10 per cent. The two scenarios of growth show the problem. In the second case, the poor are absolutely better-off but relatively worse-off— meaning there has been pro-poor growth; but, the growth is still not inclusive. Some rigorous methods of measuring these have been developed (Ravallion and Shen 1999). The details of these measurements are not provided as a methodological necessity because this article is only a general analysis of challenges. Meaningful inclusive growth which by definition is pro-poor should see both absolute and relative poverty reduced. It is thus a complex issue which has ultimately settled around three meanings: 1) the poor's incremental income is greater than their current share; 2) the change in the average income of the poor is greater than the change in the average income of society; or 3) the change in the income of the poor is above a certain international norm expressed as a percentage. But, even this distinction of growth, which is pro-poor, is not enough. In this regard the meaning of inclusive growth as distinct from the broader sense of inclusive development should be clear.

As noted earlier there are also qualitative aspects of development such as gender empowerment, attributes of health and education and rights protections that characterise the overall meaning of inclusive development. Inclusive development is defined as improvement in distribution of well-being along the dimensions beyond growth as, at the same time, average improvement in achievements is realised. It has now ushered in the use of various indices that reflect on measuring inclusive growth. These are in particular the human opportunity index, gender index, indicators of shared prosperity and disaggregated unemployment data (Klasen 2010). Measurement takes into consideration economic growth, changes in structure of production, and changes in spatial distribution of population such as urbanisation and improvement in social indicators. In Eastern and Southern Africa, it is not adequate to characterise the emergence of the countries by their economic growth, pro-poor growth and performance over the last 15 years alone. A number of indicators of lack of inclusive growth are given in the next main section. In the meantime it can be said that inclusive development is only a part, apparently separable, but a necessary element of a holistic meaning of sustainable development currently in use internationally. Inclusive growth is about having 'all on board' (OECD 2014).

The conceptualisation of sustainable development has also passed through a number of stages (Sachs 2015). In the 1970s, sustainability referred to an economy in equilibrium with the basic ecological support system (Stivers 1976). Sustainable Development can be regarded as a generic definition of the principle of sustainability (Cornwall and Eade 2013). The Brundtland Commission (WCED 1987, 8) offered the first and most famous definition of sustainable development as 'development that meets the needs of the present without compromising the ability of future generations to meet their own needs". The environment became a global lobby through World Summits such as those in Rio de Janeiro 1992 and in Durban 2002. But sustainable development has not involved the environment alone. Sustainable development includes not only economic development and poverty reduction but also issues of social inclusion, and governance (UN 2013). The world is facing sustainability problems not only because of the environment but also due to a complex set of problems hindering real change to people. These are multiple problems of poverty, inequality and inequity, food insecurity, effects of climate change, social exclusion and gender, environmental degradation, cities, energy needs, water crisis and migration among others (WSSC 2013). In September 2015, world leaders endorsed Sustainable Development Goals (SDGs) as the successor of the Millennium Development Goals (MDGs) that ran from 1990 to 2015. The SDGs will run from 2016 to 2030. It has been noted that we are entering the Age of Sustainable Development (Sachs 2015). In this sense inclusive development can be regarded as part of the broader meaning of sustainable development. But in practice scholars, institutions and networks use it also as a standalone concept emphasising the need to address poverty and inequality. Recently it has tended to include issues broader than economics.

Norton and Rogerson (2011) have pointed out that challenges of inclusive development today also include climate change, violence and conflict. Climate change is a global challenge but it's the poor of Africa that are the most vulnerable to its impacts. Floods and droughts affect agriculture, the mainstay of the majority of the poor in Africa. Although conflict in Africa dropped dramatically, in sub Saharan Africa conflict has been identified with poverty and deprivation (Draman 2003, Verstegen 2001).

The institutions for inclusive development in Africa are also weak and not working properly. The role of the state, private sector, aid and other stakeholders need to be transformed (INCLUDE 2014). Oxfam (2014) talks of "ensuring benefits for all". Inclusive development is driven by people, through open dialogues between country governments and their citizens. Inclusive development is a pro-poor approach that equally values and incorporates the contributions from all stakeholders— including marginalised groups— in addressing development issues. It promotes transparency and accountability, and enhances development cooperation outcomes through collaboration between the civil society, governments and private sector actors. Sachs (2014) notes that inclusiveness also means that form of development which encompasses civil, civic and political rights. In this sense a distinction is made between development as a process and development as the outcome of economic activity only. Norton and Rogerson (2011) have noted that inclusiveness means poverty reduction but also rights. Power and empowerment also need to come out as objectives of development. While development has been regarded as non-inclusive because of lack of opportunity, there is still evidence of social exclusion related to discrimination by age, religion, gender, disability, poverty and ethnicity (OXFAM 2014). Inclusive development is also expanded to include human rights, participation, non- discrimination and accountability (OXFAM 2014). The right phrase under the newly inaugurated SDGs is development that does not leave any one behind.

3. A Review of Indicators of the Challenges from Eastern and Southern Africa

The conceptual distinctions are important in looking at the African experience now. Recently, about 23 countries in Sub-Saharan Africa have graduated to middle income countries. Africa has had the fastest growing economies in the world in the last 10 years. It has been said Africa is rising. In this section we offer some indicators of the challenges. But as noted in the previous section indicators of inclusiveness and sustainable development are multiple. In this section we refer to Eastern and Southern Africa as part of the larger Sub Saharan Africa because preliminary growth data includes most of the countries in the OSSREA outreach. It is also noteworthy that most of the countries in the region such as Ethiopia, Rwanda, Kenya, Uganda and Mozambique are among those considered to be emerging or with considerable rapid growth rates. The region includes middle income countries like South Africa, Botswana, and Mauritius.

Like in the rest of Africa, the starting point is the remarkable performance of the countries on the economic growth front. This has been regarded as the indication of the emergence of Africa. At regional level Africa is regarded as rising because of a number of attributes (Musahara 2015). GDP growth of Africa is expected to accelerate to 4.6 per cent in 2015 and 4.9 per cent in 2016 (UN 2015). The least developed countries (LDCs) in Africa will continue to exceed the global average with expected acceleration from 5.3 per cent in 2014 to 5.7 per cent in 2015 mainly due to an improving external environment (World Economic Situation and Prospects 2015). Foreign direct investment (FDI) in 1998 was USD 110 billion and rose to USD 554 billion in 2010 (ACET 2014)

If Africa was a country, it would, with per capita of USD 1500, be classified as a middle income country. By 2050 Africa will have a larger and younger workforce than China or India. Africa will continue to transform its economies through exploiting land and natural resources, economic diversification, enhancing competitiveness, raising the share of manufacturing, use of technology and reducing dependency on foreign assistance. Figure 1 is the general trend of the whole of Africa for 50 years from 1961. The general picture is that Africa has experienced rising growth rates in the past 15 years. This is also generally true with the nine selected countries of Eastern and Southern Africa. Figure 2 is the general growth trends of the 9 select countries in recent years. With the exception of Zimbabwe the positive growth trends are visibly all above zero. Botswana experienced negative growth in one year; but, as noted, it is the only one among the countries the only one that can be classified as middle income. Of course this emergence of Africa or African rising is not by definition an end in itself. The argument is that the concept of emergence of Africa will make meaningful change and shift the global position of Africa if the economic growth will lead to inclusive and sustainable development. Otherwise stated, economic growth is good but it is less meaningful if it is still accompanied by social and economic challenges. Let us now look generally into the indicators of the challenges in some 9 countries randomly selected from Eastern and Southern Africa for availability of the indicative data. Of course just like Sub Saharan Africa as whole, each country and region is influenced by context and background.

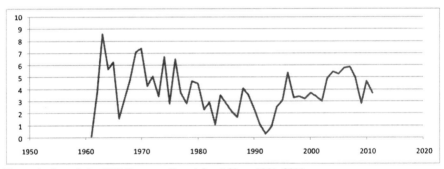

Figure 1. Growth in GDP Per cent Trend for Africa, 1961–2011
SOURCE: WDI (2015)

Table 1. Recent annual growth rates of GDP in Eastern and Southern Africa

Country	2005	2006	2007	2008	2009	2010	2011	2012	2013	2014
Botswana	5	8	9	-8	9	6	5	9	4	4
Burundi	1	5	5	5	3	4	4	4	5	5
Ethiopia	12	11	11	11	9	13	6	9	10	10
Kenya	6	6	7	0	3	8	8	5	6	5
Rwanda	7	9	8	11	6	7	8	9	5	7
Tanzania	8	5	8	6	5	6	8	5	7	7
Uganda	6	11	8	9	7	5	10	4	3	5
Zambia	7	8	8	8	9	10	6	7	7	6
Zimbabwe	-6	-3	-4	-18	6	11	12	11	4	3

SOURCE: WDI (2014).

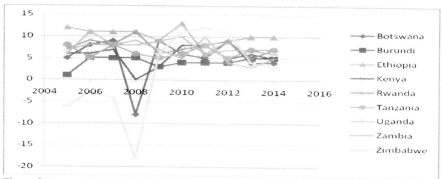

Figure 2. Annual Growth Rates Trends, 2015–2014 for Selected Countries
SOURCE: WDI (2014).

A general trend discernible from Table 1 and Figure 2 is that generally in Africa growth has been positive in the last 10 years. A noticeable negative trend was recorded for Zimbabwe up to 2008 but there is a rebound in growth up to 2014 with double digit growth rates in 2010, 2011 and 2012. Despite being a middle-income country, Botswana registered negative growth in 2008. But, Ethiopia, Rwanda, Uganda and Tanzania showed remarkably positive and high growth rates. None of the rest in the selected countries had a negative growth rate. It is clear that the average growth rate for all the countries was above 5 per cent per year. In brief, since there is no other time Africa had experienced such an economic growth episode in the past, the current years have been regarded as the years of emergence of Africa. Nonetheless the first challenge has been whether this rising trend has been accompanied by economic transformation. The first exhibits are Table 2 and Table 3.

Table 2. Contribution of of agriculture to GDP (%)in Eastern and Southern Africa

Country	2005	2006	2007	2008	2009	2010	2011	2012	2013	2014
Botswana	2	2	2	3	3	3	3	3	3	2
Burundi	44	44	37	41	41	40	40	41	40	39
Ethiopia	45	46	45	48	49	45	45	48	45	39
Kenya	27	23	23	25	26	28	29	29	29	42
Rwanda	38	39	35	33	34	33	32	33	33	30
Tanzania	37	31	29	31	32	32	32	31	33	33
Uganda	27	26	24	23	-	28	-	-	-	-
Zambia	16	14	13	13	12	10	10	10	10	-
Zimbabwe	19	20	22	19	15	15	13	13	12	14

SOURCE: WDI (2014)

Table 3. Contribution (%) of industry to GDP in Eastern and Southern Africa

Country	2005	2006	2007	2008	2009	2010	2011	2012	2013	2014
Botswana	48	49	47	41	32	36	40	35	37	38
Burundi	18	17	18	16	17	17	17	17	17	18
Ethiopia	13	13	12	11	10	10	10	10	12	15
Kenya	19	22	22	21	21	21	21	21	20	19
Rwanda	12	12	12	13	12	13	14	14	15	14
Tanzania	26	22	22	22	20	22	24	23	24	25
Uganda	25	24	27	27	20	-	-	-	-	-
Zambia	30	33	35	34	32	36	38	34	34	-
Zimbabwe	29	32	33	31	30	31	33	32	31	30

SOURCE: WDI (2014).

Table 2 shows that major contribution to GDP in terms of value addition in the countries is still from agriculture. Data is given for both agriculture and industrial contribution to GDP over the period 2005 and 2014. Except for Botswana and despite the high growth rates mentioned, there is no indication of countries tending towards a higher composition of industrial value added (Table 3). Understandably the high contribution of industry value added in Zambia is mainly because of minerals. Ideally, an economy undergoing structural transformation would see a bigger contribution coming from industry and preferably from manufacturing (Sutcliffe 1980). It is possible to argue that it is too early to see meaningful transformation of African economies; but it is also not too late to point out that emergence should lead to a permanent transformation of African economies after all. The question of sources of growth also raises the question of how sustainable the emergence of Africa is, as most of the economies (as can be seen from Table 2) are still dependent on agriculture which is still vulnerable to vagaries of weather and international market. It has been noted for instance that Total Factor Productivity had risen since the 1980s and was 4 times higher than it was 25 year earlier. The point is that by global standards productivity in agriculture in terms of output per hectare and per worker is still low (Block 2010). AGRA (2013) points out that productivity in the agricultural sector lags behind other areas and is below the regional potential explaining why agriculture provides 65 per cent of the labour force and yet contributes only about 35 per cent of the GDP. Thus the emergence of Africa in terms of growth rates in recent years needs to be accelerated in order to lead to changes in the sectoral compositions of African economies.

Table 4. The most current HDI and poverty rates

Country	HDI 2014	MDPI
Botswana	106	-
Burundi	184	80.8(2010)
Ethiopia	174	87.3(2011)
Kenya	145	47.89(2008)
Rwanda	163	69(2010)
Tanzania	151	65.6(2010)
Uganda	163	69.9(2011)
Zambia	151	.6(2013/2014)
Zimbabwe	163	29.792014)

SOURCE: HDI (2015).

Note: MDPI is Multi Dimensional Poverty Index

It has also been argued that growth has not been inclusive enough because there is still rampant poverty in these countries. Despite notable growth rates in most of Eastern and Southern African countries, poverty by different measures is still high. It is true that over the years poverty has declined in many African countries. Indeed, figures vary by individual countries. But, poverty rates in Africa, by any measure, are still the highest globally and rates of change in human development are still low. In Table 4 the Multi Dimensional Poverty Indices of the select countries show that poverty is still high above 47 per cent in all countries except Zambia and Zimbabwe for the most recent years. All the countries in the group are classified as 'Low Human Development' countries except Botswana. This means that they still have low levels of Human Development Indices (HDIs) and rank mostly above 100 out of 188 countries. Even Botswana, which is a middle-income country, is 106th and the least developed Burundi is 184th. The HDI is a composite index that includes economic growth, life expectancy and education outcomes. In Table 5 with the exception of Rwanda that has registered the highest rates of change in HDI globally, no other country in the region experienced an average growth rate of HDI above 2 per cent.

Table 5. Rates of change in Human Development over the last 25 years

Country	Average HDI Change, 1990–2014
Botswana	0.74
Burundi	1.28
Kenya	0.62
Rwanda	2.89
Tanzania	1.44
Uganda	1511.89
Zambia	1.57
Zimbabwe	0.08

Another indicator of non inclusive development is levels of inequality. Inequality is, however, a general concept. There is inequality in assets and gender; inequality is between individuals and between households; inequality is within countries and between countries. Therefore, there are multiple indicators of inequality. On another hand, in the case of poverty, it is important to look at changes over time. Using general indicators it has been stated that using economic indicators related to income inequality in Africa has been falling since the 1990s. But, as noted already this has to be looked at carefully. For example, among our selected countries, it increased in Uganda and Zambia, while it generally decreased in Ethiopia and Kenya during the same period. A new interest is also going beyond Gini coefficients and looking at indices other than Gini coefficients and other forms of non-income inequalities. From Table 6 through Table 8 a number of different indices are used to give an overview of the challenge of inequality in Africa using the selected countries as cases. Table 6 shows incomes held by the highest and lowest 20 per cent of the population in Eastern Africa. Data available is mostly for 2010 and 2011. With the exception of Ethiopia, which has 27.5 per cent of income held by the highest 10 per cent, the rest have more than 30 per cent of total income held by the highest 10 per cent of the population.

Table 6. Levels of inequality by income of the population

Country	Income held by highest 10%	Income held by lowest 20%
Ethiopia	27.5(2011)	8.0(2011)
Rwanda	43.2(2011)	5.2(2011)
Tanzania	31.1(2012)	7.4(2012)
Uganda	35.8(2013)	5.8(2013)

SOURCE: UNDP (2014)

Table 7. Gender inequality and ranking

Country	GII	Ranking
Botswana	0.488	106
Burundi	0.492	109
Ethiopia	0.558	129
Kenya	0.552	126
Rwanda	0.4	80
Tanzania	0.547	125
Uganda	0.538	12
Zambia	0.587	132
Zimbabwe	0.504	112

SOURCE: UNDP (2015)

Another indicator is gender inequality. The Human Development Report includes Gender Inequality Index and the ranking of countries in its report. For 2015 only Rwanda among the countries under study improved from its previous rank of 100th to 80th in the world with a GII of 0.4 (Table 7). Indeed as an outcome of the experience with the MDGs gender equality has been given   due priority as crosscutting in most Sustainable Development Goals (SDGs).

But, as noted inequality is complex and can be looked at using different indices and over periods of time. Table 8 provides the most common measure of inequality Gini Coefficient in the last column. The Gini coefficient is an average over the period between 2005 and 2013. From 2005 to 2013, the average Gini coefficient had been higher than 0.40 per cent in 5 of the 9 countries. The most developed of the countries has the highest level of inequality among the selected countries. Even countries that we noted to have been doing well in GDP growth, such as Rwanda and Zambia have levels of inequality above 0.5. But, it also compares the index of human inequality for 2014 and two other types over a period of time where data is available. The Palma Index is a ratio between the richest 20 per cent and the lowest 40 per cent while the Quintile Ratio is the ratio of the richest 20 per cent to the poorest 20 per cent. Thus, you can see that on both quintile ratio and the Palma Index Botswana has the highest levels of inequality. The ratios of incomes of the rich to the poor are highest in both cases with 22.9 and 5.8 on the quintile and Palma indices respectively. The rates in the rest of the countries show levels of inequalities that are a concern even if it is argued that they have been generally declining. For example the richest 20 per cent have about 12 times and 11 times more than the poorest 20 per cent in Kenya and Rwanda respectively. On the Palma index Rwanda's rich 20 per cent have about 3 times more income than 40 per cent of the poor for 2005 to 2013. In Kenya it is about 2.8 times and the figure is even the highest in Zambia (excluding Botswana).

Table 8. Inequality under different indices and over time

Country	Co-efficient of human inequality 2014	Quintile ratio 2005–2013	Palma Ratio	Gini Index 2005–2013
Botswana	36.5	22.9	5.8	60.3
Burundi	31.5	4.8	1.3	33.3
Ethiopia	28	5.3	1.4	33.6
Kenya	36	11.8	2.8	47.7
Rwanda	30.2	11	3.2	50.8
Uganda	30.2	8.8	2.4	44.6
Zambia	33.9	17.4	4.8	57.5
Zimbabwe	-	6.2	1.7	37.8

SOURCE: HDR (2015).

Human inequality calculated from the Human Development estimates shows all the countries, with the exception of Ethiopia, to have above 30 per cent human inequality. This as expected would generally be including all non-income inequalities. This means that although inequality may have been declining, it is still considerable. We should finally note also that there are all sorts of discrimination based on religion, ethnicity, and region, as well as all sorts of social exclusion that are not captured by these statistics. All these are concerns of inclusive and sustainable development.

Sustainability is mainly about considering environment in matters of promoting economic growth. There are so many attributes of environment.

One aspect we can see from Table 9 is the amount of area under degraded land. With the exception of Zambia, the study countries are environmentally vulnerable with degraded land sizes between 18.5 for Burundi and a high of 72.5 per cent for Ethiopia. Table 10 shows scores of countries on environment. Rwanda is the only country that has ever scored 4 on a scale of 1 to 6 in terms of considering environment in their policies. The most pervasive challenge to all countries is, of course, adapting to and mitigating the effects of climate change.

Table 9. Estimates of population under degraded land, in 2014

Country	Per cent of population living on degraded land
Botswana	22.0
Burundi	18.5
Ethiopia	72.3
Kenya	31.0
Rwanda	10.1
Tanzania	25.0
Uganda	23.5
Zambia	4.6
Zimbabwe	29.4

SOURCE: HDR (2015)

Table 10. Scores on countries' consideration of environmental matters

Country	2010	2011	2012	2013
Kenya	3.5	3.5	3.5	3
Uganda	4	3.5	3.5	3.5
Tanzania	3.5	3.5	3.5	3.5
Rwanda	3.5	3.5	3.5	3.5
Ethiopia	3	3.5	3.5	3.5

Low =1   high=6
SOURCE: UNDP (2014)

Employment and unemployment pose another challenge of inclusive and sustainable development. Table 11 presents the general aspects of formal employment vis-a-vis total population and agriculture and services. In Table 12 are the rates of youth unemployment. Most of the countries have considerable rates of youth unemployment with the highest rates in Botswana which is already a middle-income country and Zambia which has also experienced rapid growth of the economy. But, of course, the concept of 'jobless growth', which has featured the most recent criticism of African growth, is deeper than this indication. First the actual situation of unemployment— open and disguised— has depended on the type of measures used. It is, for example, today common to talk of the 'working poor'. It means people who numerically are employed but have jobs that are not decent enough to provide a decent living which in fact is a form of disguised unemployment. Figure 2 indicates trends of unemployment from available data sets from 2004 to 2013. Althoug there is no country with a falling trend despite rapid economic growth, most have had high rates, constant or growing for several of the years.

Table 11. Different employment aspect in the selected countries

Country	E2P	E2A 1999	2012	E2S 1990	2012
Botswana	62.6		29.9	31.4	54.9
Burundi	76.9				
Ethiopia	79		79.3		13
Kenya	61.1		61.1		32.2
Rwanda	85.4		78.8	6.7	16.6
Tanzania	8		76.5		19.2
Uganda	74.5		65.6		28.4
Zambia	68.8	49.8	72.2	20.8	20.6
Zimbabwe	81.9		64.8		15.3

SOURCE: HDR 2015 E2P is employment to population per cent, E2A is employment in agriculture and E2S is employment in the services sector

Table 12. Unemployment in 2014

Country	Youth unemployment
Botswana	36
Burundi	-
Ethiopia	7.3
Kenya	-
Rwanda	4.5
Tanzania	5.8
Uganda	2.6
Zambia	15.2
Zimbabwe	8.7

SOURCE: WDI 2014

Table 13. Rates of unemployment

Country	Total as % population	Long term as % population	Youth as % of youth labour force
Botswana	17.9	10.4	36
Ethiopia	4.5	1.3	7.3
Rwanda	3.4		4.5
Tanzania	3.5		
Uganda	4.2		2.6
Zambia	7.8		15.2
Zimbabwe	11.1		4.5

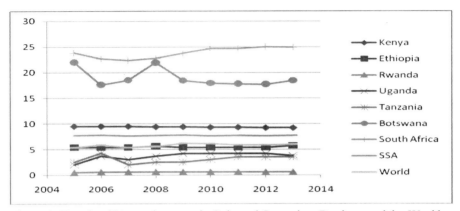

Figure 3. Trends of Unemployment in Selected Countries, Regions and the World
SOURCE: Drawn from WDI data adopted from Musahara 2015

Table 14. Annual growth of population 2005–2013

Botswana	Average Annual growth 2005–2013	Average annual growth 210–2015
Botswana	1.3	0.9
Burundi	3	3.2
Ethiopia	2.9	2.6
Kenya	2.7	2.7
Rwanda	2.3	2.7
Tanzania	2.6	3
Uganda	3.4	3.3
Zambia	2.5	3.2
Zimbabwe	0.3	2.8

SOURCE: WDI (2014)

But, considering the region as a whole and each country individually, it is certainly fair to state that the growth has not been inclusive. Burundi presents an example where not only high levels of poverty challenges inclusive and sustainable development but also where the impact of good growth rates of GDP gets easily dampened by political instability. Burundi also has a limited size of arable land and the majority of the poor (almost 70 per cent) live in rural areas compared to 35 per cent who live in urban areas. This contrast means that there is a considerable amount of disparity or inequality among the different classes of the poor.

Ethiopia has one of the largest economies in Africa and a population in excess of 90 million. It has experienced a very good growth rates with real GDP growing at an average of 11 per cent in the past 15 years. But, as in the rest of the region, the growth has not managed to employ the available labour force and the urban areas have not become the drivers of growth.

Kenya has managed to make the economy depend more on services. More than 60 per cent of the GDP comes from services and about 16 per cent from industry. This is not an adequate structural transformation as expansion of manufacturing would contribute to a more durable development. The Gini coefficient has been under 0.5, which is, but stil quite high. The inequality in Kenya is attributed to past neglect of some regions of the country. It is estimated that 12.7 per cent of the youth are unemployed.

Rwanda is another success story on the growth front. Despite suspension of aid to it, Rwanda continued to realise growth rates of GDP above 5 per cent. Between 2001 and 2013, industry has grown faster than agriculture, but the economy is still dependent on agriculture. Rwanda has the best improvement in gender equality and equity. However, although Rwanda has the lowest rate of recorded unemployment, it is believed that 42 per cent of the youth are under-employed.

Tanzania was noted to be one of the fastest growing economies in Africa with an average economic growth of 6.9 per cent between 2010 and 2013. Tanzania has discovered deposits of natural gas and gets a lot of its growth from trade. But Tanzania has what is called notable basic needs poverty that, though going down, is still high. The poverty rate declined to 28.2 per cent in 2012 from the 33 per cent in 2007. Also Tanzania has not undergone structural transformation and depends on agriculture.

Uganda also discovered natural resource and, although it is investing in oil, its contribution to the economy has continued to be too little— less than 0.5 per cent. Poverty has declined in Rwanda but not as much as the economy has grown by more than 8 per cent over the last 10 years. This means that the growth has been less inclusive as well. For inclusive growth, there is still need to make some legislation that strengthens women's rights to land assets and inheritance.

Botswana is by definition a middle-income economy among our selected countries. We have, however, noted how the rate of unemployment is one of the highest. It is thus one thing to record high growth rates and another to ensure inclusive growth that provides adequate employment. The argument was further strengthened by data on Burundi, Zambia and Zimbabwe. As noted earlier, these are studies in the individual countries. For each of the challenges, more evidence on the drivers and policy options are required, as will be illustrated in the next section. But, first, a few emerging challenges are discussed below.

The first one is economic diversification. Many African countries are still dependent on one or a limited number of resources. Several Africa countries have got their rapid growth from oil or gas (Carbone 2015). It has been estimated that a third of the recent spurt in economic growth by African countries is commodity-based. The commodity sector (oil, gas, and minerals) accounts for 40 per cent of Africa's GDP but absorbs less than 1 per cent of the workforce (Havnevik 2015) UNECA (2013) has pointed out that the impressive growth story has not translated into economic diversification, commensurate jobs or faster social development. On the other hand, most Eastern African countries have not reaped their growth from oil and gas although the challenge for diversification is generally applicable to these countries, as well.

A second aspect is the challenge of illegal capital flight. It is estimated that capital flight is increasing by 12 per cent per annum. This is almost twice the volume of development assistance (Havnevik 2015). Thus, what would look like an emergence can easily degenerate into a new form of exploitation. Thirdly there is also an apparent lack of a coherent strategy. It is important for Africa to look for a sound strategy that has many pillars involving productive sectors and with backward and forward linkages. It is also noteworthy that Africa has generally overlooked smallholder agriculture on which the majority of the population relies on (Havnevik 2015).

A fourth area is trade. Trade has contributed significantly to the recent economic growth. The most spectacular has been trade with China. In the decade 2003 to 2013, it grew from USD 11 billion to USD166 billion (Havnevik 2015). A number of remarks can be made. First, the tremendous growth of trade with China does not mean links with the traditional trade partners have been replaced. In the same period, trade between Africa and the USA and EU had grown from USD 243 billion to USD 673 billion. The bulk of the trade is still focused on natural resources, minerals and fossil fuels. In relative terms, Africa's trade has not improved as dramatically as the economic story. In 1950, Africa's share of world trade was 5 per cent dropping to 1.8 per cent today and still 0.5 per cent for manufacturing (Havnevik 2015).

A fifth challenge is investment. FDI has fluctuated over the last decade (Op. Cit. 2015). FDI stagnated at USD 17 billion a year between 2000- and 2004. It rose rapidly to USD 60 billion between 2005 and 2008 and then declined to USD 40 billion between 2008 and 2010. It rose slightly to USD 46 billion in 2012. It has been very visible in only a few African countries, such as Nigeria, South Africa, Ghana, DRC, Algeria, Morocco, Mozambique and Zambia. The current sectors of investment are likely to continue to be natural resources, oil and gas, minerals (including diamond), food and energy (Op. Cit. 2015).

4. The Challenge of Evidence-based Research Analysis

The need to sustain the growth of Africa and to promote inclusive and sustainable development means that policy interventions are needed at national regional and certainly continental levels. In this section we argue that social science research and think tanks have an important role of providing evidence- based research based analysis for an inclusive and sustainable Africa. Social science research and think tanks have an important role to analyse the duo narratives of African development in the post-2015 era into a single process analysis of where Africa is in the next 50 years. These are, on the one hand, narratives of a rising Africa and on another hand narratives of Africa still struggling with poverty, inequality, diseases, environmental degradation, conflict, and exclusion.

Firstly a number of the Millennium Development Goals (MDGs) specifically meant for the region have not been reached specifically and for the region in particular. This in itself corroborates the challenges generally outlined. The most binding challenge cutting across all goals is poverty (Aworti and Musahara 2015). Poverty has been carried forward to the Sustainable Development Goals (SDGs) and is appropriately SDG number one. Secondly, SDGs were announced in September 2015. There will be 17 goals and 169 targets. Thirdly and as pointed out earlier the SDGs have been agreed upon after a 3 year debate and almost represent what was missing in MDGs (SDSN 2015). These are areas that need social science research to provide evidence and timely advice on action and pathways. Thirdly, many countries and regions have set up their own targets and visions. Africa has set up Agenda 2063, which is guiding its growth path in the next 5 decades. Social science research is needed in planning, studying and measuring capacity needs. Fourthly, the era after 2015 will apparently need social science interventions as that major actions, such as climate change mitigation require works aimed at change of behaviour. Finally, social science will be required to provide the human behaviour inputs in a multidisciplinary and multi dimensional search for solution to poverty reduction and sustainable development which is inclusive. A big challenge will be how these fronts will be taken up and which institutions will be engaged in the process.

In the age of sustainable development, the biggest challenge that social science has to address is developing tools and methods of research that will give results that can influence the change in human behaviour. Discrimination by gender, religion, ethnicity, age and other constructs are generally governed by individual, community and societal behaviour. The drivers, barriers and practices are all areas requiring social science research interventions. For instance the current challenge of effects of climate change has a large behavioural component that renders social science research relevant. Agricultural practices, what leads to environmental degradation, and excessive carbon emissions can be mitigated by changing behaviour. Social science research has to provide research products that can influence the change in practices and behaviours over the short- and long-run.

An example of the conceptualisation of the role of social sciences in the global dialogue on environment has been given by the World Social Science Report (2013). Another source of information on the role of social sciences can be derived from the so called 'Age of Sustainable Development' (Sachs 2014). In the World Social Science Report (2013) Hackman and St Clair (2012) have identified six cornerstones of social research. These are the historical and contextual complexity, identifying and mapping consequences, conditions and visions of change, interpretations, responsibilities, and governance and decision-making.

Jeffrey Sachs (2013) has indicated four areas where social sciences are important in sustainable development research. The first of these are epistemic such as poverty, hunger, climate change, access to health, education and food security. The second area is new research and demonstration. The third is improved understanding and design of global social, economic and technological change, such as eradication of poverty, or heading environmental catastrophes, such as tools of advocacy, analysing ways of addressing delayed action against hazards of climate change and designing sustainable development goals. The fourth area is research on how social scientists organise themselves. Irina Bokova (2013, 3) in introducing the WSSC report summarises the role of social science research today as follows: '*Human activity is the major force shaping the planetary system...we shape our environment as it shapes us...social sciences has the role to contribute to social transformation*'. Berkley Earth (2013), as pointed earlier, has correctly asserted that human behaviour is important in understanding and averting global crisis and social sciences are uniquely positioned to help shift the current development paradigm.

On a more specific level, the evaluations of MDGs and the current SDGs show areas where more evidence and knowledge products are required. These, as mentioned above, can be summarised as: poverty, dynamics and drivers of inequality, non-income inequalities and inequities, employment and jobless growth dynamics and quality of education. Other areas that have continued to be advocated in SDGs include climate-smart urbanisation, infrastructure, good governance and security, and issues of gender. But understanding and measuring climate change effects and financing them still needs some fundamental studies. Human rights, dynamics of conflict and conflict resolution, as well as social protection are other areas where social science research will be required to provide evidence for inclusive and sustainable development. For all these areas, we need to design methodologies and come up with new ideas on bringing about social and institutional innovations for change.

It should, however, be noted that this is a supply side analysis. These are areas where the challenges may demand social science research. Most social sciences research and especially think tanks have to supply the required disciplinary and interdisciplinary inputs to guide inclusive and sustainable development. Their institutional set up and missions shall determine how they can provide research and knowledge products. Think tanks in Africa are becoming more relevant because the challenges of inclusive and sustainable development are made more important by the pressures of democratisation, accountability of institutions and maturing political systems. Arinaitwe (2010) suggests three roles. Firstly, think tanks can assist in establishing relative priorities. Secondly, they can assist in offering policy choices and advice to chosen recipients and thirdly they can indicate the implications on the implementation of policies. Think tanks can do this as academic institutions or what is called 'universities without students, in terms of contract research or providing advocacy for all sorts of activities on promoting inclusive and sustainable development. It's Think Tanks that will be the custodians of openness to ideas of governments and institutions in the quest for inclusive and sustainable development. A considerable amount of evidence has been compiled on how think tanks influence policy (Transparify 2014) and how, in Africa, they have a role in influencing development (Mugambe 2014, Leautier 2014 and Mendizabal 2014).

Adopting Arinaitwe's (2010) analysis of the role of think tanks in Africa to inclusive and sustainable development the following are 8 possible roles of social science think tanks:

1. To make expertise and talents available to governments by convening professionals together to share new ideas and create a common understanding of inclusive and sustainable development challenges;

2. To facilitate policy dialogue between the government, academia, civil society and other groups on specific issues related to inclusive and sustainable development;

3. To engage the public through education and capacity building to enrich the culture of embracing inclusive and sustainable development;

4. To act as lobby groups for democratic, open and accountable processes and institutions through policy analysis, research, decision-making, and evaluation;

5. To provide evidence from research that will inform agricultural development, security regulation, economic policy, policy innovations in welfare, education, health care, taxation, environment and climate change policies and reforms;

6. To do advocacy work in social policy and political strategy, economy, issues of science and technology issues and industrial and business policies;

7. To engage the public to accelerate and understand the dynamics of globalisation, integration, global events and institutions, and to bridge differences in areas of conflict; and

8. Assessing the validity and utility of ideals that form the basis of policy and develop new ideas upon which the policies of the future might be based.

The social science research agenda may be easy to conceptualise in the context of inclusive and sustainable development. Indeed the role of Think Tanks and social science organisation is clear but complex. It is complex in that it is shaped by the environment, the resources and the rules of engagement of policy makers and other stakeholders. It is complex also because of the competition with other institutions inside and outside individual countries and regions. The one that has the funds for such interventions may also be the one who defines the scope and perspective of social science research. Indeed the challenge for social science research will also be the provision of timely and quality knowledge products that are useful and needed. Think Tanks may for example trade off quality, impartiality and demand for funding. A continuous learning process should be how this role is relevant and can attract demand and support from all research constituencies especially countries and economies that appreciate the role of knowledge in nation building. Obviously, research organisations and think tanks in the social sciences also need to build their capacities to play their roles effectively.

5. Conclusion

The terms inclusive and sustainable refer to complex complex concepts and run the risk of being buzz words. It is important that conceptual distinctions are made so that in content and policy making the terms are not used interchangeably. It is true that economic growth alone cannot explain development. Growth that leads to meaningful development is that which reduces poverty. This is growth which is pro-poor. But it can be shown that what is in economic terms pro poor is not necessary inclusive growth even within economics itself. Growth may have been favourable to the poor as well as the rich but with variant inequality that leaves the poor worse off. Thus, within inclusive growth, it must be seen that both absolute and relative poverty are reduced in growth episodes. But, again, even if the two forms of poverty were reduced, inclusive growth is not synonymous to inclusive development because there are several forms of exclusion that are not captured by the economic measurements of income and consumption. These may be based on race, gender, geography, ethnicity and religion.

It can be shown that a dialogue has evolved since World War II to clarify the meaning of development required by major nations. The concepts of inclusive and sustainable development have come after a long decade of dialogue on both human and sustainable development. The call for sustainable development has involved world lobby for the environment and now the climate change. Ultimately in 2015 the Sustainable Development Goals have replaced Millennium Development Goals. Thus Sustainable Development in addition to the condition of being inclusive has embraced economic growth and poverty reduction, social inclusion, environment and climate change sensitivity, and good governance.

The concepts find currency in Africa with those of 'emergence of Africa' and 'Africa rising'. In the last decade, Africa, including Eastern and Southern Africa, has experienced fast growth. But the chapter has demonstrated that despite this reversal of the former position of Africa the same rapid growth is happening against rampant poverty levels, inequality, environmental stress, and gender imbalances. Data for the nine countries in Eastern and Southern Africa have been used generally to show the challenges faced. These are challenges that Africa, through the SDGs and Agenda 2063, has to address. There are emerging works challenging the Africa rising narrative on the grounds of economic diversification, foreign direct investments and varying degrees of capital flight. Finally, it has been argued that social sciences and think tanks have the opportunity to provide evidence based research for policy makers to work for more inclusive and sustainable development. On the supply side African Think Tanks need to align themselves to the needs for building inclusive and sustainable development and to provide the required knowledge inputs.

References

ACET. 2014. African transformation report 2014. Growth with depth. Accra viewed on 22.12.2015 http://acetforafrica.org/wp-content/uploads/2014/03/2014-African-Transformation-Report.pdf.AGRA.2013. Annual report. visited on 6.1.2016 https://www.google.com/url?sa=t&rct=j&q=&esrc=s&source=web&cd=2&ved=0ahUKEwi96ZTa7pnKAhXC1iwKHZ37Au0QFggjMAE&url=http%3A%2F%2Fwww.agra.org%2Fdownload%2F53a9751217556%2F&usg=AFQjCNEtDCwq9LwuTYX3V3xLIcGm-0DSBg.

Alesina, A. and Rodrick, D. 1994. Distributive politics and economic growth. *Quarterly Journal of Economics, Volume 109(20).pp. 465– 490.*

Amaceoglu, D. and Robinson, J. 2013. Why nations fail. The origins of power, prosperity and poverty. Available online viewed on 22.12.2015 http://norayr.arnet.am/collections/books/Why-Nations-Fail-Daron-Acemoglu.pdf.

Arinaitwe, R. 2010. The role and place of think tanks in decision and policy making in Africa. Consulting for development. CAFRAD. Available online viewed on 22.12.2015 http://tasam.org/Files/Icerik/File/_96f09336-2efb-46af-a52f-166e947f9f69.pdf.

Aworti, N. and Musahara, H. 2015. *Implementation of the Millennium Development Goals. Progress and challenges in selected eastern and southern African countries*. OSSREA. Addis Ababa.

Berkley Earth. 2013. About Berkeley Earth. Berkeley. California HTTPS//:berkeleyearth.org.

Brundtland Commission Report. 1987. *Our common future*. Report of the Commission on Environment. UN General Assembly. New York

Block, S. 2010.The rise and fall of agricultural productivity in Sub Saharan Africa from 1961. *NBER working paper* 16481. National Bureau of Economic Research. Cambridge.

Bokova, I. 2013. Preface to the World Social Science Report 2013. International Social Science Council. Paris.

Carbone, G. 2015. Africa still rising? Italian Institute for International Political Studies. Milano.

Cornwal, A. and Eade, D. 2013. *Deconstructing development discourse.* Buzzwords and Fuzzwords.

Dollar, D. and Kraay, A. 2001. Growth is good for the poor. World Bank e library Washington.   see   summary   at http://elibrary.worldbank.org/doi/abs/10.1596/1813-9450-2587.

Domar, E. 1946. Capital expansion, growth and employment. *Econometricak,* 14. pp 137–147.

Draman, R. 2003. Poverty and conflict in Africa. Explaining a complex relationship. Expert Group on Africa-Canada on Parliamentary Strengthening Programme. Final Paper. Addis Ababa http://www.harep.org/ifaapr/semi.pdf.

Grosse, M. Harttgen, K. and Klassen, S. 2005. Measuring pro poor growth in non income dimesnaions. *World Development Report,* Vol. 36. Elservier.

Hackmann, H. and St. Clair, L. 2012. Introducing the World Social Science Report. Transformative cornerstones for social science resaerch for global change. WSSC 2013. Paris.

Harrod, R. 1939. An essay in dynamic theory. *The Economic Journal,* Vol. 49(193): 14–33.

Havnevik, K. 2015. The current Afro optimism. A realistic image of Africa? *Scandinavian Journal of Intercultural Theory and Policy,* Vol. 2 No. 2 NAI Uppsala.

INCLUDE. 2014. Inclusive Development Knowledge Platform Network. Leiden.

ISSC/UNESCO. 2013. *World Social Science Report 2013: Changing Global Environments.* Paris: OECD Publishing and UNESCO Publishing.

Kakwani, N. and Pernia, E. 2000. What is pro-poor growth? Policy innovations. *Asian Development Review,* Vol. 8 No 1.

Kanbur, R. and Rauyinar, G. 2010. Inclusive development: Two papers on conceptualization and application. ADB.

Klasen, S. 2010. *Measuring and monitoring inclusive growth.* Mandaluyong City, Phillipines. Asian Development Bank.

Kraay, A. 2004. When growth is pro-poor? Cross country evidence. *IMF WP/4/47.*

Kuznets, S. 1955. Economic growth and income inequality. *American Review,* Vol XLV Number 1 pp. 1–28.

Leautier, F. 2014. Think tanks in Africa as catalysts for ideas and action. Key note speech to the First Regional African Think Tank Summit. Pretoria.

Mendizabal, E. 2014. A quick and dirty transparify like assessment of TTI think tanks blog. https://onthinktanks.org/articles/a-quick-and-dirty-transparify-like-assessment-of-tti-think-tanks/.

Mugambe, B. 2014. Maximising the role of think tanks in policy making. World Economic Forum Uganda. http://www.devinit.org/maximising-the-role-of-african-thinkMusahara, H. 2015. African emergence, inclusive and sustainable development and the role of social science research. Forthcoming Chapter 10 of *Integration, currency union, and sustainable and inclusive growth in East Africa.* Springer.

North, D. 1990. Institutions, institutional change and economic performance. Available on amazon. http://www.amazon.com/Institutions-Institutional-Performance-Political-Decisions/dp/0521397340.

OECD. 2014. All on board. Making inclusive growth happen. Paris.

———. 2001. Promoting pro-poor growth. Social protection. OECD Report. Paris.

OECD. 2005. Annual Report. Paris.

OXFAM. 2014.What is inclusive growth. CAFOD discussion paper viewed 26.12.2015 file:///C:/Users/ossrea/Downloads/Inclusive%20Growth%20full%20paper.pdf.

Norton, A. and Rogerson, A. 2012. Inclusive and sustainable development. Challenges, opportunities, policies and partnerships. ODI Paper prepared for International High Level Conference on 5o[th] Anniversary of DANIDA.

Ravallion, R. and Shen, S. 2003. Measuring pro-poor growth. *Economics Letter,* 78. World Bank: Development Research Working Group.

Rostow, W.W. 1960. *Stages of economic growth. A non-communist manifesto.* Cambridge University Press.

Sachs, J. 2013. The challenge of sustainable development and the social sciences. *In:* World Social Science Report, 2013. Changing Global Environments. P. 79 ISSC. UNESCO. Paris.

Sachs, J. 2014 . Sustainable Development Solutions Network. New York.

Sachs, J. 2015. *Age of sustainable development.* New York: Columbia University Press.

SDSN. 2015. *Sustainable development goals.* Working group. New York.

Sen, A. 1988. The concept of development. *In* Rodrick, D. and Rosenzweig, M. (Eds.), *Handbook of development economics.* Amsterdam: Elservier.

Sen, A. 1999. *Introduction. Development as Freedom.* First Anchor Book Edition. New York.

Schumpeter, J 1961. Theory of economic development. Translated from German. Oxford: Oxford University Press.

Stivers, R. 1976. The sustainable society. Ethics and Economics. Amazon book. http://www.amazon.com/The-sustainable-society-Ethics-economic/dp/066424789X.

Solow, R. 1956. A contribution to the theory of economic growth. *Quarter 1 Journal of Economics,* 70(1): 65–94.

Swan, T. 1956. *Economic growth and capital accumulation.* Economic Record (Wiley) 32 pp 334–361.

Stuart, E. 2011. Making growth inclusive. Oxfam Research Reports

Streeten, P. 1979. *Basic needs. Premises and promises*. World Bank Reprint series. Originally from Journal of Policy Modelling.

Sutcliffe, R. 1980. Industry and underdevelopment. Addison-Wesley. Massachusets.

Transparify. 2014. Think tanks articles. at www.transparify.org.

UN. 2000. *Millennium Declaration*. New York: United Nations.

UN. 2013. Sustainable Development Solutions Network. New York: United Nations.

UN. 2015. Sustainable Development Goals. New York. http://www.un.org/sustainabledevelopment/sustainable-development-goals/.

UNDP. 1990. Human Development Report. Concepts and measurement. UNDP, New York.

UNDP. 2015. *Human Development Report*. New York.

UNECA. 2013. *Economic Report on Africa*. Addis Ababa.

Verstegen, S. 2001. *Poverty and conflict*. Entitlement Perspective Conflict Prevention Network. Berlin.

World Bank. 2000/1. *Attacking poverty*. Washington D.C.: World Development Report.

World Economic Situation and Prospects. 2015. http://www.unescap.org/resources/presentation-world-economic-situation-and-prospects-2015.

CHAPTER TWO

Trade and Inclusive Development in Mauritius: Evidence from a Dynamic Framework

Sheereen Fauzel

Abstract

Trade openness has always been viewed as an important element in Mauritius. Trade not only increases a country's access to a wide variety of goods and services but also acts as a vehicle through which there is a transfer of knowledge and technology; it serves an engine that boosts entrepreneurship in the private sector; it is a variable that attracts foreign capital; it creates employment, reduces distortions in price relatives, increases foreign earnings, and encourages the production of goods and services with comparative advantages (WTO 2008). These benefits obviously have various advantages to the country in the sense that economic growth is promoted and social welfare is enhanced. The aim of this study is to investigate the extent to which trade openness has led to inclusive development in Mauritius during the period 1980 to 2013. For inclusive development to take place, the economy should grow and there should be an increase in social welfare, or alternatively there should be a reduction in poverty level. Hence, focusing on this aspect, this study has used a dynamic Vector Error Correction Model (VECM) to investigate the issue. The results provide indicative evidence that trade openness plays an important role in generating gains in terms of economic growth both in the short and in the long run. Referring to the results, it is further noted that trade openness has also contributed towards boosting social welfare in the country. Moreover, the Granger-causality results show that there is a uni-directional causality flowing from trade openness to welfare variables.

Keywords: Trade, inclucive development, ..., dynamic framework

1. Introduction

An open economy has been considered an important engine for growth by many economists as compared to a closed one. However, many policy makers have also feared that trade openness might come to harm those down the income ladder. For instance, many African countries have been experiencing important improvements in trade liberalisation but still the continent is classified among the poorest in the world. Hence, significant gains expected from adopting trade openness policies have been partial in Africa, mainly for those down the income ladder (Le Goff and Singh 2013).

Since independence in 1968, Mauritius has advanced from a low-income, monoculture economy to a middle-income, well diversified economy.

Mauritius has also been formulating policies to open up the economy, adopting a mixed strategy of import substitution together with incentives for exports through the export processing zone (EPZ). Mauritius' economy was mainly based on agriculture However, there has been significant diversification in the economy whereby other sectors such as industrial, financial, and tourism sectors have flourished. Moreover, the economy has registered a high growth over the last several decades. As a result, several improvements have been observed in the economy such as more equitable income distribution, increased life expectancy, lower infant mortality, and a much-improved infrastructure.   The main drivers of growth for the economy have been the sugar, tourism, textiles and apparel, and financial service sectors. The fish processing, information and communications technology, hospitality and property development sectors have also played a big part. In 2014, Mauritius was classified as an upper middle-income country with a gross national income per capita of $9710.   Mauritius has been devising policies to ensure poverty reduction through the creation of jobs and the provision of better quality of life for its population by maintaining social cohesion (Ramessur and Durbarry 2009). The poverty rate today is lower than in some other sub-Saharan African countries.

2. Evolution of HDI in Mauritius

Mauritius has achieved sustained progress in the past decades. Also, the level of inequality has been decreasing. The economy has been progressing mainly because of the development in the export processing zone (EPZ). Furthermore, the government has been adopting various policies which benefitted the economy to a great extent.

The human development index (HDI) has also been improving throughout the past years. In fact, it is a composite measure of three basic dimensions of human development: health, education, and income. According to the United Nations Development Programme, the Human Development Index of Mauritius was 0.771 in 2014, which was quite close to the HDI of the North African economy at 0.784. Mauritius was ranked second in Africa after Libya on human development, with the two countries achieving global ranks of 63rd and 55th, respectively, in the high human development category, out of 187 countries which were ranked on the Human Development Index in 2014.

According to the Global 2014 Human Development Report of the United Nations entitled "Sustaining Human Progress: Reducing Vulnerabilities and Building Resilience", there are categories into which countries are classified: very high, high, medium and low. Mauritius has been classified under the 'high' category, which it has maintained since 2013.

Figure 1 shows the evolution of HDI for Mauritius compared to sub-Saharan Africa and the world. It can be noted that Mauritius has a higher score on HDI as compared to sub-Saharan Africa.

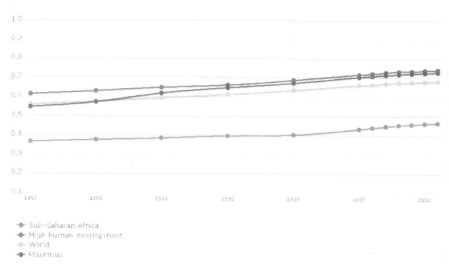

Figure 1. Evolution of HDI for Mauritius Compared to Sub-Saharan Africa and the World
SOURCE: http://www.wikiprogress.org/

Table 1 below summarises the selected indicators of welfare for Mauritius.

Table 1. Selected indicators on education and employment, Republic of Mauritius - 1990, 2000 and 2011

	1990	2000	2011
Illiteracy rate[1] (%)	19.2	14.5	9.9
Percentage of population aged 6 to 11 years not attending school (%)	3.4	1.0	0.2
Percentage of population aged 12 to 19 years not attending school (%)	51.4	36.9	19.1
Percentage of population aged 18 years and over without an O-level qualification (%)	83.1	77.0	65.3
Unemployment rate[2] (%)	5.3	8.9	7.5
Percentage of employed persons aged 16 years and over engaged in low[3] occupations	47.7	39.9	27.8

SOURCE: Housing and Population Census 1990, 2000 and 2011

The illiteracy rate declined between 1990 and 2011 from 19.2% to 9.9% showing an improvement in the educational attainment of the population. Being a key ingredient for economic growth and development, education has benefited the island throughout this period. However, over the same period, the unemployment rate has increased from 5.3% to 7.5%. Hence, though the illiteracy rate has fallen, this has not really contributed to the creation of jobs in the country. Hence, one can claim that there is a mismatch between education and employment needs in Mauritius.

3. Growth in Trade in Mauritius

Since 1975, Mauritius has been undergoing a record growth in international trade and this has mainly been due to the signing of trade agreements and the removal of trade barriers. Mauritius is a member of a number of regional trade agreements including AGOA (African Growth and Opportunity Act), COMESA (Common Market for Eastern and Southern Africa), IORA (Indian Ocean Rim Association), SADC (Southern African Development Community) and interim EPA (Economic Partnership Agreement) with EU (European Union), and is also a member of the GSP (Generalised Scheme of Preferences) scheme and WTO (World Trade Organization) for multilateral trade agreements. Moreover, Mauritius has bilateral trade agreements with the USA, Pakistan, and Turkey (Mauritius Trade Easy 2015).

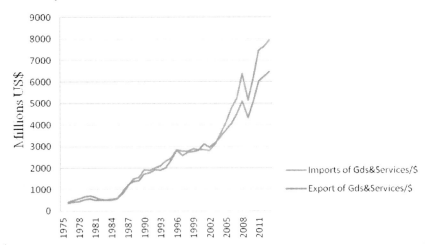

Figure 2. Trends in Exports and Imports of Goods and Services (US $) for Mauritius from 1975–2013
SOURCE: Computed from World Bank database

Mauritius imports mainly manufactured goods, capital goods, foodstuffs, oil, and chemical products from India, China, France, and South Africa. The country is also highly dependent on oil. The main export partners are the European market, Madagascar, and the USA, amongst others, to which

Mauritius exports clothing, sugar, flowers, molasses, and fish. Watches and diamonds are thriving exports. Mauritius is also making efforts to diversify its exports to other sectors including the seafood industry and jewellery. The above figure shows the trend in exports and imports of goods and services (US $) for Mauritius from 1975 to 2013.

4.   Literature Review

4.1. Review of the Theoretical Literature

Trade openness can have important influences on the welfare of the poor through various channels (Bannister and Thugge 2001):

1) **Trade can change the price of tradable goods:**   For example, it lowers the price of imports for poor consumers.

2) **Trade facilitates the importation of technologies and processes** in low income countries. This can help poor consumers and producers, for example, when low-cost technologies for packaging perishable foods or better quality seeds and fertilisers are imported. Also, trade can aid anti-poverty programs and social policies by facilitating the importation of products and technologies used in these programs.

3) **Trade leads to an improvement in the economic welfare of a country**. A number of economic models have linked trade, growth, and poverty for developing countries and shown that increased trade can contribute to economic growth and poverty reduction. The international liberalisation of markets can improve economic growth. It enhances the free movement of goods and increases specialisation and the production of goods by countries in which they have a comparative advantage. This leads to an increase in total output, income, and employment, thereby benefitting consumers.

4) **Trade and Employment Creation:** Trade can have significant effects on wages and employment. Stolper-Samuelson (SS) theorem, for example, states:

> A rise in the relative price of a commodity leads to a rise in the real return to the factor used intensely in producing that commodity. Thus, for a developing country with a highly protected production structure, liberalization will result in a rise in the relative price of unskilled workers.   As the market for labour-intensive products expands; so the demand for unskilled workers will raise leading to higher returns to unskilled labours in general (Stolper and Samuelson (1941) as quoted in Bannister and Thugge 2001).

So, with trade liberalisation we would expect more unskilled workers to be employed and real wages to rise. However, this theorem does not always apply in practice as it is based on restrictive assumptions about technologies, labour markets, and the number of products and factors.

5) **The impact of trade on government revenues and programs for the poor:** Trade openness and trade reforms may lead to lower government revenues as trade taxes are reduced. Given such a situation, governments may reduce social expenditures or even introduce new taxes to maintain macroeconomic stability. Both of these policies would affect the poor. However, when a country first adopts trade liberalisation policies, it might replace non-tariff barriers with tariffs, thereby generating revenues for government. If initial tariffs are excessively high, lowering them can result in higher trade flows and/or reduce the incentives for smuggling and corruption, which could increase revenues. Also, implementing simpler tariff regimes can increase fiscal revenues.

6) **Investment, innovation, and growth:** Trade openness has the potential to boost economic growth as it can reduce the anti-export bias of a country's trade policy and, thus, leads to a more efficient allocation of resources. In the long run, trade liberalisation can lead to higher growth by creating incentives to boost investment; better trade regime usually stimulates foreign direct investment. Hence, the country benefits from the advantages of the inflow of foreign capital and from technological and managerial spillovers which can increase the overall productivity and growth of local firms.

7) **Vulnerability to negative external shocks:** Better trade policies can lead to more trade openness and extend economic integration with other countries. This will enable a country to diversify its exports and be less dependent on a single export market. Also, trading on the foreign markets helps a country become less dependent on the local market and, thus, local economic recessions or downturns are counterweighed by the growth of the international economy. However, openness may also make an economy become very susceptible to external shocks, such as abrupt changes in the terms of trade that can significantly reduce growth. If the shocks directly affect agricultural or informal sectors, they can have significant adverse effects on the poor.

4.2. Review of the Empirical Literature

From both a theoretical and empirical point of view, the investigation of the impact of trade openness on welfare is far from being conclusive. Research on the link between trade and poverty is limited mainly to case studies. Some analyses have employed computable-general-equilibrium (CGE) models to trace the effects of trade reform on the poor. The general consensus in the literature is that, in the long run, trade openness benefits the aggregate economy more than the closed economy. Trade liberalisation policies have also been found to significantly contribute to economic development. In the short run, however, trade may not be pro-poor as they are seen to affect the poorer actors in the economy.

For instance, there are studies like Bhagwati and Srinivasan (2002) which examined how freer trade affects poverty, taking resources and technology as given, and the growth effects and the evolution of poverty over time. In general, studies like Winters (2000a) found that trade reform generally increases the income of the poor as a group and that the transition costs are generally small relative to the overall benefits. Nonetheless, there are circumstances where the short-run effects of trade liberalisation on the poor are negative. The significant benefits from liberalisation come from dynamic gains such as more efficient patterns of investment and technological diffusion. Also, they do not include the effects of complementary policies that facilitate adjustment to the new free-trade equilibrium. Given these explanations, the studies are likely to significantly exaggerate liberalisation's costs and minimise its benefits, even for the poor. Over the medium term, changes in investment and economic growth can significantly exceed the negative distributional effects of changes in prices that result from trade liberalisation (Bannister, and Thugge 2001).

Another strand of the literature argues that economic growth is crucial for poverty alleviation and that trade liberalisation has the potential to boost productivity and economic growth. In light of this discussion, Bhagwati (2004) argued that trade helps to foster economic growth, thereby leading to higher incomes and in turn to a reduction in poverty. Studies like Berg and Krueger (2003); Grossman and Helpman (1991), and Lucas (1988) contended that freer trade boosts investment and favours more openness to new ideas and innovations. Also, the studies pointed out that, for comparative advantage to boost the incomes of unskilled workers, these workers should be able to move from shrinking to expanding sectors. However, some studies like Davis and Mishra (2006), Goh and Javorcik (2006), and Topalova (2006) advocated that labour is rather immobile in the real world and there are too many barriers for firms to come into or get out of countries, and too many barriers for workers to move from one country to another. Hence, the anticipated benefits from freer trade may not happen.

Several cross-country studies on poverty, which did not deal with trade explicitly, have incorporated trade openness as a control variable and shown that the benefits of greater trade openness seem to have bypassed the poor (Beck, Demirgüç-Kunt, and Levine 2007; Dollar and Kraay 2001; Guillaumont-Jeanneney and Kpodar 2011; Kpodar and Singh 2011; Singh and Huang 2011). Other studies, for instance, Dollar (1992), Sachs and Warner (1995), and Edwards (1998), using various cross country studies and different measures of openness, have shown a positive link between trade and economic growth. However, the studies mentioned have been criticised on their openness and protection measures, their econometric techniques, and the problem to establish the direction of causation between the main variables.

4.2.1 Trade, Employment and Poverty

An important mechanism by which trade openness is translated into poverty impacts is through job creation. Certainly, securing employment is one of the best ways to come out of poverty. The structure of the labour market is important to how trade liberalisation induces changes in wages and employment (Ramessur and Durbarry 2009). Referring to empirical evidence, Rama (1994) applied a model of monopolistic competition to a panel of 39 sectors in Uruguay over 1979-86 and reported a significant and positive relationship between protection and employment in manufacturing but no significant effects on real wages. Also, Revenga (1997) did not find any effect of tariff cuts on employment in Mexico. Likewise, minor employment effects were reported elsewhere in Latin America as stated by, for example, Marquez and Pages-Serra (1998) for Latin America and the Caribbean in general, Levinsohn (1999) for Chile, and Moreira and Najberg (2000) for Brazil.

By analysing the literature on trade, it is noted that most studies have been focusing on the impact of trade liberalisation on economic growth. However, this study will investigate the role of trade openness on economic development. The focus of the present study is to investigate the link between trade openness and economic development and social welfare of the country.

5. Gaps in the Literature

As previously stated, most research has focused mainly on the role of trade liberalisation and its impact on economic growth (Dollar and Kraay 2004; Lee and Vivarelli 2004). However, the focus of this study is on the role of trade openness on the economic development of Mauritius for the period 1980 to 2013. The major novelty of this study is that it does not link economic development to growth only but to social welfare as well. Hence, the main objective of the study is to investigate the extent to which trade openness has led to inclusive development in the country. This paper is believed to depart from and contribute to the existing literature in various ways. A dynamic panel analysis has been employed for this investigation. Also, a Vector Error Correction Model (VECM) has been used to determine the relationship between trade openness and economic development while simultaneously allowing the identification of any bi-directional and/or unidirectional causality between the variables of interest.

Accordingly, this study also investigates trade openness, economic growth, as well as social welfare. Finally, Granger-Causality tests are performed in order to discern the exact direction of causality between the variables.

6. Methods

This section describes the models adopted and the empirical indicators of welfare, trade, and economic growth, and other control variables used in the model. Even though there is no clear assistance from theory on the choice of regressors that can be used to model the investigation in this study, it leads to the possibility of using a wide set of specifications. However, referring to the basic specification of the papers discussed in the empirical review, the econometric models take the following functional forms:

Model Specifications
Model 1:

$$GDP = \beta_0 + \beta_1 OPENt + \beta_2 EMPLOYMENTt + \beta_3 CPIt + \beta_4 GOVT\ EXP + ut \text{-----}(1)$$

Model 2:

$$HDI = \beta_0 + \beta_1 OPENt + \beta_2 EMPLOYMENTt + \beta_3 CPIt + \beta_4 GOVT\ EXP + ut \text{------}(2)$$

The variables are described in Table 2.

Table 2. Description of Variables

Variables*	Definition	Measurement
Emp	Employment level	In employment
Inf	Inflation Rate	In CPI
Gov Exp	Govt expenditure on social aid	In real government expenditure on social aid
Real Growth	Real economic growth	In real GDP
Open	Trade Openness	In Trade openness: Export + imports/GDP

Note: However, because of the variance stabilising properties of log transformation, the logvalues of the variables are used. In fact, logged variables yield a more clear-cut interpretation of the coefficients in terms of percentage change.

The variables adopted are economic growth (proxy for economic welfare), inflation, employment rate (refer to Blank and Blinder 1986; Cutler and Katz 1991; Powers 1993), HDI (proxy for welfare), (refer to Gohou and Soumare 2010), and government expenditure on social aid (see Agenor 2005 and Castro-Leal *et al.* 2000). To account for trade, the variable trade openness (ratio of imports and exports to GDP) (refer to Loko 2007) has been adopted. The variables are further defined below:

HDI: There have been various welfare measures used in the literature to assess the economic development of countries. Mostly, the GDP per capita and the poverty headcount ratio have been used as welfare indicators. On the one hand, while GDP per capita is widely used, it should be noted that GDP captures only the economic dimension of progress made by countries. However, economic development is a multi-dimensional phenomenon and it depends on various influences including heath care and education, among other things. Alternatively, poverty incidence is a more accurate measure of well-being in a country as it considers all facets of an individual (health, education, access to basic services, food, etc.) and measures these facets against the minimum needed for a good standard of living (Gohou and

Soumare 2010). However, this study has used a more suitable indicator of wellbeing, which is the Human Development Index (HDI), as provided by the United Nations Development Programme (UNDP). HDI is considered as the best available measure of a country's human development. Hence, the main welfare indicator used in this study is HDI, and according to the UNDP, "The HDI – human development index – is a summary composite index that measures a country's average achievements in three basic aspects of human development: health, knowledge, and a decent standard of living. Health is measured by life expectancy at birth; knowledge is measured by a combination of the adult literacy rate and the combined primary, secondary, and tertiary gross enrolment ratio; and standard of living by GDP per capita (PPP US$)." Following Gohou and Soumare (2010), HDI is used as a proxy for welfare and poverty alleviation.(Refer to the technical note of the Human Development Report available on the UNDP website at http://hdr.undp.org/en/media/HDR_20072008_Tech_Note_1.pdf   for   a better understanding of the variable HDI).

Economic Growth: Many studies have been associating economic growth as an indicator of welfare for a particular country. Economic growth does contribute towards the economic development of a particular country both through direct and indirect channels. However, the major criticism towards using economic growth as a welfare indicator pertains to the fact that growth of a country mainly relates to economic welfare. In fact, higher growth does not always mean higher social welfare. Hence, if a country is experiencing an increase in its GDP, it does not really indicate that standard of living of the population has increased as well. Referring to the economy of Mauritius, however, it is noted that real GDP has increased during the period from 1980 to 2013, and within the same period, the income of the average Mauritian has also increased. Besides, according to the poverty analysis report as provided by Statistics Mauritius, poverty incidence has been decreasing in the country.

Employment: It is crucial to note that the economy of Mauritius has grown mainly because of the development of the EPZ sector in the country during the 1980's. This sector was mainly labour-intensive, and, thus, one can argue that employment has played a significant role in boosting the income level of the population. Also, it has contributed towards achieving economic growth in the country as well. Furthermore, employment is an important regressor that will certainly influence welfare in the country. In order to capture the employment effect, the aggregate (economically active) level of employment is used in the present study and the data is extracted from the database of Statistics Mauritius. Employment is computed on the Continuous Multi-Purpose Household Survey (CMPHS). Studies using this proxy include Blank and Blinder (1986), Cutler and Katz (1991), and Powers (1993).

Inflation: The consumer price index is used to measure inflation. On average, Mauritius has been recording a one-digit level of inflation throughout the last decade. The level of inflation in the country has been fluctuating, though not widely, but still with negative repercussions on the poor. Mauritius is a country which is highly dependent on imports for its basic necessities like rice, milk, and petroleum products. Hence, given that the poor spend a large proportion of their income on basic foods, rising prices of food are seen as taxes on the poor and, thus, it becomes very important to investigate the impact of inflation on welfare in the country.

Government Expenditure on Social Aid: Mauritius has introduced policies to maximise social welfare in the country. These policies include the provision of free education; free health facilities; and social aid to widows, orphans, and other vulnerable groups. Moreover, there is a well-established basic retirement plan also known as basic retirement pension, which is given to people above the age of 60 years. The public expenditure on social aid and social welfare has always been given tremendous importance by policy makers in Mauritius. However, policies regarding investment in social welfare, such as free education, may take time to have their full effect on the economy. Hence, one would expect the positive effect of government expenditure to show in the long-run, not in the immediate future. Data is extracted from Statistics Mauritius.

Trade Openness: To capture the effect of trade openness, the ratio of imports and exports to GDP has been used. The expected sign for this variable is ambiguous and the changes in the long run may be different from those in the short run. Table 3 shows the expected signs for each coefficient of the variables.

Table 3. Expected signs on controlled variables

Variables	Expected Signs Model 1	Expected Signs Model 2
Employment	+	+
Inflation	-	-
Expenditure on social aid	+	+
Trade openness	?	?

6.1 Estimation Issues
Before proceeding with the estimation of the model, it is important to investigate the time series properties of all the individual data series. Firstly, the unit roots properties of the time series are investigated, and, once the order of integration has been determined, the likelihood of a long-run link among the variables of interest is also studied.

6.2 Tests for Stationarity
Applying regression on time series data may generate spurious results (Granger and Newbold 1974; Philips 1986), given the possibility of non-stationarity data. As such, undertaking a check as to the stationarity of data is a prerequisite for applying the co-integration test. As a result, the

Augmented Dickey-Fuller (ADF) test (Dickey and Fuller 1979) and the Phillips-Perron test (Phillips and Perron 1988) were applied.

To test the presence of co-integration, the Johansen Maximum Likelihood test is used. This test will enable the detection of any long-run relationship between variables which are integrated at the same order. This concept was first put forward by Engle and Granger (1987). It was, then, expanded by Stock and Watson (1993), Johansen (1988), and Johansen and Juselius (1990). Also, in contrast to the two-step estimation approach by Engle and Granger (1987) by which only one co-integrating vector can be found, Johansen (1988) and Johansen and Juselius (1990) suggest maximum likelihood testing procedure to find out the number of co-integrating vectors in the Vector Autoregressive (VAR) representation. The general form of VAR is as follows:

$$x_t = \alpha + \beta_t x_{t-1} + \ldots\ldots + \beta_k x_{t-k} + \varepsilon_t$$

Where X_t is an (n x 1) column vector of k variables, that are integrated of order 1, α is an (n x 1) vector of intercepts, $\beta_t \ldots\ldots \beta_{t-k}$ are parameters and ε_t is an independently and identically distributed error term. The general VAR model presented above can also be reformulated in the following alternative form of vector error correction model (VECM).

$$\Delta x_t = \alpha + \sum_{i=1}^{p-1} \Gamma_i \Delta x_{t-i} + \Pi x_{t-1} + \varepsilon_t$$

Where X_t is an (n x 1) column vector of ρ variables, α is an (n x 1) vector of constant terms, ε_t is an (n x 1) vector of usual error term, Δ is difference operator, and Γ and Π represent coefficient matrices. The coefficient matrix Π is also termed as impact matrix and it explains the long-term equilibrium relationships of the variables, while the coefficient matrix Γ captures the short-run impact.

A VAR approach is used to delineate the relationship between trade and economic development. One can argue that such an approach does not impose *a priori* restriction on the dynamic relations among the different variables. It is like a simultaneous equation modelling, whereby several endogenous variables are considered together. Hence, the VECM linking short-term and long-term causality between trade and economic development is set as follows:

Model 1:

$$\Delta gc \sum\nolimits_{j}^{n} \alpha_0 + \sum\nolimits_{j=1}^{n} \alpha_1 \Delta open_{t-j} + \sum\nolimits_{j=1}^{n} \alpha_2 \Delta employment_{t-j} + \sum\nolimits_{j=1}^{n} \alpha_3 \Delta cpi_{t-j} + \sum\nolimits_{j=1}^{n} \alpha_4 \Delta \ln govtexp_{t-j} + \eta ECT_{t-1} + \varepsilon_t \text{-------------------------------(3)}$$

Model 2:
$$+ \sum_{j=1}^{n} \alpha_1 \Delta\, open_{t-j} + \sum_{j=1}^{n} \alpha_2 \Delta\, employment_{t-j} + \sum_{j=1}^{n} \alpha_3 \Delta\, cpi_{t-j}$$
$$+ \sum_{j=1}^{n} \alpha_4 \Delta\, \ln govtexp_{t-j} + \eta\, ECT_{t-1} + \varepsilon_t \text{---}$$
(4)

The coefficient of the error correction term (ECT_{t-1}) indicates whether there exists a short-run relationship among the time series variables. Referring to Banerjee *et al.* (1998), if the error correction term is negative and significant, it implies that there exists a rather long-run equilibrium in the model.

7. Analysis of Data

From the application of the augmented Dickey-Fuller (ADF) (1979) and Phillips-Perron (PP) (1988) unit-roots tests, it is observed that the variables are integrated of order 1 and stationary in first difference.

The Johansen Maximum Likelihood approach is subsequently used to test the presence of co-integration in a vector error correction model in both specifications. Trace statistics and maximal eigenvalue confirm the presence of co-integration and, thus, it can be concluded that a long-run relationship exists in both of the above specifications.

7.1 Empirical Results
The long-run coefficients of the analysis are reported in the equations below:

gdp = 22.778 – 1.2547*cpi + 1.6638***employment + 0.1577** govtexp
social aid + 0.077*open---(5)

hdi = 1.1074 – 0.0225 employment –0.1158* cpi + 0.0136*** govtexp
social aid + 0.0869*open---(6)

*Indicates the significance at 10%, ** significance at 5% and
***significance at 1%

The long-run equation yields very interesting results. For instance, it is observed from equation 5 that trade openness has contributed towards boosting the economic growth of the country; a 1% increase in trade openness has led to an increase in economic growth of 0.08%. This result is in line with Sachs and Warner (1995); Edwards (1998); Frankel and Romer (1999); Dollar and Kraay (2004); Lee and Vivarelli (2004). These empirical investigations showed that, in the long run, more outward-oriented countries register higher economic growth. Hence, one can argue that trade has really benefitted the economy of Mauritius. Relating this result to Mauritius, it is observed that the island has been categorised as a well-known economic success, mainly due to a well-established EPZ sector. The success of the Mauritian EPZ is based on a number of factors. The Mauritian government has devised various policies conducive to investment and several trade liberalisation policies have been adopted. As documented by Johansson and Nilsson (1997), out of a number of studied EPZs, it was normally those economies that have applied trade liberalisation measures that registered positive effects in their economies. Accordingly, it was argued that the EPZ can be considered as a stepping stone towards a generally more open economy, which was the case for Mauritius.

However, the main objective of the study was to analyse whether trade has led to the economic development of the country. Thus, apart from economic welfare, the study investigated the extent to which trade openness has contributed towards improving the social welfare of the country. A measure of social welfare applied in this study is HDI. From the results reported in equation 6 above, it is observed that an increase in trade openness has led to an increase in HDI in the long run as well. Therefore, it can be concluded that trade openness in the country has led to economic development. Hence, according to the results obtained, trade openness has contributed to both economic development and social welfare of the country.

Employment is included in the model to capture its effect on the dependent variables. Employment has had a positive impact on the economy. This is in line with theory postulating that an increase in employment will lead to an increase in output, thereby generating growth. It should be noted that with trade openness, and subsequently with the success of the EPZ sector, there was significant job creation in the country. Employment was created mostly for female labour, which ultimately led to a better standard of living in the country.

As far as inflation is concerned, it can be observed that it negatively affected growth and welfare in the country as expected. Inflation has a negative impact on real wages and it is mostly low income earners who suffer from increasing prices. Another important observation from the long-run results relates to the coefficient on real government expenditure on social security and welfare. Here, it can be observed that the social aid has benefitted the population in terms of boosting social welfare but the coefficient is relatively small. In Mauritius, various categories of people benefit from social aid from the government, including widows, orphans, the handicapped, and people who cannot take jobs due to health problems. However, the major criticism against the social aid provided is that it is very limited and not always sufficient for the needy.

7.2 The Short-run Regression
In the presence of co-integration, the next step is to estimate a VECM, including the error correction term, which should allow for an investigation of the dynamic nature of the model. The VECM specification forces the long-run behaviour of the endogenous variables to converge towards their co-integrated relationships, which accommodates short-run dynamics. The

empirical results of the short-run estimates of the VECM are displayed in table 4.

Table 4. Short run Estimates

Regressors	Model 1 Δgdp_t	Model 2 Δhdi_t
Δhdi_{t-1}		1.0585***
Δreal growth$_{t-1}$	0.2805*	
Δemployment$_{t-1}$	0.9391*	-0.0119
Δcpi_{t-1}	-0.5696	-0.0193**
$\Delta open_{t-1}$	0.0494*	0.0004***
Δge_{t-1}	0.3069	0.0010**
Constant	0.0559**	0.0008***
ECT (-1)	-0.809*	-0.088*
R^2	0.80	0.98

*Indicates the significance at 10%, ** significance at 5% and ***significance at 1%*

SOURCE: Author's computation

Table 5 is a composite table, where each column can be analysed as an independent function. Results of the short-run estimates turned out to be different from the long-run ones. Column one gives an insight on the impact of trade openness on economic growth while column two allows for an investigation on the impact of trade openness on social welfare in the short run.

Analysing the short-run results in column two with HDI_t as the dependent variable, it can be observed that trade openness has contributed to boosting social welfare in the country, but the magnitude of the coefficient is very small. This can be explained by the fact that trade policies take time to have their full effect on social welfare in a country. Looking at column one with real GDP as the dependent variable, it can be seen that trade openness has a positive impact on economic welfare in the country in the short run. However, trade openness has contributed more to economic development in the long run than in the short run.

Furthermore, the coefficient for real government expenditure on social aid and welfare does not have a significant impact on economic growth but does boost social welfare in the short run. Moreover, employment has a positive and significant effect in model 1. This shows that the labour market is important for boosting welfare. Further analysis of the results for inflation shows that it worsens welfare. This result is in line with Mocan (2005) and Easterly and Fischer (2000), who argue that inflation makes the poor worse off as they have difficulties to insulate themselves from the effect of increases in prices.

7.3. Granger Causality Based on VECM

To investigate whether any causal relationship exists between trade openness and economic development and social welfare, the Granger-

Causality test is adopted. Granger-Causality tests are adopted in order to detect the direction of causality between trade and welfare. The Granger-Causality test allows for the test of the null hypothesis: variable X does not Granger-Cause variable Y, against the alternative that variable X does Granger-Cause variable Y. The results are presented in the Table 5, where the symbol '→' indicates the direction of Granger Causality.

Table 5. Results of the Granger-Causality test

	F-Statistic	Prob.	Direction of causality
Open → Social Welfare	4.64660	0.0184	Open→Social Welfare
Social Welfare → Open	1.54476	0.2316	
Economic Welfare → Open	0.00681	0.9932	Open→Economic Welfa
Open →Economic Welfare	3.17642	0.0577	

The findings show a unidirectional causality between trade openness and economic development and social welfare. The causality direction runs from trade openness to the welfare variables.

8. Conclusion

This paper investigated the relationship between trade openness and economic development in Mauritius for the period 19980–2013. The study has used a rigorous vector error correction model to explore the interaction among trade openness, economic growth, human development index, employment, inflation and real government expenditure on social aid. Although openness induced a relatively higher positive impact on economic welfare, the magnitude of the coefficient was quite small in the short run.

The employment level in the country has a positive effect on economic growth. With trade openness, and subsequently with the success of the EPZ sector, a lot of jobs were created in the country. Employment, mostly for female labour, was created, which ultimately led to a better standard of living in the country. Moreover, inflation was observed to have a negative impact on economic development in the long run. The results for real government expenditure on social security and welfare were seen to help those down the income ladder but by a marginal rate only. Results from the analysis also indicated the presence of a unidirectional causality between openness and economic development and social welfare.

The findings have various policy implications for the government to strengthen economic development. This study is important as it has been able to show the complexity of economic development. Indeed, the interactions between employment, inflation, real government expenditure on social aid and welfare, and human development, according to models 1 and 2, allow growth dynamics to be stabilised and deepened. The Mauritian government should further adopt trade policies that help to boost growth and development in the country. Also, trade policies should be incorporated together with other development strategies.

Regarding the development path of Mauritius so far, one can ascertain that it has recorded a successful development path. However, several challenges remain. The external shocks have demonstrated that the country has heavy reliance on a few sectors and markets. Mauritius is not yet ready to fully take advantage of the worldwide re-balancing of export markets. It is not yet well integrated in the production chain and final markets of those countries which are bound to increase domestic absorption. The main challenges of the country are in terms of the infrastructure system, whereby there are major problems of road congestion and water supply. Also, there is scarcity of skilled human resources due to limited capacity to reform the traditional education system, the country's brain-drain, and large and relatively inefficient public companies and parastatals.

Moreover, Mauritius is engaged in setting various reforms to diversify the economy further, both in terms of climbing the value chain and diversifying exports towards emerging markets. Several reforms including the educational sector, infrastructure, and trade barriers are high on policy makers' agenda. However, there is also a need to speed up fiscal consolidation in order to attain considerable efficiency improvements in the budget and also to ensure effective expenditure in priority areas. More precisely, there is a need to strengthen the social safety net system in the country (World Bank 2014).

References

Agenor, P-R. 2005. The macroeconomics of poverty reduction. *The Manchester School*, 73(4): 369–434.

Banerjee, A., Dolado, J. and R. Mestre. 1998. Error correction mechanism test for co-integration in single equation framework. *Journal of Time Series Analysis,* 19(3): 267–283.

Bannister, G. J., and K. Thugge. 2001. *International trade and poverty alleviation.* Vol. 1. International Monetary Fund.

Beck, T., A. Demirgüç-Kunt, and R. Levine. 2007. Finance, inequality and the poor. *Journal of Economic Growth,* 12: 27–49.

Berg, A., and A. Krueger. 2003. Trade, growth, and poverty: A selective survey. *IMF Working Paper,* WP/03/30. Washington, DC.

Bhagwati, J. 2004. *In defense of globalization.* New York: Oxford University Press.

Bhagwati, J., and T. N. Srinivasan. 2002. Trade and poverty in the poor countries. *AEA Papers and Proceedings* 92 (2): 180–83.

Blank, R., and A. Blinder. 1986. Macroeconomics, income distribution, and poverty. *In:* Danziger, S. and D. Weinberg (Eds.), *Fighting poverty: What works and what doesn't.* Cambridge, MA: Harvard University Press.

Castro-Leal, F., J. Dayton, L. Demery,, and K. Mehra. 2000. Public spending on health care in Africa: Do the poor benefit? *Bulletin of the World Health Organization*, 78: 66–74.

Cutler, D. M., and L. F. Katz. 1991. Macroeconomic performance and the disadvantaged. *Brookings Papers on Economic Activity*, vol. 2, pp. 1–61.

Davis, D., and P. Mishra. 2006. Stopler-Samuelson is dead and other crimes of both theory and data. *In:* A. Harrison (ed.). *Globalization and poverty*, Chicago: University of Chicago Press.

Dollar, D. 1992. Outward-oriented developing economies really do grow more rapidly: Evidence from 95 LDCs, 1976–1985. *Economic Development and Cultural Change,* 40(3): 523–44.

Dollar, D., and A. Kraay. 2004. Trade, growth, and poverty. *The Economic Journal*, 114(493), F22-F49.

— 2001. Trade, growth and poverty. Mimeo, Development Research Group, World Bank, Washington, DC.

Edwards, S.. 1998. Openness, productivity and growth: What do we really know? *The Economic Journal* 108(447): 383–98.

Easterly, W., and S. Fischer. 2000. Inflation and the poor. *Policy Research Working Papers* 2335.

Frankel, J., and D. Romer. 1999. Does trade cause growth? *American Economic Review,* 89(3): 379–399.

Goh, C., and B. S. Javorcik. 2006. Trade protection and industry wage structure in Poland. *In:* A. Harrison (ed.). *Globalization and poverty*, Chicago: University of Chicago Press for NBER.

Gohou, G., and I. Soumaré. 2010. Does foreign direct investment reduce poverty in Africa and are there regional differences? *Working Paper, World Development*, 40(1), 75–95.

Grossman, G. M., and E. Helpman. 1991. *Innovation and growth in the global economy.* Cambridge, M.A., and London: MIT Press.

Guillaumont-Jeanneney, S., and K. Kpodar. 2011. Financial development and poverty reduction: Can there be a benefit without a cost? *Journal of Development Studies,* 47 (1): 143–63.

Johansen, S. 1988. Statistical analysis of co-integration vectors. *Journal of Economic Dynamics and Control*, 12(2): 231–254.

Johansen, S., and K. Juselius. 1990. Maximum likelihood estimation and inference on co-integration with applications to the demand for money. *Oxford Bulletin of Economics and Statistics*, 52(2): 169–210.

Johansson, H., and L. Nilsson. 1997. Export processing zones as catalysts. *World Development*, 25(12): 2115–2128.

Kpodar, K., and R. Singh. 2011. Does financial structure matter for poverty? Evidence from developing countries. *World Bank Policy Research Working Paper* WPS5915, Washington, DC.

Le Goff, M., and R. J. Singh. 2013. Does trade reduce poverty? A view from Africa. *World Bank Policy Research Working Paper* 6327, Washington, DC.

Lee, E., and M. Vivarelli (Eds.). 2004. *Understanding globalisation, employment, and poverty reduction.* New York, NY: Palgrave Macmillan.

Levinsohn, J. 1999. Employment responses to international liberalisation in Chile. *Journal of International Economics*, 47(2): 321–344.

Lucas, R. E. 1988. The mechanics of economic development. *Journal of Monetary Economics*, 22(1): 3–42.

Marquez, G., and C. Pagés-serra. 1998. Trade and employment: Evidence from Latin America and the Caribbean. *Working Paper* 366. Washington, D.C.: Inter-American Development Bank

Mauritius Trade Easy. 2015. www.mauritiustrade.mu.

Mocan, H. N. 2005. Income inequality, poverty, and macro-econometric conditions. Paper presented at the American Economic Association Meetings, Washington, D. C.

Moreira, M. M. and S. Najberg. 2000. Trade liberalisation in Brazil: Creating or exporting jobs? *Journal of Development Studies*, 36(3): 78–100.

Philips, P. C. B. 1986. Understanding spurious regression in econometrics. *Journal of Econometrics*, 33(3): 311–340.

Powers, J. 1993. The report on rural women living in poverty. International Fund for Agricultural Development. Rome.

Rama, M. 1994. The labour market and trade reform in manufacturing. In: M. Connolly and J. De Melo (Eds.), *The effects of protectionism on a small country*. World Bank Regional and Sectoral Studies, Washington, D. C.

Ramessur, T. and R. Durbarry. 2009, Labour market effects of trade liberalization: The case of Mauritius. *Estey Centre Journal of International law and trade policy*, Vol. 10, No. 2.

Revenga, A. 1997. Employment and wage effects of trade liberalisation: The Case of Mexican Manufacturing. *Journal of Labour Economics*, 15(3): 520–543.

Sachs, J. D., and A. M. Warner. 1995. *Economic convergence and economic policies*. (No. w5039), National Bureau of Economic Research.

Singh, R., and Y. Huang. 2011. Financial deepening, property rights, and poverty: Evidence from sub-Saharan Africa. *IMF Working Paper*, WP/11/196, Washington, D. C.

Stock, J. H., and M. W. Watson. 1993. A simple estimator of co-integration vectors in higher order integrated systems. *Econometrica: Journal of the Econometric Society*, 783–820.

Stopler, W. F., and P. A. Samuelson. 1941. Protection and real wages. *Review of Economic Studies*, 9(1): 58–73.

Topalova, P. 2006. Trade liberalization, poverty and inequality: Evidence from Indian districts. *In:* A. Harrison (Ed.). *Globalization and poverty*. Chicago: University of Chicago Press for NBER.

Winters, L. A. 2000a. Trade policy and poverty: What are the links? *CEPR Working Paper Series*, No 2382. London Centre for Economic Policy Research.

World Bank. 2004. Working for a world free of poverty.

World Trade Organisation. 2008. Trade in a globalised world.

CHAPTER THREE

Rural-Urban Divide in Ethiopia: A Challenge for Inclusive Growth and Development

Muluadam Alemu

Abstract

Rural and urban areas exhibit a myriad of interactions that are key strategic elements for inclusive growth and development. To nurture this potential, the two spaces should complement each other. In this regard, research suggests that inclusive rural-urban development should form critical parts of development policies. However, to date development policies and empirical inquiries have treated the two areas independently. In fact, the situation cannot be any worse when it comes to developing countries like Ethiopia where stereotyped development policies are developed at the expense of inclusiveness. Despite the wider rural-urban divide in the country, there exists only little empirical evidence on the challenges it poses to inclusive development. Thus, the purpose of this chapter is to address the question: 'While Ethiopia has achieved a track record in economic growth, why are large numbers of people (about 27 million) in the country trapped in poverty, exclusion, high levels of inequality, and undefined mechanisms of social protection and marginalisation?' To achieve its purpose, the study has scrutinised a mix of extensive desk research and examined official data collected from data sets of the Ministry of Finance and Economic Development, the Ministry of Education, the Ethiopian Development Research Institute, the National Planning Commission, the Central Statistical Authority, and the Ethiopian Road Authority. Data were analysed using descriptive statistics and presented in tables and graphs. A synthesis of policy documents was conducted as keeping track of the policy framework for economic transformation and growth is essential for transcending the divide. The study reveals that disparity in terms of urban and rural poverty increases the rural-urban divide, on the one hand, and undermines efforts of inclusive growth and development, on the other. It is also found out that the persistent inequality in income and the disparity in access to health, education and infrastructure services between rural and urban areas have serious implications on inclusive growth and development as these influence the distributional impacts of policies and external shocks on maximising welfare. Finally, the study shows that, though development policies and strategies implemented in Ethiopia for a decade and half have been pro-poor, in practice they have not resulted in a narrowing of the urban-rural divide.

Keywords: rural-urban divide, inclusive growth, inclusive development, Ethiopia

1. Introduction

1.1. Background

The evolution of rural-urban divide can be traced back to the Industrial Revolution (Jongereden 2010). According to mainstream development theory (Jerve 2001), modernisation has given birth to conceptually and materially distinct urban and rural worlds (Peet and Hartwick 2009). There is indisputable evidence as well as on-going debate in the literature that helps to understand how the divide impacts inclusive development (UNDP 2000; Lynch 2005a). For Jongereden (2010), the rural-urban divide is anticipated as a "specific form of spatial division of labour and material". Friedmann (1996, 129) argues that "...rural-urban divide pits cities against the countryside as two incompatible social and physical formations". Likewise, Zhihong and Xiaoying (2013) succinctly illustrate it as the most blatant problem the world faces at the expense of inclusiveness. Thus, "breaking the analytical, policy silos" is essential to promote inclusive development. In this regard, there is ample evidence in the scientific literature on how important it is to transcend the divide to promote inclusive development (Berdegué *et al.* 2014).

Debates on inclusive development begin with strong criticisms on urban-based industrialisation policies of the 1950s/60s (Anders 1992; Parr 1999) that were championed by modernisation theorists (Perroux 1950; Hirschman 1958; Rostow 1960). They considered towns as centres of agglomeration economies and advocate to bring about development via the triggering influence of towns acting on the countryside as a catalyst of inclusiveness (Hughes and Holland 1994). The result was a widened divide that put rural people at a structural disadvantage by twinning industry and trade with the urban areas and traditional agriculture with the rural ones (Dabson 2012). They finally proved to be in vain due to the strong tendency of urban bias (Lipton 1977; Gore 1984; Willis 2005) and were later replaced by the Integrated Rural Development Program (IRDP). IRDP was put forward to reverse polarisation impacts of previous policies on rural areas by generating a series of changes in rural areas: improving living conditions and creating social infrastructure (Mulongo *et al.* 2010). The main trust of the strategy, as described by Baker and Pederson (1992), spins over agricultural change, with little, if any, attention to the role of urban centres in rural development. Thus, IRDP has failed to bring inclusive development as it neglects the urban aspects in the development process (Lynch 2005a).

Beyond the theoretical explanations, one manifestation of the divide lies in conceptualisation of the terms 'urban' and 'rural' (Dabson *et al.* 2012). In the contemporary thought, academia lacks fixed delineations of what is urban and rural (Scott *et al.* 2007). So, using either or combinations of criteria as standards to demarcate between the two spaces is no more adequate (Dabson 2012). They all are difficult to measure and vary both over space and time, making generalisations problematic (van Leeuwen 2010). One could argue that in a more intricate pattern of settlement, no theorist could come up with an objective measure that represents distinct aspects of the two settlements. Dabson (2012, 9) suggests that "the way definitions are applied has sizeable policy implications for resource distribution and development". Thus, the current paradigm moves away from hard-and-fast distinctions and measures to designs of complementary development policies (Cristóbal 2009). It is, therefore, vital to note that clearly demarcating urban and rural areas is difficult due to blurring borders that call for systematic approaches to properly conceptualise the dynamics of their interaction. Besides, most of the definitions and theories used so far are often inconsistent, non-analogous, perplexing, and irreconcilable. To subvert the problem, researchers need to pay more attention to issues intersecting along the rural-urban continuum by offering contextual definitions (Scott *et al.* 2007). In this regard, Tacoli (2006, 49) says: "Defining rural and urban areas for the purpose of research and development agenda is not somewhat mechanical; nonetheless, it should be given more attention to reconcile with local context." Despite the fact that the divide has narrowed down possibilities for inclusive development (Jongereden 2010), it did not linger uncontested. Circa the first half of 19th century, surmounting the divide has been a continuous but largely unrealised nightmare (Friedmann 1996). However, failure to fully realise these dreams did not hold back the forward-looking theorists from devising mechanisms on how to excel the divide.

To date, there is no difference of opinion among scholars on the importance of closing the divide (Korie *et al.* 2007). Thus, the challenge in bringing inclusive development is how to bridge the divide by incorporating this fact into development and policy frameworks for mutual benefits (Tostensen 2004; Momen 2006). The situation is at its worst in developing countries (Baker and Pederson 1998). Concomitant to sub-Saharan African reality, the policy framework adopted for growth and transformation in Ethiopia from 1950 – 2000s fails to take into account the need to close the divide. The persistence of the divide is not due to the absence of policy; instead, it is not fit for the purpose as it is shared between rural and urban issues that fatally undermine the role of linkages for inclusive development (Mohammed 2007; Aynalem and Asefa 2011). As a result, the policy framework adopted for growth and transformation in Ethiopia during the Imperial[1] and *Dergue*[2] regimes failed to promote inclusive development (Dorosh *et al.* 2011). Similarly, even if there are good beginnings, contemporary policy framework adopted for growth and transformation in Ethiopia, with the exception of the Plan for Accelerated and Sustained Development to End Poverty (PASDEP)[3] (2005/06-2009/10) (MoWUD 2009) and the Growth and Transformation Plan (GTP)[4] (2010/11-2014/15) policy initiatives (MoFED, 2010), remains rural-cantered with minimal opportunities to strengthen linkage for inclusive development. Though partly designed to fit for the purpose of closing the divide, both PASDEP and GTP show wide policy implementation gaps (Miheret 2008 2014). Consistent with the realities in several parts of Eastern and Southern Africa (Owuor 2006), there is still lack of adequate, evidence-based research and literature in Ethiopia describing the challenges posed by the persistent rural-urban divide on inclusive development. Besides, in the Ethiopian context, it is also not known how far the divide affects inclusive growth and development, which calls for more research. It needs to be investigated as it is important in evaluating the adequacy of government policy for bridging the divide. Thus, the purpose of this chapter is to assess challenges posed by the persistent rural-urban divide on inclusive growth and development in Ethiopia.

1.2. Research Methods

Taking Ethiopia as a case, the study has used a mix of extensive desk research as it allows the researcher to collect data from reliable sources like published reports and statistics (Rickinson and May 2009). Thus, the study has examined official data collected from data sets and reports of accredited national and international organisations like the Ministry of Finance and Economic Development, the Ministry of Education, the Ethiopian Development Research Institute, the National Planning Commission, the Central Statistical Authority and the Ethiopian Road Authority. Besides, for the purpose of triangulating data reliability and accuracy, secondary data from recent and peer-reviewed publications were used. Data were analysed by making use of descriptive statistics and presented using tables, graphs and charts. Finally, the chapter is organised into four parts. The first part consists of the background while the second part presents the literature review; the third and fourth parts present the results and the conclusion, respectively.

2. Review of Related Literature

This section provides a bird's eye view of the related literature. Concepts, measures, and indicators that are important and come in handy in the chapter are elucidated. Definitions of key concepts like 'pro-poor growth', 'inclusive growth', and 'development' are given with justifications on how each concept is useful in understanding the urban-rural divide, analysing the data and helping to make meaning of the findings. Finally, the literature on the implications of the policy environment to transcend the rural-urban divide in Ethiopia is reviewed.

2.1. Pro-poor Growth

There is a lively debate on the role of the pro-poor growth agenda in closing the rural-urban divide. Some writers view growth as pro-poor if it leads to any reduction in poverty (Ravallion and Chen 2003), while others view it as pro-poor only if it leads to a disproportionate increase in the incomes of the poor with declining inequality (Kakwani and Pernia 2000). Likewise, OECD (2006, 10) conceptualises it as "a pace and pattern of growth that enhances the ability of the poor to participate, contribute and benefit from growth". Specifically, Klasen (2009, 196) describes it as "growth that maximizes the income gains of the poor by eradicating extreme poverty and hunger". There are two approaches of pro-poor growth: absolute and relative (World Bank 2009). While the former focuses on the pace of rural and urban poverty reduction measured by the increase on average income of the poor, the latter focuses on income distribution between the poor and the non-poor that is achieved when the income of the poor grows faster than that of the non-poor, with declining income inequality. Pro-poor growth analysis should be seen as a toolbox for studying country-specific determinants of rural-urban growth (Klasen 2009) in terms of reduced regional inequality, improved asset base for the poor, reduced gender inequality, and political commitment to pro-poor policies. Empirical evidence in Africa and Latin America in the 1990s and 2000s shows that pro-poor growth was accompanied by pro-poor distributional change (Klasen 2009) and rising inequality (Ravallion 2005). All in all, there is a lively debate about what pro-poor growth is (Ravallion and Chen 2003; Klasen 2009). These debates centre on whether pro-poor growth means that the poor benefit differentially from growth. Like other low income counties, Ethiopia has been implementing pro-poor policies deemed to transcend the divide for a decade and half. However, these policies have not resulted in narrowing the divide (Alemayehu and Addis 2014). Thus, in this paper, the concept of pro-poor growth is used to explain why the pro-poor development policies and strategies implemented in Ethiopia in the last two decades have failed to narrow the rural-urban divide.

2.2. Inclusive Growth

Inclusive growth is a recently introduced concept that has become a buzz-word in policy circles and in academia (Chang 2014). Whereas the World Bank (2009) aligns its definition of inclusive growth with absolute pro-poor growth, Klasen (2010), on the other hand, relates it to the relative definition of pro poor growth. For Khan (2012, 15), growth is inclusive "if it supports high levels of employment and rising wages"; for Ali and Zhuang (2007, 19), it is inclusive "if it increases the social opportunity function"; and for AfDB (2012, 2) it is inclusive "if it results in wider access to sustainable socio-economic opportunities". Though it is possible to generalise that unlike pro-poor growth, inclusive growth should be broad-based to benefit everyone in the society, the lack of a unanimously established definition makes exultant measurement of inclusive growth policies challenging (Alexander 2015). However, there are different criteria and approaches to measuring inclusive growth. For instance, opportunity curve and opportunity index are used to analyse access to and equity of opportunities in education and health (Kjøller-Hansen and Sperling 2013). Likewise, income growth and distribution are also used to integrate equity and growth in a unified measure (Anand *et al.* 2013). More comprehensively, de Haan and Thorat (2013) propose a wide range of indicators measured in terms of average progress, distribution, and participation. Some theorists are trying to relate inclusive growth with either absolute (Anand *et al.* 2013) or relative pro-poor growth (Dollar and Kraay 2002). On the other hand, the two approaches are also different mainly in their targets (Kozuka 2014)) and criteria of measurement (Alexander 2015). One could argue that inclusive growth is vital in bridging the rural-urban divide by benefiting not only the poor but also other groups excluded from the process of growth. Like other sub-Saharan African (SSA) countries, Ethiopia experiences a widening rural-urban divide. Thus, in the context of this paper, I use the concept of inclusive growth to assess the challenges posed by the divide in ensuring inclusive outcomes from growth as measured by access, quality, and equity of education, health, and infrastructure services.

2.3. Inclusive Development

Inclusive development involves comprehensive dimensions and theoretical underpinnings. It is the amalgam of two key concepts: inclusiveness and development, which make it the broadest development agenda. Kanbur and Rauniyar (2009b) use it to refer to improvement on the distribution of well-being along education and health dimensions. Kozuka (2014, 110) describes it as "development that enhances people's well-being by advancing the equality of opportunity for all members of society". Likewise, Madhur and Menon (2014) posit inclusive development as a process in which the fruits of development are shared equitably among the diverse segments of the population in a society. Unlike the two approaches, inclusive development refers to progress on the distribution of well-being along non-income dimensions concomitant with the improvements in the average achievement (Kanbur and Rauniyar 2009a). Thus, it has been promoted as a rights-based development model with the vision to advance equality and participation of the largest possible part of society. It is, therefore, unthinkable to bring inclusive development in a world that is classified as urban and rural with widening divides. One means to promote inclusive development as part of the effort to bridge the rural-urban divide is by strengthening the linkage along the rural-urban continuum. In line with this, there is rich evidence in the literature that bridging the divide via inclusive development entails the achievement of mutually reinforcing pillars like education, health, infrastructure, employment, asset building, business investment, and fiscal transfers (Samans *et al.* 2015). Based on the research context and nature of data that each pillar requires, in the context of this paper, the most important pillars that are assumed to underpin the concept of inclusive development along the rural-urban continuum in Ethiopia include: access, quality, and equity of education; access to health services; and wider and equal access to road infrastructures.

2.4. Debates on Indicators beyond the GDP

The fact that inclusive development aspires to measure quality of life using new indexes more than economic quantity fuels the contemporary academic debates on indicators beyond GDP. Since 1934, change in GDP has been a widely accepted indicator of progress and well-being, but it was never meant to serve that purpose (Heloisa 2012). Thus, the debate on how and for what purpose GDP should be used began in the 1930s (Sen 1999). Its ascendancy as an indicator is being challenged and its limits are being questioned (Cassiers and Thiry 2014). It is now clear that using it to measure quality of life and progress has problems as it has nothing direct to say about distribution, inequality, and poverty (Costanza *et al.* 2009). So, new ways of measuring national-level progress that are grouped into four categories were developed to address pitfalls of GDP (Chancel *et al.* 2014). The first category consists of indexes that correct GDP: Index of Sustainable Economic Welfare, the Genuine Progress Indicator, Green GDPs, and Genuine Wealth. Given that these measures are based on much of the same economic data as GDP, they still have limitations (Costanza *et al.* 2009). The second category includes indexes that measure aspects of well-being directly: Ecological Footprint (Wackernagel and Rees 1996), Subjective Well-Being (Diener and Suh 1999; Stiglitz *et al.* 2009), and Gross National Happiness (Ura and Galay 2004). The third consists of composite indexes that combine all of the alternatives to GDP (and GDP itself) including: Human Development Index (UNDP 1990), the Living Planet Index (Hails 2006), and Happy Planet Index (Abdallah *et al.* 2006). Finally, the fourth index consists of 'indicator suites': National Income Satellite Accounts, Calvert-Henderson Quality of Life Indicators (Lickerman *et al.* 2000) and MDGs Indicators (UN DESA 2007). Though the academia has gone a step forward to propose numerous alternative measures by identifying problems with GDP, there are still significant methodological barriers to developing, implementing, and using better measures of real progress (Costanza *et al.* 2009). Thus, due to lack of comprehensive data and clear methodological underpinnings, beyond-GDP indicators are not used in this paper to explain the nature of rural-urban divide. The reason I have discussed them is to contribute to the debate, which might help to shape inclusive growth and development indicators.

2.5. Implications of the Policy Environment to Transcend Rural-Urban Divide in Ethiopia

The growing body of scholarship shows that in the SSA region, there has been failure to close the rural-urban divide (Owuor 2006). In this paper, I want to explore if this is the case in Ethiopia, which has had policies to reduce the divide and promote inclusive development. In doing so, I am going to use policy synthesis to investigate what the outcomes of the policy have been. Thus, this section presents implications of policy environment to reduce the divide for inclusive development. Arguably, this could help to examine whether there is policy failure or a policy that has not sufficiently addressed the issue. It also helps to identify meaningful policy lessons on inclusive development endeavours in Ethiopia and in the Eastern and Southern African region. Though Ethiopia started to adopt explicit development policies circa the 1950s, in this paper more attention has been given to assessing implications of policies implemented since 2000.

In the early 1990s, ADLI[5] had been officially affirmed as the mainstream development strategy of Ethiopia with the objective of increasing agricultural production and creating sectoral linkages that would finally fuel industrialisation (Tegegne 2005). Since it anticipates urbanisation to be the derivative of the rural sector, it was highly criticized for neglecting the role of linkages for inclusive development (Asefa 2006). The argument for and against ADLI is endless with no consensus on its appropriateness to promote inclusive development. While supporters argue that rising income in the agricultural sector would offer a huge market for non-agricultural sectors, critics on the other hand argue that urbanisation should be a prerequisite to narrow down the divide. In this regard, Dessalegn (2008, 129) succinctly described ADLI as a strategy that "walks in one leg". Since 2000, Ethiopia has implemented three consecutive five-year development plans under the umbrella of ADLI: Sustainable Development and Poverty Reduction Program (SDRP)[6] (2000/01–2005/06), PASDEP (20005/06–2009/10), and GTP (2010/11–204/15). Principally, the ADLI concept was highly incorporated in the first two development plans.

SDPRP was a pro-poor strategy enacted with special emphasis for rural areas where poverty, food security, and agriculture have remained among the highest priorities. It has made no mention of the role played by towns in facilitating rural-urban interactions to narrow the divide. Although the arguments included in SDPRP are sensible, it has failed to achieve its objectives due to weak rural-urban connection (Assefa 2006). While SDPRP addresses many policy concerns in Ethiopia, the problem of rural-urban divide and the demand side of production did not receive much attention (Workrneh 2008; Getnet and Mehrab 2010). As a result, the effectiveness of SDPRP in transcending the divide for inclusive development has been dismal as it was not fit for the purpose (Asefa 2006). This has served as a basis for the emergence of a more accommodative pro-urban view that was crystallised with the adoption of PASDEP. It underscored the need to strengthen the urban agenda by promoting strong linkages between agriculture and industry to effectively tackle challenges of the rural-urban divide on inclusive development (Gete 2006; Miheret 2008; MoWUD 2009). Though PASDEP has brought significant achievements in GDP growth (UN-Habitat 2014), discouraging results were recorded on overall wellbeing and equity (Getnet and Mehrab 2010).

Following its relative success, PASDEP was replaced by GTP with its emphasis on infrastructure development and export expansion. Through the GTP, as in its predecessor, significant results have been registered in poverty reduction and changes in GDP (MoFED 2013). However, unemployment and inflation, which menace Ethiopia's attempt to nurture inclusive development, still remain high. Even though government reports show that progress in social development has also been inspiring, empirical verification by independent scholars like Miheret (2014) reveals that government sources can only be described as mixed, with some sectors showing remarkable progress, while in other sectors the outcome has been discouraging. Overall, in the plan periods, inclusive growth and development between urban and rural areas has not been achieved sufficiently due to the wider rural-urban divide. In sum, the policy synthesis on major development strategies like SDPRP, PASDEP, and GTP implemented in Ethiopia from 2000 to 2015 reveals that there has been a failure generally to close the rural-urban divide and to promote wellbeing.

2.6. Research Questions

Based on the synthesis presented above, I would argue that though some encouraging achievements are recorded in the last decade and a half, Ethiopia has failed to close the rural- urban divide and promote inclusive growth and development. My explanation for the failure is that even though development policies and strategies implemented in Ethiopia in the last decade and a half were pro-poor, in practice they have not resulted in a narrowing of the divide. One important lesson that can be learnt for inclusive sustainable development is that designing development policies that theoretically fit to the existing situation is not an end by itself. It is now logical to ask three basic questions as to why these policies have failed. First, while Ethiopia has a good track record in economic development, why are large numbers of people trapped in poverty, exclusion, high inequality, and undefined mechanism of social protection? Second, to what extent does Ethiopia create an enabling environment that provides high quality education and health with broad participation of all members of society? Third, to what extent does Ethiopia provide its citizens access to quality road infrastructure that enables productive engagement in the national economy and contributes to a higher standard of living?

3. The Rural-urban Divide in Ethiopia: A Challenge for Inclusive Growth and Development

Conventionally, GDP, poverty indices, and Gini Coefficient are common quantitative indicators of the rural-urban divide (Eshetu 2004; Ravallion 2005; Stifel and Tassew 2013). Lately, qualitative indicators have started to be used widely after the introduction of multidimensional poverty measures including Alkire and Sarwar (2009), How is Life (OECD 2011), capability approach (Sen 1999), and Inclusive Post Dependent Framework (Bookwalter and Koehn 2014). Recently, in describing the basic characteristics of inclusive development, Samans *et al.* (2015) have developed a comprehensive benchmarking framework that comprises indicators of performance and enabling environmental conditions in six principal policy pillars. The six basic pillars are education; employment and labour compensation; asset building and business investment; corruption and rents; fiscal transfers; and basic service and infrastructure. Samans *et al.* (2015) argue that while all of these characteristics are likely to be important for ensuring inclusive outcomes from growth, they are not mutually exclusive; hence, two or more of them can be significant at the same time, as shown in the economic literature. Although a range of indicators are discussed in this paper, the extent of applying all in this paper is limited by data availability. Accordingly, the challenge of rural-urban divide on inclusive development in Ethiopia was examined with respect to some selected pillars like education, health, poverty, inequality and infrastructure.

3.1. Poverty, Inequality and Inclusive Development in Ethiopia

At the turn of the 20th century, Ethiopia experienced one of the highest poverty rates in the world. In 2000, the population living on less than US$1.25 Purchasing Power Parity (PPP) per day was 56 per cent while 44 per cent of the population was living below the poverty line (World Bank 2015). In 2011, 30 per cent (27 million) of the people lived below the poverty line and 31 per cent lived on less than US$1.25 PPP per day (Alemayehu and Addis 2014). As shown in Table 1, in 2000, 51.9 per cent of the population was poor, compared to 44.5 per cent in 2005, and 30.0 per cent in 2011. The change over time from 2000 to 2011 was 21.9 per cent. At the beginning of the 21st century, poverty in Ethiopia was definitely higher by 13 per cent in rural areas, with 53.7 per cent of the rural population living below the poverty line in 2000, compared to 40.8 per cent in urban areas (Table 1).

Table 1. Rural-urban divide on poverty in Ethiopia, 2000-2011

	Poverty level over time			Change in poverty over time		
	2000	2005	2011	2000-2005	2005-2011	2000-2011
National						
$P_{0\,Index}$	51.9	44.5	30	(7.4)	(14.5)	(21.9)
$P_{1\,Index}$	14.6	11.7	8.2	(2.9)	(3.5)	(6.5)
$P_{2\,Index}$	5.7	4.2	3.3	(1.5)	(0.9)	(2.4)
Urban						
$P_{0\,Index}$	40.8	21.7	13.9	(19.1)	(7.8)	(26.9)
$P_{1\,Index}$	11.9	4.4	3.4	(7.5)	(1.0)	(8.5)
$P_{2\,Index}$	4.7	1.4	1.3	(3.3)	(0.1)	(3.4)
Rural						
$P_{0\,Index}$	53.7	48.2	33.2	(5.5)	(15.0)	20.5
$P_{1\,Index}$	15.1	13.0	9.1	(2.1)	(3.9)	(6.0)
$P_{2\,Index}$	5.8	4.7	3.7	(1.1)	(1.0)	(2.2)

SOURCE: MoFED (2013)

Note: P_0 = Headcount Ratio[7]; P1= Depth of Poverty[8]; P2= Severity of Poverty[9]

While the rural headcount ratio fell by an extraordinary 20.5 per cent, urban areas as a whole saw even greater declines in poverty, as the urban poverty rate fell by 26.9 per cent in 2011. Most of the decline in urban poverty took place in the first half of the decade, falling by just over 19.1 per cent. Conversely, rural poverty fell only marginally by 5.5 per cent from 2000-2005, with the majority of gains (15.0 per cent) occurring after 2005. The depth of poverty was 14.6, 11.7, and 8.2 per cent in 2000, 2005, and 2011, respectively. Depth of poverty was 11.9 per cent for urban areas in 2000, while it was 15.1 per cent in rural areas. It shows significant improvement both in rural and urban areas from 2000 to 2011 with 6.0 per cent and 8.5 per cent changes, respectively. Likewise, severity of poverty was 4.7 per cent for urban areas in 2000, while it was 5.8 per cent in rural areas. Whereas severity of poverty in urban areas shows a major change from 4.7 per cent in 2000 to 1.3 per cent in 2011, the change in rural areas is relatively small from 5.8 per cent in 2000 to 3.7 per cent in 2011 (see Table 1).

Besides poverty indices, rural-urban income (consumption) inequality in Ethiopia is another challenge to promote inclusive growth and development. Figure 1 shows that since 1995/96, urban inequality had been increasing, reaching 0.44 in 2004/05. But the increasing trend was halted during the PASDEP period due to the change in urban development policy. In 2010/11, the Gini coefficient for urban and rural areas became 0.37 and 0.27, respectively. Akin to the years before, income inequality is higher in urban areas than in rural areas.

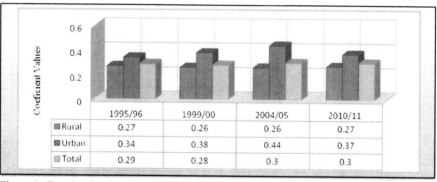

	1995/96	1999/00	2004/05	2010/11
Rural	0.27	0.26	0.26	0.27
Urban	0.34	0.38	0.44	0.37
Total	0.29	0.28	0.3	0.3

Figure 1. Trends of national, rural, and urban Gini coefficients (1995/96-2010/2011)
SOURCE: Author's own calculation of data from MoFED (2013)

However, rural inequality slightly increased from 0.26 in 2004/05 to 0. 27 in 2010/11, while urban inequality declined substantially from 0.44 in 2004/05 to 0.37 in 2010/11. Despite this, the national Gini coefficient has remained unchanged. The decline in income inequality in urban areas has resulted in a colossal decline in poverty attributed to the urban-focused development activities carried out in Ethiopia. On top of the disparity in the level of urban and rural income inequality, the analysis shows the existence of frequent oscillation that makes it difficult to make precise academic prophecy on the growth performance of the country towards inclusive growth and development by closing the rural-urban divide.

Decomposing changes in poverty into growth and inequality components can help to understand the dynamics of the rural-urban divide over time. Figure 2 shows that, of the total 9 percentage-point reduction in headcount poverty between 2005 and 2011, five percentage points were due to growth, and four were due to redistribution. However, the pattern between urban and rural areas is reasonably different, although the fall in the headcount was almost the same. The result shows a clear disparity on changes in poverty over time between urban and rural areas. For instance, in urban areas, growth contributed negatively to poverty reduction, and it was redistribution, or the fall in inequality, that contributed to poverty reduction. Unlike this, the six percentage-point changes in rural areas are mainly due to average growth.

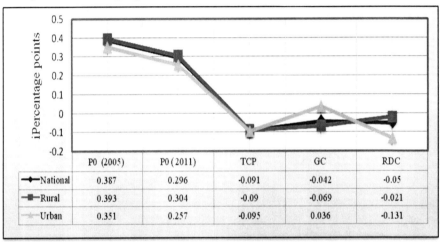

	P0 (2005)	P0 (2011)	TCP	GC	RDC
National	0.387	0.296	-0.091	-0.042	-0.05
Rural	0.393	0.304	-0.09	-0.069	-0.021
Urban	0.351	0.257	-0.095	0.036	-0.131

Figure 2. Decomposition of Change in Headcount Poverty between 2005 and 2011

SOURCE: Author's construction based on data from MoFED (2013)

P_0 = Headcount poverty; TCP = Total change in poverty; GC = Growth Component; RDC = Redistribution component.

To assess the impact of the persistent income poverty and inequality on household consumption distribution among the Rural Poor (RP), Rural Non-Poor (RNP), Urban Poor (UP), and Urban Non-Poor (UNP), the National Input Output Table and Social Accounting Matrix of Ethiopia has been used (EDRI 2009). In view of that, when the urban poor are compared with their rural counterparts in terms of their share in the total marketed and non-marketed goods and services, we observe a huge disparity between the two groups (see Table 2). Since non-marketed home-consumed outputs are primarily food products with limited manufactured outputs, the large share of non-marketed consumption among poor households both in urban and rural areas show the disparity in consumption patterns across the different income groups. These differences have serious implications on inclusive growth and development by influencing the distributional impacts of policies and external shocks on maximising welfare.

Table 2. Household consumption distribution

Goods and services	Consumption demand, by household (%)				
	RP	RNP	UP	UNP	PC
Share in total marketed	14.3	49.9	5.3	30.5	100
Share in total non-marketed	26.2	71.5	0.7	1.5	100
Share in Total PC	18.3	57.2	3.8	20.7	100
	Composition of consumption, by household				
Marketed	51.5	57.5	93.3	97.5	66.0
Non-Marketed	48.5	42.5	6.7	2.5	34.0

SOURCE: National Input Output Table and Social Accounting Matrix, EDRI (2009, 27)

In sum, the above discussion on poverty, inequality, and inclusive development in Ethiopia clearly affirms that, though Ethiopia has made immense progress in poverty reduction in the last decade and a half, there exists a wider rural-urban divide in terms of the level of poverty and inequality between rural and urban areas. Thus, a wide gap persists since poverty reduction (and presumably economic growth) has not resulted in a marked closing of the urban-rural divide.

3.2. Access, Quality, and Equity of Health and Education Services in Ethiopia

As discussed in the review of literature, inclusive development indicators go beyond income poverty and inequality to include non-monetary measures of wellbeing (see Sen 1999; Stiglitz *et al.* 2009; OECD 2011; Bookwalter and Koehn 2014; Samans *et al.* 2015). In line with this pursuit, Figure 3 shows under-five child stunting, wasting and underweight rates in Ethiopia between 2000 and 2011.

Figure 3 shows that 51.5 per cent of children were stunted in 2000, which decreased to 46 and 44.4 per cent in 2005 and 2011, respectively. It also reveals that stunting was 42.3, 29.8, and 31.5 per cent in urban Ethiopia while it was 52.6, 47.9, and 46.6 per cent in rural parts in 2000, 2005, and 2011, respectively. The decline in stunting rates is found to be high in the first half of the 2000s compared with what has been achieved in the second half. The stunting rates are lower in urban areas, and declined by 25.5 percentage points, which is relatively more than the 12.2 percentage point decrease in rural areas. Figure 3 also presents the proportion of children who are too light to their weight. In Ethiopia, 10.5 per cent of the children were wasted (below 2SD Weight-for-height Ratio) in 2000 and 2005. This declined to 9.7 per cent in 2011. The incidence of wasting was 5.5, 6.3, and 5.7 per cent in urban Ethiopia while it was 11.1, 10.9, and 10.2 per cent in rural parts in 2000, 2005, and 2011, respectively. Wasting rate has also remained relatively higher in rural areas in the last decade.

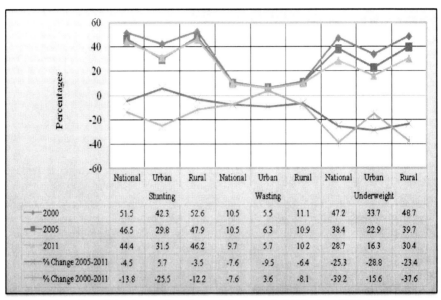

Figure 3. Stunting, Wasting and underweight rates in Ethiopia, 2000–2011
SOURCE: Author's own calculation of data from NPC (2013)

When we look at the proportion of children who are too light for their age, Figure 3 shows that the prevalence of underweight level was 47.2, 38.4, and 28.7 per cent in 2000, 2005, and 2011, respectively, at the national level while it was 33.7, 22.9, and 16.4 per cent in urban and 48.7, 39.7, and 30.4 per cent in rural areas for the same years. Compared to rural areas, urban areas experience lower underweight rates but with a higher rate of decline. Despite some changes seen in the last decade, there is a clear rural-urban divide on the stunting, wasting, and underweight rates in Ethiopia.

Since school enrolment rate in above primary levels of schooling is one of the proxy indicators for inclusive growth and development, the net primary and secondary schooling enrolment rates are calculated based on the data set from the National Planning Commission (NPC) (2013) and surveys carried out by CSA (2007).

The primary enrolment rate rose from 33.7 per cent in 2000 to 62.3 per cent in 2011. As shown in Figure 4, the issue of rural-urban divide is also prevalent in school enrolment rates achieved so far in the country. In this regard, while primary enrolment rates rose faster in rural areas than in urban areas, the level remained lower in rural areas (59.1 per cent) than in urban areas (84.7 per cent) in 2011.

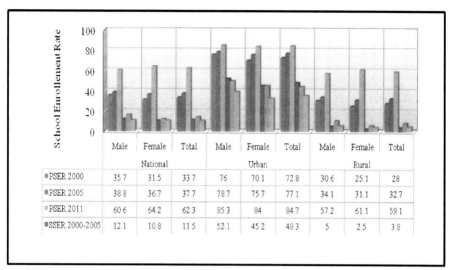

	Male	Female	Total	Male	Female	Total	Male	Female	Total
		National			Urban			Rural	
PSER 2000	35.7	31.5	33.7	76	70.1	72.8	30.6	25.1	28
PSER 2005	38.8	36.7	37.7	78.7	75.7	77.1	34.1	31.1	32.7
PSER 2011	60.6	64.2	62.3	85.3	84	84.7	57.2	61.1	59.1
SSER 2000-2005	12.1	10.8	11.5	52.1	45.2	48.3	5	2.5	3.8

Figure 4. Primary and Secondary Net School Enrolment Rates in Ethiopia (2000–2011)

SOURCE: Author's own calculation of data from CSA (2007), MoFED (2013) and NPC (2013).

PSER: Primary school net enrolment rate and SSER: secondary school net enrolment rate

Comparatively, primary enrolment rates for girls rose faster than for boys from 2000-2011 as Ethiopia has been working in line with the Millennium Development Goal of equal access to education for girls. Secondary school net enrolment rates, which are much lower than primary school enrolment rates, showed some improvement in 2005 compared with those of 2000; but they then appear to have fallen below the 2000 rate by 2011. The secondary school net enrolment rate remains a huge source of rural-urban disparity, which poses daunting challenges to inclusive growth and development. Whereas the rural part of the country that hosts 85 per cent of the total population exhibited only 4.8 per cent secondary school net enrolment rate in 2011, the urban part that hosts only 15 per cent of the total population achieved 35.6 per cent in the same year, which is seven times more than its rural counterpart.

The literacy rate is a broad-based measure of basic educational attainment that is not sensitive to changes in the formal education restructuring system. The trends and changes over time on the literacy rate in Ethiopia for people 10 years of age and older show substantial progress between 2000 and 2011 (see Figure 5).

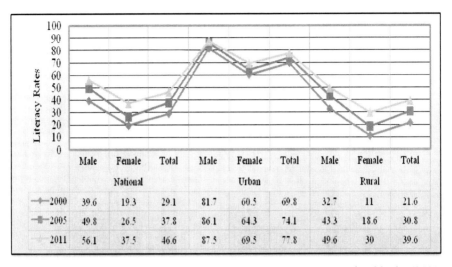

	Male	Female	Total	Male	Female	Total	Male	Female	Total
	National			Urban			Rural		
2000	39.6	19.3	29.1	81.7	60.5	69.8	32.7	11	21.6
2005	49.8	26.5	37.8	86.1	64.3	74.1	43.3	18.6	30.8
2011	56.1	37.5	46.6	87.5	69.5	77.8	49.6	30	39.6

Figure 5. Trends and Changes Over time in Literacy Rates of Ethiopia (2000–2011)

SOURCE: Author's own calculation of data from CSA (2007), MoFED (2013) and NPC (2013).

A comparison of the level of literacy between urban and rural areas reveals an increase over time in both spatial units regardless of sex. Surprisingly, most of the increase in literacy level took place in rural areas with an 18 per cent increase, against 8 per cent in urban areas, where rates at the beginning were very low at 21.7 per cent in 2000. Despite the encouraging improvement recorded in rural literacy rate for the last decade, the general literacy rate that is yet below 50 per cent appears to be one source of rural-urban literacy disparity with 77.8 and 39.6 per cent in urban and rural areas, respectively. Thus, literacy rates were much higher in urban compared to rural areas in 2000, and while there has been a narrowing of the urban-rural gap, the differences remain wide. To measure whether or not education is accessible, of high quality, and inclusive in terms of attainment and learning outcomes, analysis was made on the data set from the NPC (2013) and CSA (1994, 2007) (see Figure 6). Figure 6 shows that there was a wide disparity in terms of educational access at all levels across regions in Ethiopia for a decade and a half (2000–2013). For instance, while Addis Ababa had 82.5 and 85.3 per cent literacy rate in 1994 and 2007, respectively, Afar as a lagging rural region, on the other hand, had achieved only 8.7 and 17.3 per cent in the same period. The levels and trends of literacy rate across the nine regions and two city administrations shows the inaccessibility of education especially for the remotest rural pastoralist regions like Afar and Somali compared with the urban areas like Addis Ababa and Dire Dawa (see Figure 6).

Figure 6 shows that there was a wide disparity in terms of educational access at all levels across regions in Ethiopia for a decade and a half (2000– 2013). For instance, while Addis Ababa had 82.5 and 85.3 per cent literacy rate in 1994 and 2007, respectively, Afar as a lagging rural region, on the other hand, had achieved only 8.7 and 17.3 per cent in the same period. The levels and trends of literacy rate across the nine regions and two city administrations shows the inaccessibility of education especially for the remotest rural pastoralist regions like Afar and Somali compared with the urban areas like Addis Ababa and Dire Dawa (see Figure 6).

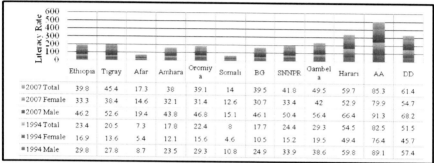

	Ethiopia	Tigray	Afar	Amhara	Oromiya	Somali	BG	SNNPR	Gambela	Harari	AA	DD
■2007 Total	39.8	45.4	17.3	38	39.1	14	39.5	41.8	49.5	59.7	85.3	61.4
■2007 Female	33.3	38.4	14.6	32.1	31.4	12.6	30.7	33.4	42	52.9	79.9	54.7
■2007 Male	46.2	52.6	19.4	43.8	46.8	15.1	46.1	50.4	56.4	66.4	91.3	68.2
■1994 Total	23.4	20.5	7.3	17.8	22.4	8	17.7	24.4	29.3	54.5	82.5	51.5
■1994 Female	16.9	13.6	5.4	12.1	15.6	4.6	10.5	15.2	19.5	49.4	76.4	45.7
■1994 Male	29.8	27.8	8.7	23.5	29.3	10.8	24.9	33.9	38.6	59.8	89.1	57.4

Figure 6. Access to Education and Literacy Trends in Ethiopia (1994 and 2007)
SOURCE: Author's own calculation of data from CSA (1994, 2007).

As literacy measures only if an individual can read and write a few words, it is not a very good measure of educational attainment. Instead, a much better internationally accepted proxy for functional literacy is primary school completion rate. Figure 7 shows the primary school completion rates at grade five (survival rates) and grade eight, by regions, in Ethiopia.

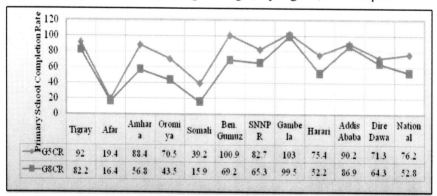

	Tigray	Afar	Amhara	Oromiya	Somali	Ben. Gumuz	SNNPR	Gambela	Harari	Addis Ababa	Dire Dawa	National
◆G5CR	92	19.4	88.4	70.5	39.2	100.9	82.7	103	75.4	90.2	71.3	76.2
■G8CR	82.2	16.4	56.8	43.5	15.9	69.2	65.3	99.5	52.2	86.9	64.3	52.8

Figure 7. Primary School Completion Rates of Grade Five and Eight, by Region
SOURCE: Author's own calculation of data from MoE (2013)
G5CR = Grade 5 completion rates G8CR = Grade 8 completion rates

Figure 7 shows that, compared to grade eight completion rates, grade five completion rates (survival rates) are relatively higher in all regions. While Gambella and Benshangul Gumuz regions have achieved the highest primary school completion rates, primary school completion rates remain low in Afar and Somali regions. Primary school completion rates in Ethiopia vary not only across regions but also over time. So in Figure 8 it is indicated that, whereas the primary school completion rate of grade 8 has increased consistently in the five-year period, the survival rates (primary school completion rate of grade 5) has shown a decline.

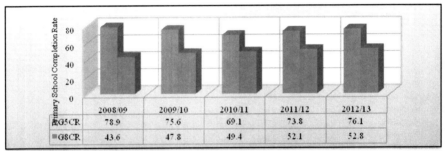

Figure 8. Trends of Primary School Completion Rates of Grade Five and Eight (2008/09–2012/13)

SOURCE: Author's own calculation of data from MoE (2013)

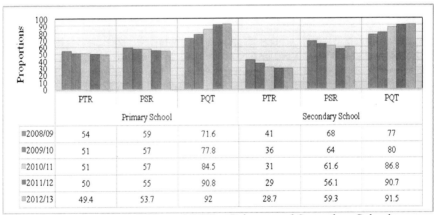

Figure 9. Trends of PTR, PSR, and PQT at Primary and Secondary Schools (2008/09–2012/13)

SOURCE: Author's own calculation of data from MoE (2013, 2012, 2011, 2010)

In addition to survival and primary school completion rates, Pupil-Teacher Ratio (PTR), Pupil-Section Ratio (PSR), and Proportion of Qualified Teachers (PQT) are proxies to measure quality of education. In Ethiopia, the standard set for PTR is 50 at primary (1-8) and 40 at secondary levels. The PTR values indicated in Figure 9 above reveal that the country did not meet the minimum criteria of 50 PTR except in 2012/13. A good PTR has been recorded in secondary school except in 2008/09. Besides, a wide regional disparity is reflected by the low PTR in urban areas like Addis Ababa (23) and a relatively higher PTR in the remotest rural Somali region (65) at primary level.

In terms of PSR, the highest ratio was observed in 2008/09, which declined to 53.7 and 59.3 in 2012/13 at primary and secondary schools, respectively. Whereas there has been a gradual improvement in the PSR ratio, the results recorded indicate overcrowding, which affects the quality of education. The proportion of qualified teachers has shown gradual increase over time at primary and secondary schools. But the disaggregated data reveals that, compared to major urban centres in the country, low PQT is affecting quality of education in the remotest rural regions of Somali, Afar, Gambela, and Benshangul Gumuz.

Finally, to measure the inclusiveness of education in Ethiopia in terms of equity, the Gender Parity Index (GPI) has been calculated using an eight-year data set from NPC and MoE. As can be seen from Figure 10, GPI in Ethiopia has shown a continuous improvement both at primary and secondary schools. In 2005/06 the GPI at primary school was 0.78, which increased to 0.94 in 2012/13. The GPI at secondary school in 2005/06 was 0.57, which was lower than the GPI at primary school by 21 percentage points. However, the GPI gap between primary and secondary schools was narrowed down to two percentage points in 2012/13 when the GPI at secondary school reached 0.92. One can observe that the relatively better GPI at primary school is a symptom that the country should do more to raise GPI closer to one at secondary school level.

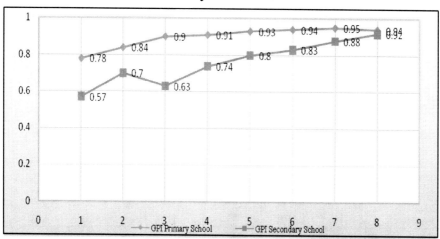

Figure 10. Gender Parity Index at Primary and Secondary Schools (2005/06–2012/13)

SOURCE: Author's own calculation of data from MoE (2013, 2012, 2011, 2010)

3.3. Challenges of the Rural-urban Infrastructure Divide on Inclusive Development in Ethiopia

Infrastructure plays a principal role to transcend the divide for inclusive development. Particularly those that are related to roads, water, and communication are the main forms of infrastructure that integrate rural and urban areas to close the divide through improved linkages. Due to constraints with data availability, the current discussion on the role of infrastructure to bridge the rural-urban divide for inclusive growth and development is limited to road infrastructure. Prior to the 1990s, the role of road infrastructure in closing the divide in Ethiopia was limited due to poor road quality and low density. Therefore, recognising the essential roles of transport system to link urban and rural areas in the country, Ethiopia has made the road sector development central in its development strategy and has implemented four large-scale road sector development programs during 1997/98-2014/15. The role of road infrastructure in the country has also been acknowledged in ADLI as well as in SDPRP, PASDEP, and GTP. In line with these development policies, the Road Sector Development Program (RSDP) and the Ethiopian Rural Travel and Transport sub-Program (ERTTP) were formulated as parts of the particular road sector policy.

For administrative purposes, roads are classified into three categories as Federal Roads, Rural Roads, and District Roads. In the last decade, the road network in Ethiopia has shown progress where the average growth rate has increased from 1.3 in 2001 to 15.8 in 2014. Table 3 shows that the total stock of road network, which was 44,359 km in 2007/08, has reached 99,522 km in 2013/14; of this, 26,857 km was federal road (roads administered by the central government), 33,609 km was rural road (roads administered by regional rural roads authorities), and 39,056 km was district road (roads administered by local governments).

Table 3. Classification of road networks in Ethiopia (Length in km; Growth Rates in percentage)

Year	Federal roads Asphalt		Gravel		Rural roads		District roads		Total	
	Length	Rate	Length	Rate	Length	Rate	Length	Rate	Length	Rate
2007/08	6,066	11.3	14,363	-1.8	23,930	7.1	70,038.1	21.3	44,359	4.5
2008/09	6,938	14.4	14,234	-0.9	25,640	7.2	85,767.0	22.5	46,812	5.5
2009/10	7,476	7.8	14,373	1.0	26,944	5.1	100,384.9	17.0	48,793	4.2
2010/11	8,295	11.0	14,136	-1.6	30,712	14.0	854.0	-	53,997	10.7
2011/12	9,875	19.1	14,675	3.8	31,550	2.7	6,983.0	717.7	63,083	16.8
2012/13	11,301	14.4	14,455	-1.5	32,582	3.3	27,628.0	295.6	85,966	36.3
2013/14	12,640	11.8	14,217	-1.6	33,609	3.2	39,056	41.4	99,522	15.8

SOURCE: Author's own calculation of data from ERA (2011) and NBE (2014)

The total stock of road network administered by the Federal Government in 2007/08 was 20,429 km, of which 6,066 km (27 per cent) was asphalted and the remaining 14, 363 km (73 per cent) was gravel. In 2013/14, the share of federal roads reached 26,857 km, of which 12,640 km (47 per cent) was asphalted and the remaining 14, 217 km (53 per cent) was gravel. In Ethiopia, rural and district roads lack quality due to financial and technical constraints. Thus, the fact that 72.9 per cent is covered by rural and district road shows that the country has a long way to go to increase the proportion of asphalted and gravel roads to close the rural-urban divide.

Table 4 shows the progress made against selected indicators during the period of the RSDP. The proportion of the total road network in good condition, which was 22 per cent at the beginning of the RSDP in 1997, rose to 56 per cent at the end of the third RSDP in 2010. In this regard, the proportion of asphalted, gravel, and rural road networks in good condition, which was 17, 25, and 21 per cent, respectively, in 1997 showed an impressive increase reaching 73, 53, and 53 per cent in 2010. In 1997, the road density per 1000 sq.km, which was as low as 24.1 km per 1000 sq.km, increased to 44.4 km per 1000 sq.km in 2010. Likewise, the road density per 1000 population, which was 0.46, increased to 0.58 in 2010. The distance of more than 5km from all-weather roads decreased from 79 per cent in 1997 to 64.2 per cent in 2010. In the same manner, the average distance to all-weather roads decreased from 21.4 km in 1997 to 11.3 km in 2010. Despite all these positive changes, low road density can be witnessed from the fact that over 64.2 per cent of rural people are more than five km away from an all-weather road, which affects inclusive development efforts.

Table 4. Improvements in road infrastructure between 1997 and 2010

Selected indicators	1997	2007	2009	2010
Asphalt roads in good condition (%)	17	64	70	73
Gravel roads in good condition (%)	25	49	54	53
Rural roads in good condition (%)	21	46	50	53
Total road in good condition (%)	22	49	50	56
Road Density per 1000 sq. km	24.1	38.6	42.6	44.4
Road Density per 1000 population	0.46	0.55	0.57	0.58
Area more than 5km from all-weather road (%)	79	68	65.3	64.2
Average distance to all-weather road (km)	21.4	13	11.8	11.3

SOURCE: Author's own calculation of data from NBE (2014) and ERA (2011)

The level of physical linkage can be measured by the level of connectivity on the road network. In line with this, a graph theory analysis of the road network using the ERA data set shows extreme underdevelopment and wide divides, mainly due to lack of connection between urban and rural areas in Ethiopia. Table 5 reveals that the beta index, which describes linkages per place or node, is only 0.9 against a maximum of 3.0. Owing to the radial nature of road connectivity in Ethiopia, the index value is found to be lower for regions. Remote and emerging regions like Afar, Soamli, Benishangul, and Gambella have a very low linkage and high rural-urban divide. Besides, the regional variation in average travel distance (km) covered during a one-hour drive (1996-2008) is also higher in these remote and emerging regions where the road infrastructure is yet minimal. Correspondingly, the value for the gamma index (which measures the degree of connectivity) was found to be 30 per cent for the country as a whole, which indicates that 70 per cent of the centres of the population have no connection to the road network.

Table 5. Estimated beta index for regional network/rural-urban linkages of Ethiopia

Regions	Vertices* (e)	Edges (v)	Beta Index (e/v)	MPLs 3(v-2)
Tigray	74	62	0.84	216
Afar	28	20	0.71	78
Amhara	208	200	0.96	618
Oromiya	305	350	0.93	1119
Somali	69	36	0.52	201
Ben. Gumuz	16	12	0.75	42
SNNPRS	149	140	0.94	441
Gambella	14	9	0.64	36
National	933	829	0.89	2793

SOURCE: Author's own calculation of data from ERA (2003, 2009)

*Vertices considered are only those over 3000 people

Nb: Regions with one urban centre like Harari are purposefully excluded from this calculation.

To sum up, following the road sector development program, improvements were seen in terms of access, density, and travel time. Nevertheless, the current level is below that of SSA regions, which indicates that Ethiopia should double its effort to improve road infrastructure today more than ever before. Besides, there is a wide gap on road infrastructure development between urban and rural areas. Except for the major highway roads that cross the rural areas in connecting one urban centre with another, most of the rural roads are not found in good condition due to technical and financial constraints. Thus, Ethiopia's current capacity to close the rural-urban divide by creating reasonable basis for inclusive growth and development is limited, and this has an adverse impact on poverty reduction efforts, access to education and health services, development of the non-farm economy, labour productivity, capital transfer, and production and consumption linkages. As a result, the issue of rural accessibility still remains far from the desired target level that Ethiopia needs to have and poses a serious challenge to inclusive growth and development. Therefore, the country needs to further strengthen its efforts, first, to transcend the inherent rural-urban divide and, second, to graduate to a middle-income country status in terms of road network development, quality, and improved accessibility. Based on the results discussed above, the next section presents the conclusion and policy implications.

4. Conclusion

Inclusive growth and development, as the antithesis of exclusion in development and increased poverty, has gained immense attention after the Copenhagen Summit in 1995. The change in paradigm can be attributed to several reasons. One reason is the search for clarity on the different conceptual frameworks of development: pro-poor growth, inclusive growth, and inclusive development. The other facet is related with the non-stop scholarly search for unanswered questions such as: where there has been considerable growth and development across different parts of the globe, why are large numbers of people trapped in poverty and excluded from the fruits of development and prosperity? In this regard, there is clear evidence in the growing body of scholarship that the persistent rural-urban divide has been posing challenges on inclusive growth and development. Most importantly, the impact of the rural-urban divide on inclusiveness is more serious when it comes to the sub-Saharan Africa region.

This chapter attempted to address three questions. First, while Ethiopia has a good track record in economic development, why are large numbers of people trapped in poverty, exclusion, high inequality, and undefined mechanisms of social protection? Second, to what extent does Ethiopia create an enabling environment that provides high quality education and health with equal/broad participation of all members of society, including vulnerable or marginalised groups? Third, to what extent does Ethiopia provide its citizens access to quality road infrastructure that enables productive engagement in the national economy and contributes to high standard of living? To address the three questions, the study began by reviewing the literature to identify what we already know about the problem. Then, to add to what we know, the study examined the official data that had been collected for almost a decade and a half starting from 2000. In view of that, first, it attempted to synthesise the nature of the rural-urban divide, poverty, and inequality from inclusive growth and development perspectives. Second, it examined how the persistent divide posed challenges to inclusiveness by affecting people's wellbeing in terms of access, quality, and equity of health and education services. Finally, the study synthesised challenges posed by the road infrastructure divide on inclusive growth and development.

Beyond the many theoretical explanations forwarded by development scholars, one manifestation of the divide lies in the conceptualising and understanding of the terms 'urban' and 'rural'. To date, the theoretical and conceptual debate persists and at present even the academia lack fixed delineations of what is urban and what is rural. The accepted wisdom in the contemporary thought divulges that using either or a combination of social, economic, and ecological criteria as standards to differentiate between urban and rural is no more adequate. They are all difficult to measure and vary not only between countries but over time, which makes generalisations problematic. I argue that in a more intricate pattern of settlement, no theorist could come up with a single objective measure that could represent all distinct aspects of urban and rural settlements. Concomitant to this argument, the current development paradigm moves away from hard-and-fast distinctions and degrees of measure in ways that calls for the design of complementary development theories and policies for inclusive development. Therefore, the search for a common theoretical ground within inclusive development frameworks is to move towards intensified synergies that transcend the divide to nurture fruits of linkages for inclusiveness.

The study reveals that the continued divide in Ethiopia poses serious policy challenges to inclusive growth and development. Hence, the main argument I forward from my analysis with respect to the discrepancies and debates on the conceptualisation of rural and urban areas is that clearly defining rural and urban areas is difficult as the two units have increasingly blurring borders that call for a systematic approach to properly conceptualise the dynamics of their interaction from inclusive development perspectives. The inconsistent and irreconcilable definitions and theories lead nation states to enact development policy frameworks that separate rural and urban agendas that scantily address quite a lot of the social, cultural, economic, and environmental issues. To subvert such problems, researchers and policy makers need to pay attention to subtle issues intersecting along the rural-urban continuum and use them as means to nurture inclusive development by reconciling them with local contexts.

The field of development saw the proliferation of dozens of conceptual and theoretical frameworks. Right in the first decade of the 21st century, the concept of inclusive development became a buzzword and a pressing issue and has since been thoroughly discussed in development theories and policy circles. Despite the fact that it has been gathering impetus as a global development agenda, there has not been conceptual clarity on the issue. It has been synonymously used with terms like 'pro-poor growth' and 'inclusive growth' which are actually different. Furthermore, though there are cases where concepts like inclusive growth and development have been extensively discussed in the mainstream development theories, what has become ever more frightening is the fact that the explanations given to them vary and in some cases even contradict each other. Thus, what is important in such academic exercises is to distinguish between inclusive development and pro-poor growth and inclusive growth. I argue that this paves the way to formulating a clear conceptual framework for the growing body of scholarship by reducing the ambiguity in the current debate on these concepts. What is important to note here is that, besides developing a clear conceptual explanation for each concept, scholars in the field of development should be determined to identify the genesis in line with the specific rationale and context in which each development approach can be used.

In the post-independent period, pro-poor growth is conceptualised as a pace and pattern of growth that enhances the ability of the poor to participate in, contribute to, and benefit from growth. In some cases, pro-poor growth is more closely related to the notion of inclusive growth when it is meant to refer to the idea that poverty falls more than it would have if all incomes had grown at the same rate. This study identifies two approaches of pro-poor growth - absolute and relative - and poses one important question that needs to be taken as the centre of current and future theoretical debates: Which sub-classification is closely related to inclusive growth and development? The debate is ongoing and will continue in search of conceptual clarity. What is important is that, while the pro-poor growth approach has more affinity to poverty reduction, inclusive growth, on the other hand, is broad-based and tends to benefit everyone in the society. The author argues that both pro-poor growth and inclusive growth are interrelated but different strategies. We see a stronger relationship between the two if we are trying to relate inclusive growth with either absolute or relative pro-poor growth, but they are also different mainly in their targets and criteria of measurement.

Unlike the two approaches, inclusive development involves comprehensive dimensions with complex theoretical underpinnings. The study contends that, while 'development' tries to bring into play dimensions of well-being beyond income, 'inclusiveness' focuses attention to the distribution of well-being in society. Inclusiveness can be measured simply by the reduction in poverty, by the fall in the overall inequality with growth, and by the improvement in the average level of literacy and life expectancy. Thus, the study confirms that a move from just growth to inclusive development involves, first, a move to evaluate the distribution as well as the average level of well-being along with any dimension considered, and second, it involves a move to include dimensions other than income in assessing performance. In light of this, what is important to note is that, while inclusive growth takes only the first step, staying focused on the income dimension, inclusive development as a concept and practice invites and requires that both steps be put to use.

In this study, inclusive development has been conceptualised as a development process that enhances people's well-being by advancing the idea that all opportunities are equally available to all members of society. Besides, the contemporary development agenda promotes inclusive development as part of the rights-based development model with the vision to advance equality and the participation of the largest possible parts of society, including urban and rural people. Hence, it is unthinkable to bring about inclusive development in a world that is classified as urban and rural with widening gaps. One means to promote inclusive development as part of the effort to bridge the divide is by strengthening the linkage along the rural-urban continuum. In line with this, there is rich evidence in the literature that closing the divide via inclusive development entails the achievement of broad and mutually reinforcing pillars. Therefore, the author argues that the most important pillars that underpin inclusive development along the rural-urban continuum in Ethiopia shall include:

wider and equal access to basic infrastructure; access to social services such as education and health beyond the primary levels; greater access to financial services and employment opportunities; and reduced poverty, inequality and exclusion.

Being one of the few researchers in Ethiopia to investigate the challenges posed by the rural-urban divide on inclusive growth and development, the author argues that understanding the nature and challenges of the rural-urban divide, poverty, and inequality in the country could help to scientifically investigate the reasons why these development anomalies remain long lasting while the country has registered double digit growth rates. The author also believes that the result from such academic scrutiny is important when designing national and or regional development policies to promote inclusiveness. The study reveals that at the turn of the century, Ethiopia is experiencing one of the highest poverty rates in the world. In 2000, the population living on less than US$1.25 PPP per day was 56 per cent, and 44 per cent of the population was below the national poverty line. In 2011, 30 per cent (about 27 million) of the population lived below the national poverty line and 31 per cent lived on less than US$1.25 PPP per day. The study attests the prevalence of rural-urban divide in the country. For instance, urban areas witnessed the greatest growth gains from 2000 to 2005 while rural areas appeared to benefit more from 2006 to 2011. Furthermore, other monetary and non-monetary measures of well-being confirm the general pattern of persistent improvements, though the large declines in poverty are not entirely supported by the magnitudes of change in other measures of equality and equity. Notwithstanding the decline in poverty incidences and the narrowing gaps in both rural and urban areas, poverty in Ethiopia is still more of a rural phenomenon. The disparity in terms of urban and rural poverty excels the divide while, at the same time, it undermines efforts of inclusive growth and development.

In a country where pro-poor policies have been implemented for more than a decade, the prevalence of unrelenting rural poverty has something to inform policy makers to hold back for a moment and evaluate the results that have been achieved so far from inclusive development perspectives. Regardless of the fact that the number of people living in poverty has fallen, there is still a worrying concern that the figure that indicates severe poverty has not fallen since 2004/05; rather, it has risen. This shows that the poorest of the poor are not benefiting significantly from the double-digit growth that has been recorded for at least a decade. Relatively, they were worse off in 2011 than in 2005. Therefore, further coordinated efforts should be exerted by all development stakeholders so as to assimilate the poorest of the poor into the development process via an inclusive approach. This can protect the poor from being liable to further poverty if poverty reduction policies and strategies do not specifically target and reach them. The study shows that all measures of inequality in urban areas prove substantial increase in inequality from 1996 to 2005 and substantial reduction in inequality from 2005 to 2011. In rural areas, all measures of inequality suggest that there has been little change in inequality over time although inequality fell marginally from 1996 to 2005 and increased from 2005 to 2011. The analysis on the level of urban and rural inequality shows the existence of frequent oscillation that makes it difficult to make precise academic prophecy on the growth performance of the country towards inclusive development. When the urban poor are compared with their rural counterparts in terms of their share in the total marketed and non-marketed goods and services, we observe a huge disparity. Since non-marketed home-consumed outputs are primarily food products with limited manufactured outputs, the large share of non-marketed consumption among poor households in both urban and rural areas shows the disparity in consumption patterns across the different income groups. These differences have serious implications on inclusive growth and development by influencing the distributional impacts of policies and external shocks on maximising welfare.

Access to quality education and health services with a broad participation of all members of society helps to measure whether or not these services are accessible, of high quality, and inclusive. The study indicates that there is a clear rural-urban divide on the stunting, wasting, and underweight rates observed in urban and rural Ethiopia for a decade. The study reveals that, in terms of education, Ethiopia's problems have been three-fold. These are related to access, quality, and equity. The levels and trends of literacy rates across the nine regions and the two city administrations show that education is inaccessible especially for the disadvantaged rural pastoralist regions. When quality of education across the different regions is measured by PTR, in 2011, a wide regional disparity was reflected by the low PTR in urban areas like Addis Ababa (23) and the relatively higher PTR in the disadvantaged rural Somali region (65). Likewise, the result on the inclusiveness of education in Ethiopia in terms of equity using GPI shows that education is not inclusive at secondary school level. The result in this study has a clear message to the academia and policy makers to devise ways on how to transcend the rural-urban education divide across the country.

Physical infrastructure plays a principal role to transcend the rural-urban divide for inclusive development. The finding on the role of road infrastructure to promote inclusive development in Ethiopia, however, reveals that the country's current capacity for transcending the divide by creating a reasonable basis for inclusive growth and development is limited. This has an adverse impact on poverty reduction efforts, access to education and health services, productivity of labour and land, transfer of capital, and production and consumption linkages. As a result, the issue of rural accessibility still remains far from the desired target and poses a serious challenge to inclusive growth and development. Therefore, the country needs to put forth more effort, first, to transcend the inherent rural-urban divide and, second, to graduate to a middle-income-country status in terms of road network development, quality, and improved accessibility.

Finally, the study shows that, though the development policies and strategies implemented in Ethiopia for a decade and a half have been pro-poor, in practice they have not resulted in a narrowing of the rural-urban divide.

Notes

1. Emperor Haile Sellasse ruled Ethiopia from 1930 to 1974. His Majesty, Emperor *Haile Sellassie*, gave the country its first written constitution in 1931, which was revised in 1955, on the occasion of the Silver Jubilee of his coronation.

2. *Dergue* is an *Amharic* term meaning "committee". This committee (of soldiers) ruled Ethiopia from 1974 to 1991 under the socialist ideology of the Eastern bloc. The Ethiopian People's Revolutionary Democratic Front (EPRDF) is the party of the incumbent government that took power right after the downfall of the *Dergue* regime in 1991.

3. Plan for Accelerated and Sustained Development to End Poverty (PASDEP), 2005/6-2009/10, was the most consolidated policy framework in the country's history. PASDEP states that "rural-urban linkages need to be strengthened to maximise the poverty impacts and to take full advantage of the synergy for inclusive development".

4. The Growth and Transformation Plan (GTP) is a five-year development plan (20101-2015) developed based on Rosenstein-Rodann's theory of a big push approach, with emphasis on infrastructure development and export expansion. In the GTP, Ethiopia has accorded top priority to accelerated industrialisation in order to create jobs and lift workers from low-productivity agriculture and informal sectors into higher-productivity activities. In Ethiopia, more than 85% of the population lives in the rural area earning basic needs from the traditional agricultural sector. In the last two and a half decades, all sorts of policies and strategies including ADLI were directed to the rural agricultural sector for which the incumbent government has a strong affinity.

5. The Sustainable Development and Poverty Reduction Program (SDPRP), 2002/03-2004/05, was a strategy in which EPRDF gave its primacy to rural people. It was a poverty-reduction strategy enacted to offer special emphasis for rural areas where poverty, food security, and agriculture have remained among the highest priorities of EPRDF.

6. The Agricultural Development-led Industrialisation (ADLI) policy framework has been the mainstream development strategy of the country for more than two decades. ADLI considers the development of the agricultural sector as the engine of growth that would, in turn, fuel the process of industrialisation.

7. Incidence of Poverty (Headcount Index) is the share of the population whose income or consumption is below the poverty line, i.e., the share of the population that cannot afford to buy a basic basket of goods.

8. Depth of Poverty (Poverty Gap) provides information regarding how far households are from the poverty line. This measure captures the mean aggregate income or consumption shortfall relative to the poverty line across the whole population. It is obtained by adding up all the shortfalls of the poor (assuming that the non-poor have a shortfall of zero) and dividing the total by the population. In other words, it is the result of the total resources needed to bring all the poor to the level of the poverty line divided by the number of individuals in the population.

9. Poverty Severity (Squared Poverty Gap) takes into account not only the distance separating the poor from the poverty line (the poverty gap) but also the inequality among the poor; that is, a higher weight is placed on those households further away from the poverty line.

References

Abdallah, S., N. Marks, A. Simms, and S Thompson. 2006. *The (un)happy planet index: An index of human well-being and environmental impact.* London: Friends of the Earth, New Economics Foundation.

African Development Bank Group (AfDB). 2012. Inclusive growth agenda. *Briefing Notes for AfDB's Long-Term Strategy* 6. Tunis: AfDB.

Alemayehu, G., and Y. Addis. 2014. Growth, poverty and inequality, 2000-2013: A macroeconomic appraisal. *In:* Dessalegn, R. *et al.* (Eds.). *Reflections on development in Ethiopia: New trends, sustainability and challenges.* Forum for Social Studies (FSS), Addis Ababa, Ethiopia. pp. 31–66.

Alexander, K. 2015. *Inclusive growth: Topic guide.* Birmingham, UK: GSDRC, University of Birmingham.

Ali, I., and J. Zhuang. 2007. Inclusive growth toward a prosperous Asia: Policy implications. *ERD Working Paper Series,* 97. Manila: ADB.

Alkire, S., and M. B. Sarwar. 2009. Multidimensional measures of poverty and well-being. OPHI, Oxford Department of International Development, Queen Elizabeth House University of Oxford.

Anand, R., S. Mishra, and S. J. Peiris. 2013. *Inclusive growth: Measurement and determinants.* International Monetary Fund, WP/13/135.

Anders, A. 1992. The role of small towns in regional development in South-East Africa. *In:* Baker, J. and P.O. Pedersen (Eds.) *The rural-urban interface in Africa: Expansion and adaptation,* pp. 51–68. Uppsala: The Scandinavian Institute of African Studies.

Assefa, A. 2006. Development policies and their implications to rural-urban linkages in Ethiopia: Opportunities and challenges. *In:* Gete, Z., P. Trutmann and D. Aster (Eds.). Fostering new development pathways: Harnessing RUL to reduce poverty and improve environment in the highlands of Ethiopia, *In:* Proceedings of a planning workshop on thematic research area of Global Mountain Program held in Addis Ababa, Ethiopia. August 29–30, 2006. pp. 181–196. Global Mountain Program. .

Aynalem, A., and H. Assefa. 2011. Rural–urban linkages in Ethiopia: Insuring rural livelihoods and development of urban centers. *The Demographic Transition and Development in Africa,* pp. 167–186. Available at: http://link.springer.com/book [Accessed 22 January 2013].

Baker, J., and D. Pederson (Eds.). 1992. The rural urban interface in Africa: Expansion and adaptation. *Seminar proceedings No 27.* Uppsala: The Scandivian Institute of African Studies.

Berdegué, J. A., F. J. Proctor, and C. Cazzuffi. 2014. Inclusive rural-urban linkages. *Working Paper Series* N° 123. Working Group: Development with Territorial Cohesion. Territorial Cohesion for Development Program. Rimisp, Santiago, Chile.

Bookwalter, J., and P. H. Koehn. 2014. Growth post dependent rural development: Engaging and assessing rural well-being. *In:* Dessalegn R. *et al.* (Eds.). *Reflections on development in Ethiopia: New trends, sustainability and challenges,* pp. 199–218. Addis Ababa: Forum for Social Studies (FSS) .

Cassiers, I., and G. Thiry. 2014. A High-stakes shift: Turning the tide from GDP to new prosperity indicators. *IRES: Discussion Paper* 2.

Central Statistical Agency of Ethiopia (CSA). 2007. Household income, consumption and expenditure (HICE) survey 2004/05, Vol. I, Analytical report. *Statistical Bulletin 394.* Addis Ababa.

———. 2007. Welfare monitoring survey 2004: Analytical report. *Statistical Bulletin 339-A.* Addis Ababa.

———. 2007. Population and housing census of Ethiopia. Addis Ababa.

———. 1994. Population and housing census of Ethiopia. Addis Ababa.

Chancel, L., G. Thiry, and D. Demailly. 2014. Beyond-GDP indicators: To what end? *Study* N°04/14. Paris: IDDRI.

Chang, C. 2014. What is "inclusive growth"? *CAFOD Discussion Paper.*

Costanza, R., M. Hart, S. Posner, and J. Talberth. 2009. *Beyond GDP: The need for new measures of progress.* Boston University: The Frederick S. Pardee Center for the Study of the Longer-Range Future.

Cristobal, K. 2009. Development strategies and rural development: Exploring synergies, eradicating poverty. *Journal of Peasant Studies*, 36(1), pp. 103–137. Available at: http://www.informaworld.com/smpp [Accessed 26 March 2015].

Dabson, B. 2012. Overview of rural America: Past, present, and future. Research and Training Center on Disability in Rural Communities. The University of Montana. USA. Available at: *http://rtc.ruralinstitute.umt.edu* [Accessed 22 January 2013].

Dabson, B., J. Jensen, A. Kagaki, A. Blair, and M. Carroll 2012. Case studies of wealth creation and rural-urban linkages. Rural Policy Research Institute. Available at: *www.ruralfutureslab.org.* [Accessed 22 January 2013].

de Haan, A., and S. Thorat. 2013. Inclusive growth: More than safety nets. *SIG Working Paper,* No. 1.

Dessalegn, R. 2008. Ethiopia: Agriculture policy review. *In:* Taye, A. (Ed.). *Digest of Ethiopian national policies, strategies and programs,* (pp. 129–152). Addis Ababa: Forum for Social Studies (FSS), Ethiopia.

Diener, E., and E. M. Suh. 1999. National differences in subjective well-being. *In:* Kahneman, Diener and Schwarz. *Well-being: The foundations of hedonic psychology.* New York: Russell Sage.

Dollar, D., and A. Kraay. 2002. Growth is good for the poor. *Journal of Economic Growth,* Vol. 7, No. 3, pp. 195–225.

Dorosh, P., G. Alemu, A. de Brauw, M. Malek, V. Mueller, E. Schmidt, K. Tafere, and J. Thurlow. 2011. The rural-urban transformation in Ethiopia. Ethiopia Strategy Support Program II (ESSP II), International Food Policy Research Institute. Available at http://essp.ifpri.info. [Accessed 31 January 2013].

Eshetu, C. 2004. *Under development in Ethiopia.* OSSREA, Addis Ababa: Colour Steps and Print: United Printers.

Ethiopian Development Research Institute (EDRI). 2009. National input-output table and social accounting matrix. Addis Ababa, Ethiopia.

Ethiopian Roads Authority (ERA). 2011. RSDP 13 years performance and phase IV. Addis Ababa, Ethiopia.

————. 2009. RSDP performance: Twelve years later. Addis Ababa.

————. 2003. Road sector development program. Addis Ababa, Ethiopia.

Friedmann, J. 1996. Modular cities: Beyond the rural-urban divide. *Environment and Urbanization* 8(1), 129–131. Available: http://www.eau.sagepub.com [Accessed 8 February 2012].

Gete, Z. 2006. Draft conceptual framework of RUL thematic research area. In: Z. Gete, P. Trutmann, and D. Aster (Eds.). Fostering new development pathways: Harnessing RUL to reduce poverty and improve environment in the highlands of Ethiopia, pp.27– 44. Proceedings of a Planning Workshop on Thematic Research Area of GMP, held in Addis Ababa, Ethiopia. August 29–30, 2006. Global Mountain Program.

Getnet A., and M. Mehrab. 2010. Implications of land policies for rural-urban linkages and rural transformation in Ethiopia. International Food Policy Research Institute ESSP II. *Working Paper No.* 15. Accessed on 22/02/2015 from: *www.ifpri.org.*

Gore, C. 1984. *Regions in question: Space, development theory and regional policy.* London: Methuen.

Hails, C. (Ed.). 2006. *Living planet report 2006.* Gland, Switzerland: World Wildlife Fund for Nature.

Heloisa, M. 2012. Measuring economic progress and well-being: How to move beyond GDP. Oxfam America Research Backgrounder series.

Hirschman, A. O. 1958. *The strategy of economic development.* New Haven, CT: Yale University Press.

Hughes, D. W., and D. W. Holland. 1994. Core periphery economic linkages: A measure of spread and possible backwash effects for Washington economy. *Land economics*, 70(3), 364–377.

Jerve, A. M. 2001. Rural-urban linkages and poverty analysis. *In:* Grinspun, Alejandro. *Choices for the poor: Lessons from national poverty strategies.* New York: United Nations Development Program, 89–120.

Jongereden, J. 2010. Beyond the rural urban divide: New spaces for development. Paper presented at the conference on development, technology and sustainability, Universidade de Maringa, Brazil, September 23–26, 2010. Social Science Group, Wageningen, the Netherlands.

Kakwani, N., and E. Pernia. 2000. What is pro-poor growth? *Asian Development Review*, 18, 1–16.

Kanbur, R. and G. Rauniyar. 2009a. Conceptualizing inclusive development: With applications to rural infrastructure and development assistance. Asian Development Bank. Manila, Philippines. Available at: www.adb.org/evaluation [Accessed 4 March 2015].

Kanbur, R., and G. Rauniyar. 2009b. Inclusive growth and inclusive development: A review and synthesis of Asian development bank literature. Available at: www.adb.org/evaluation. [Accessed 4 March 2015].

Khan, M. H. 2012. The political economy of inclusive growth. *In:* de Mello, L. and M. A. Dutz, (Eds.). *Promoting inclusive growth: Challenges and policies*, 15-54. OECD Publishing. Available at: http://dx.doi.org/10.1787/9789264168305-en. [Accessed 4 March 2015].

Kjøller-Hansen, A. O., and L. L. Sperling. 2013. Inclusive growth in Africa: Measurement, causes, and consequences. UNU-WIDER's conference held in Helsinki on 20–21 September 2013.

Klasen, S. 2010. Measuring and monitoring inclusive growth: Multiple definitions, open questions, and some constructive proposals. *ADB Sustainable Development Working Paper Series*. Manila: ADB.

Klasen, S. 2009. Determinants of pro-poor growth. In: von Braun, J. R. Hill, , and R. Pandya-Lorch, (Eds.). *The poorest and hungry: Assessments, analyses, and action*, pp. 195–202. Washington, D.C.: IFPRI.

Korie, O., C. Eze, J. Lemchi, and U. Ibekwe. 2007. Poverty alleviation through rural urban linkages: Lessons and implications for development in Nigeria: Global approaches to extension practices (GAEP), 3(2). Owerri, Nigeria.

Kozuka, E. 2014. Inclusive development: Definition and principles for the post-2015 development agenda. *In:* JICA (Ed), *Perspectives on the post-2015 development agenda*, (pp. 109–122). Tokyo: Japan International Cooperation Agency Research Institute.

Lickerman, J., P. Flynn, and H. Henderson. 2000. *Calvert-Henderson quality of life indicators: A new tool for assessing national trends*. Bethesda, Maryland: Calvert Group.

Lipton, M. 1977. *Why poor people stay poor*: *Urban bias in world development.* Cambridge: Harvard University Press.

Lynch, K. 2005a. *Rural-urban interaction in the developing world.* London and New York: Rutledge.

Madhur, S., and J. Menon. 2014. *Inclusive development in the greater Mekong sub region: An Assessment.* Phnom Penh: CDRI.

Miheret, A. 2014. Growth and transformation plan: Opportunities, challenges, and lessons. *In:* Dessalegn R. *et al.* (Eds.). *Reflections on development in Ethiopia: New trends, sustainability and challenges,* pp. 3–30. Addis Ababa: FSS.

———. 2008. A review of the FDRE's urban development policy. *In:* Taye, A. (Ed.). *Digest of Ethiopian national policies, strategies and programs.* (pp. 451– 468). Forum for Social Studies (FSS), Addis Ababa, Ethiopia.

Ministry of Education (MoE). 2013. Education statistics annual abstract (2012/13). Addis

Ababa, Ethiopia.

———. 2012. Education statistics annual abstract (2011/12). Addis

Ababa, Ethiopia.

———. 2011. Education statistics annual abstract (2010/11). Addis

Ababa, Ethiopia.

———. 2010. Education statistics annual abstract (2009/10). Addis

Ababa, Ethiopia.

Ministry of Finance and Economic Development (MOFED). 2013. Growth and Transformation   Plan: Annual progress report for F.Y. 2011/12, Federal Democratic Republic of   Ethiopia, Addis Ababa.

———. 2010. Growth and Transformation   Plan   (GTP),   (2010– 2015). Main Text vol. 1. Addis   Ababa, Ethiopia.

Ministry of Works and Urban Development (MoWUD). 2009. Rural-urban linkage manual. Federal   Urban Planning Coordinating Bureau. Addis Ababa, Ethiopia.

Mohammed, S. 2007. Livelihood strategies and their implications for RULs: The case of   Wolenkomi town and the surrounding rural *kebele*s. Working paper on population and   land use change in central Ethiopia. Series A, No. 18 Addis Ababa.

Momen, M. S. 2006. Toward synergistic rural-urban development. The experience of the rural-urban partnership program (RUPP) in Nepal. International Institute for Environment and Development. Working paper series on rural urban interactions and livelihood strategies. *Working paper 13.*

Mulongo, L. S., B. Erute, and P. M. Kerre. 2010. Rural-urban interlink and sustainability of   urban centers in Kenya, Malaba Town. 46th ISOCARP Congress 2010, Nairobi, Kenya.

National Bank of Ethiopia (NBE). 2014. The 2013/14 annual report of NBE. Addis Ababa, Ethiopia.

National Planning Comission (NPC). 2013. Demographic and socio-economic profile of Ethiopia. Addis Ababa, Ethiopia.

Nordhaus, W., and J. Tobin. 1972. *Is growth obsolete?* New York: Columbia University Press.

OECD. 2011. *How's Life? Measuring well-being,* OECD Publishing. Available at: *http://dx.di.org/10.1787/9789264121164-en* [Accessed 24 May 2015].

————. 2006. *Promoting pro-poor growth: Policy guidance for donors*. Paris: OECD.

Ohno, K. 2009. Ethiopia: Political regime and development policies. Japan International Cooperation Agency.

Owuor, S. O. 2006. *Bridging the urban-rural divide: Multi-spatial livelihoods in Nakuru town, Kenya*. African Studies Centre. Leiden, The Netherlands.

Parr, J. B. 1999. Growth-pole strategies in regional economic planning: A retrospective view. Part I. Origins and Advocacy. *Urban Studies*, 36(7), 1195–1215. Available at: www.usi.sagepub.com [Accessed 24 December 2011].

Peet, R., and E. Hartwick. 2009. *Theories of development*: Contentions, *arguments, alternatives*. 2nd ed. New York: The Guilford Press.

Perroux, F. 1950. Economic space: Theory and application. *Journal of Economics,* 4, 90–97.

Ravallion, M. 2005. Inequality is bad for the poor. Development Research Group, World Bank, Washington, D.C.

Ravallion, M., and S. Chen. 2003. Measuring pro-poor growth. *Economics Letters* 78, 93–99. Washington, D.C. 20433, USA.

Rickinson, M., and H. May. 2009. A comparative study of methodological approaches to reviewing literature. The Higher Education Academy.

Rostow, W. W. 1960. *The stages of economic growth: A non-communist manifesto*. London: Cambridge University Press.

Samans, R., J. Blanke, G. Corrigan, and M. Drzeniek. 2015. Benchmarking inclusive growth and development. WEF.

Scott, A., A. Gilbert, and A. Gelan. 2007. The urban-rural divide: Myth or reality? Macaulay Institute. *SERG Policy Brief No. 2*.

Sen, A. 1999. *Development as freedom*. New York: Anchor Books.

Stifel, D., and W. Tassew. 2013. Utility-consistent poverty in Ethiopia, 2000–2011: Welfare improvements in a changing economic landscape. A draft version of a conference paper submitted for presentation at UNU-WIDER's conference, held in Helsinki on 20–21 September 2013.

Stiglitz, J., A. Sen, and J. P. Fitoussi. 2009. Report of the commission on the measurement of economic performance and social progress. Commission on the Measurement of Economic performance and Social Progress: France.

Tacoli, C. 2006. Rural-urban linkages research initiatives: Lessons and key issues from   international experiences. *In:* Z. Gete, P. Trutmann and D. Aster (Eds.). *Fostering new development pathways: Harnessing RUL to reduce poverty and improve environment in the highlands of Ethiopia,* pp. 45–56. Proceedings of a planning workshop on thematic research area of GMP held in Addis Ababa, Ethiopia. August 29-30, 2006.

Tegegne, G. 2005. Rural-urban linkages in Ethiopia: The need to bridge the divide. *In:* G. Tegegne and Van Dik (Eds.). *Issues and challenges in local and regional development, decentralization, urban service delivery, linkage and inequality.* Addis Ababa, Ethiopia.

Tostensen, A. 2004. Rural-urban linkages in sub-Saharan Africa: Contemporary debates and   implications for Kenyan urban workers in the 21st century. *Chr. Michelsen Institute of Development Studies and Human Right, WP,* No. 4. Available at: www.cmi.no/publications [Accessed 12 October 2013].

UN DESA. 2007. *The millennium development goals report.* New York: United Nations Department of Economic and Social Affairs.

United Nations Development Program (UNDP). 2000. Rural-urban linkages: An emerging policy priority. New York: Bureau for Development Policy.

————. 1990. Human development report. Concept and measurement of human development, Oxford University Press: New York, Oxford, 189p.

United Nations Human Settlements Program (UN-Habitat). 2014. Structural transformation in   Ethiopia: The urban dimension: Building 'economically productive, socially   inclusive, environmentally sustainable and well-governed' cities. Available at www.unhabitat.org   [Accessed   14   March 2015].

Ura, K., and K. Galay. (Eds.). 2004. Gross national happiness and development. First International Seminar on Operationalization of Gross National Happiness, Thimphu, Bhutan: The Centre for Bhutan Studies.

van Leeuwen, E. S. 2010. Urban-rural interactions: Towns as focus points in rural development. Berlin Heidelberg: Springer-Verlag.

Wackernagel, M., and W. E. Rees. 1996. *Our ecological footprint: Reducing human impact on the earth.* Gabriola Island, BC: New Society Publishers.

Willis, K. 2005. *Theories and practices of development.* New York: Rutledge.

Workneh, N. 2008. Food security strategy and productive safety net program in Ethiopia. *In:* Taye, A. (Ed.). *Digest of Ethiopian national policies, strategies and programs,* pp. 1–23. Addis Ababa: Forum for Social Studies (FSS) .

World Bank. 2015. Ending poverty and sharing prosperity. GMR, 2014/2015.

World Bank. 2009. What is inclusive growth? *PRMED Knowledge Brief,* Washington, DC: Economic Policy and Debt Department (PRMED), World Bank.

Zhihong, Z., and Z. Xiaoying. 2013. Inclusive development: The mode of equalization of basic public cultural service in China. *Cross-cultural* March 2015].

CHAPTER FOUR

The Dynamics of Poverty, Vulnerability, and Welfare in Rural Ethiopia

Degye Goshu

Abstract

This paper analyses the dynamics of poverty and vulnerability and their determinants and correlates in rural Ethiopia. The study uses the ERHS panel data for the latest two rounds in the four major regional states with a pool of 2495 households sampled from the major sedentary farming systems of the country. The paper generates new empirical evidence on the major dimensions and dynamics of poverty and vulnerability reflecting inclusive growth and development in Ethiopia. The descriptive measures indicated that welfare transition rates were relatively higher for the poor. Every five years, 33 per cent of the poor households were able to escape the poverty trap and the remaining majority (67 per cent) of poor households persisted in the same poverty status. However, nearly 48 per cent of the non-poor households descended to the poverty trap while the rest 52 per cent remained in the same status. Households were characterised by simultaneously descending into and escaping from poverty. Moreover, depth and severity of poverty were substantially reduced with increasing incidence of poverty. The major determinants and correlates of poverty and vulnerability were consistently identified by employing linear and non-linear panel data estimators (RE, RE probit and GEE PA probit). The econometric model outputs pointed out that the likelihood of households to be poor was 45.8 per cent. Vulnerability to poverty was reduced by about 5 percentage points to 41 per cent, , indicating the probability of households to gravitate to long-run better well-being. Major positive welfare changes were generally observed among the poor households which markedly suggest that growth in Ethiopia is pro-poor. But, it is evidenced that there is considerable difference in poverty reduction effects among regions. This reality calls the need for appropriate interventions designed for more inclusive and sustainable growth and poverty reduction. The speed at which the poor are escaping from poverty trap is also sluggish, which would lead to persistent poverty and prolonged period of policy intervention to tackle problems arising from idiosyncratic and covariate shocks.

Keywords: Poverty, vulnerability, random-effects probit, inclusive growth

1. Introduction

Ethiopia has been employing different poverty reduction and food security policies, strategies and programs in the last two decades (MoFED 2006; FDRE 2004). The empirical literature on the effectiveness of these initiatives is, however, confounded by a number of divergent arguments.

The first view that there are positive developments in poverty reduction since the early 1990s is advocated by the incumbent regime and some empirical studies (MEDAC 1999; Dercon 2004; Naschold 2005). On the other hand, a large majority of scholars argue that these positive developments are the effect of methodological and sampling problems resulting in less representative data and hence incorrect implications (Devereux and Sharp 2003; Günther and Harttgen 2006; Krishna 2007; Kitaw and Woldemichael 2008). Other empirical evidence falls in between the above two arguments, justifying and proposing that the divergences are created because the appropriate methods for the analysis of poverty dynamics and the data requirements for these measurements are not met by most developing countries like Ethiopia.

According to the study by the Ethiopian Ministry of Economic Development and Cooperation [MEDaC] (1999), 50 per cent of the Ethiopian population was living below the food poverty line and could not meet their daily minimum nutritional requirement of 2200 kilocalories. Using panel data from rural Ethiopia, Dercon (2004) discusses the determinants of consumption growth (1989–1997) and concluded that consumption had grown substantially, but with diverse experiences across villages and individuals. This scenario is fully supported by Naschold (2005), implying that households in rural Ethiopia do not face asset poverty traps, but instead would be expected to gravitate towards one long-run equilibrium. Accordingly, no household in rural Ethiopia would suffer permanently from short-term asset shocks, but would recover over time.

Devereux and Sharp (2003) argue against the view that poverty in rural Ethiopia has fallen significantly since the early 1990s and suggest that the apparent decline is due to methodological limitations and the measure of welfare used. Bigsten and Shimeles (2008) reported that during the 1994–2004 period households in rural Ethiopia moved frequently in and out of poverty but the difficulty of exiting from poverty, like the chance of avoiding "slipping back", increases with the time spent in that state. This nature of poverty dynamics in Ethiopia is supported by Krishna (2007) and Awel (2007) in that poverty is inherently dynamic whereby large numbers of people are escaping from poverty at any given time, but large numbers are also falling into poverty simultaneously. These implications are also verified by Günther and Harttgen (2006) for the empirical fact that households in developing countries are frequently hit by severe idiosyncratic and covariate shocks, resulting in high consumption volatility. However, the assertion that shocks have different and more durable effects on the less well-off households in rural Ethiopia is partially disproved by the results of some studies since drought shocks are insignificant in determining the dynamics of poverty status in the last decade (Carter *et al.* 2007). Kitaw and Woldemichael (2008) found that while the number of households in persistent poverty was relatively low in both urban and rural areas from 1994 to 2004 in Ethiopia, a very high majority in rural areas and a majority in urban areas were poor at least once during the period. Yesuf and Bluffstone (2009) report the presence of high risk aversion with implications for long-term poverty and links between risk aversion and poverty traps in the highlands of Ethiopia.

All these arguments on the analysis of poverty dynamics and vulnerability in Ethiopia are generally associated with methodological approach and data coverage. There is no agreed upon scenario on the dynamics and sources of poverty for common policy formulation and implementation designed to reduce poverty in rural Ethiopia. Although several measurements to analyse the dynamics of poverty and vulnerability to poverty have recently been proposed, empirical studies are still rare in Ethiopia. The above departure of views would be converged if more rigorous estimation techniques and adequate and representative data coverage are employed in analysing poverty dynamics. This would enable to speed up poverty reduction by implementation of relevant and evidence-driven policies.

This paper considers the foregoing arguments and tries to account for limitations in previous studies. It establishes a point of convergence for the above highly differentiated arguments in terms of methodology, data coverage, and representation. The study uses the Ethiopian Rural Household Survey (ERHS) panel data for the latest two rounds (2004 and 2009) with a sample size of 1149 and 1346 in the two periods to generate a pool of 2495 rural households in the dataset. It covered more than 1346 households in 15 peasant associations (among the major crop growing areas) drawn from 15 districts in the four major regional states (Amhara, Oromia, Tigray, and Southern, Nations, Nationalities and Peoples regional states) , , and more than 1346 households in of Ethiopia (Dercon and Hoddinott 2009). Three groups of more recent linear and nonlinear panel models: Random effects (RE), RE probit and generalised estimating equations (GEE) population-averaged (PA) probit (GEE PA) estimators were employed. Accordingly, the paper is designed to estimate the dynamics of poverty and vulnerability and identify their determinants and correlates for real implications of poverty situation in rural Ethiopia. Moreover, the paper investigates the welfare changes for their implications to inclusive and pro-poor growth in rural Ethiopia.

The remaining part of the paper is organised into four sections. In the second section, the study areas, the methods of data collection, the nature of the dataset and the variables used in the analysis are discussed. The third part reviews the conceptual and analytical frameworks applicable to the analysis of poverty, vulnerability, and pro-poor growth. Then, empirical findings are presented and discussed in part four. Finally conclusions and policy implications are drawn.

2. Dataset and Conceptual Framework

2.1. Survey Sites
This study used the Ethiopian Rural Household Survey (ERHS) panel data, which is a multi-topic 'national representative survey on rural households

conducted for seven rounds since 1989. It covered more than 1346 households drawn from major crop growing areas in 15 peasant associations, 15 districts in the four major regional states (Amhara, Oromia, Tigray, and Southern, Nations, Nationalities and Peoples regional states), , , and of Ethiopia (Table 1). As indicated in Table 1, 10.1 per cent, 32.5 per cent, 24.8 per cent, and 32.5 per cent of the samples were taken from Tigray, Amhara, Oromia, and Southern Nations, Nationalities and Peoples (SNNP) regional states, respectively.

The 15 survey villages of the ERHS are indicated in Figure 1. As depicted by the figure, only sedentary farming systems in the four major regional states are included. Pastoral and agro-pastoral areas in these regions and all the other regional states are not included. However, they can be considered broadly representative of households in non-pastoralist farming systems as of 1994. With only 15 communities, but relatively large samples within each village, the interpretation of the results in terms of rural Ethiopia as a whole has to be done with care.

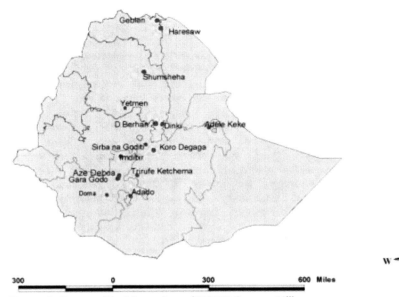

Figure 1. Geographical Location of ERHS Survey Villages
SOURCE: Dercon and Hoddinott (2009).

Table 1. Distribution of samples households across survey villages and years

District	Survey site	Survey year 2004	Survey year 2009	Total
Tsibi	Haresa	74	83	157
Saesi	Geblen	30	65	95
Regional sum— Tigray		104	148	252
Ankober	Dinki	74	79	153
Enemay	Yetmen	52	51	103
Bugna	Shumsha	112	119	231
Basonaworana	Debre Birhan Zuria	160	0	160
		0	165	165
Regional sum— Amhara		398	414	812
Adaa	Sirbana Godeti	0	80	80
Kersa	Adele	74	89	163
Dodota	Korodegaga	93	105	198
Shashemene	Triruf	83	95	178
Regional sum— Oromia		250	369	619
Cheha	Imdibir	63	62	125
Kedida	Aze Deboa	72	73	145
Bule	Adado	116	124	240
Boloso	Gara Godo	89	92	181
Darama	Doma	57	64	121
Regional sum— SNNP		397	415	812
Country sum		**1149**	**1346**	**2495**

SOURCE: Summarised from data in ERHS.

Note: Oda Dawata (Arsi), Bako Tibe (Western Shewa) and Somodo (Jimma zone) were surveyed in 1999 survey round, but there was not sufficient funding to re-survey these villages in 2004 (round 6). Hence, these three sites have been dropped from the analysis to enable comparison of rounds 6 and 7.

2.2 Variables

According to the World Bank (2005), pro-poor growth can be enhanced by resolving constraints related to population density and its degree of urbanisation; asset and income inequality; and importance of agriculture, climate, fertility, and institutions. These constraints are considerably differentiated due to country-specific heterogeneities. Accordingly, the key causes or correlates of poverty could be categorised into three as: (a) region-level characteristics, (b) community-level characteristics, and (c) household and individual level characteristics.

Region-level characteristics include vulnerability to disasters, remoteness, quality of governance, and property rights and their enforcement. The community-level characteristics encompass the availability of infrastructure (such as roads, water, electricity); services (such as health, education); proximity to markets; and social relationships. Household and individual characteristics could be demographic (such as household size, age structure, dependency ratio, gender of head); economic (such as employment status, hours worked, property owned); and social (such as health and nutritional status, education, and shelter).

Inclusive growth and development is becoming the policy imperative of most developing economies. It is a challenging objective because people could be excluded from development because of their age, educational level, occupation, gender, ethnicity, resource endowment, or poverty (McKinley 2010). Based on these related definitions, the variables considered in this study are defined, measured and their likely effects on real consumption and poverty status are hypothesised. The definitions, measurements and the expected effects of the variables are summarised in Table 2.

2.2.1. Dependent/Outcome Variables

Real consumption per capita: Real consumption per capita of households is measured in Ethiopian Birr (ETB) in 1994 constant prices. It is used as a proxy for intensity of poverty situation. Households with higher income are expected to have higher consumption per capita as a measure of wellbeing and inclusive development.

Poverty status: In this study, the consumption poverty line in 2009 in rural Ethiopia was set to be 50 ETB per day. Households falling below this threshold were considered as poor, non-poor otherwise. The intensity and dynamics of poverty and its sources in rural Ethiopia are estimated and identified from the real consumption dynamics across household and over time.

Vulnerability to poverty: The economic approach of measuring vulnerability to poverty is the probability that a household, whether currently poor or not, would find itself poor in the future. Vulnerability in this case is perceived to express the likelihood of a household to be consumption poor in the future. The vulnerability index and its correlates are determined from the real consumption and poverty dynamics in rural Ethiopia.

2.2.2. Explanatory Variables

Age of the household head: It is a continuous variable measured in years as a proxy for farm business experience. More experienced household heads are expected to be relatively more skilled and knowledgeable to enhance their household consumption and thereby to escape from the poverty trap. They are also better in identifying alternative sources of income to increase their real consumption in order to reduce depth of poverty.

Table 2. Measurement of variables and their expected effects

Definition of Variables	Measurement level	Expected effect on poverty/vulnerability
Age	Continuous (years)	+/-
Educational level	Continuous (years of schooling measured by grades completed)	-
Household size	Continuous (counts of family members)	+
Livestock holding (TLU)	Continuous (tropical livestock unit)	-
Marital status	Binary (1 if married, 0 otherwise)	+/-
Primary occupation	Binary (1 if farming, 0 otherwise)	+
Occurrence of drought	Binary (1 if occurred, 0 otherwise)	+
Ladder of life status	Categorical	
Worse-off in the ladder	Binary (1 if in the lower ladder of life, 0 otherwise)	+
Middle level in the ladder	Binary (1 if in the middle ladder of life, 0 otherwise)	-
Better-off in the ladder	Binary (1 if in the highest ladder of life, 0 otherwise)	-
Social network	Binary (1 if socially networked, 0 otherwise)	
Ethnicity/regional states	Categorical	
Tigray	Binary (1 if in Tigray region, 0 otherwise)	+/-
Oromia	Binary (1 if in Oromia region, 0 otherwise)	+/-
Amhara	Binary (1 if in Amhara region, 0 otherwise)	+/-
SNNP	Binary (1 if in SNNP region, 0 otherwise)	+/-

Educational level (years of schooling): Literacy level is one of the major dimensions and indicators of inclusive development. Human development index (HDI) is the major welfare index combining per capita income/expenditure, education, and health (measured by life expectancy) to arrive at a single index of development. Education (measured by literacy rate or grades completed) in this case could be considered as one of the major indicators or other dimensions of human wellbeing in rural Ethiopia. It can be hypothesised that more literate households are relatively more capable of increasing their household consumption and reducing poverty.

Household size: The number of household members could adversely affect real consumption expenditure available to household members. Though family size creates labour availability to households, households with more members are more likely to face poverty because the marginal product of labour in rural areas is nearly zero. Large household size may aggravate poverty in rural Ethiopia.

Livestock holding: Livestock is the major asset of households serving as a means of saving and diversification in rural Ethiopia. More asset holdings improve real consumption expenditure of households. Asset holdings of households determine their poverty situation as asset-poor households obviously consume less. Livestock holding, measured in tropical livestock unit, is hypothesised to reduce poverty and vulnerability to poverty in rural Ethiopia.

Marital status: This is a dummy variable measured as 1 if the household head is married, 0 otherwise (single, divorced, or widowed). Married households may be different from single or divorced households in earnings, asset holdings, and fertility. It is used as a proxy variable to capture this heterogeneity between the poor and the non-poor. Married households are more likely to be poor.

Primary occupation: The type of business in which the household is involved determines the expected income and the consumption expenditure available to the household because all business activities are not equally profitable and/or risky. This is a dummy variable valued as 1 if primary occupation of the household head is farming, 0 otherwise (non-farm). Households with primary occupation of farming are hypothesised to be vulnerable to poverty since farming in Ethiopia is full of multiple risks of production and marketing.

Occurrence of drought: Shocks are multiple in agricultural operations. The occurrence of drought shock within the last five years (before and after 2004 and 2009) is used to capture the effect of climatic shocks on aggravating poverty in rural Ethiopia.

Ladder of life status: Households' perception about their status of life was proxied by their response on the ladders of life status varying from 0 to 10. The top of a ladder represents the best possible life for the household. The ladders of life were further summarised into three ordinal values as worse-off (1 if the household falls in the lower ladders of life, from 0 to 3 ladders), middle-level (2 if it falls in 4 to 7 ladders), and better-off (3 if it falls in 8 to 10 ladders). Households in the lower ladders of life are expected to face persistent poverty because they could not have the capacity to escape from the poverty trap for the fact that they are challenged by serious resource constraints to break the 'vicious circle' of poverty.

Social network: Access to finance is a serious constraint among smallholder farmers in Ethiopia. Social network creates access to various services including finance. In this study, access to emergency financial need (100 ETB) is used as a proxy for social network. In the Ethiopian context, households which could get finance from others for their emergency need are assumed to be socially networked. Socially networked households are more likely to be non-poor and less vulnerable to poverty.

Ethnicity/regional states: Regions in Ethiopia are organised based on ethnicity. These regions could have differentiated aspects, such as policies, regulations, implementation capacities and resource endowments. Most of these heterogeneities are not observable. Their likely effects on poverty and vulnerability to poverty can be captured by regional dummies. The four major regions (Amhara, Tigray, Oromia and SNNP) are considered in the analysis.

2.3. Conceptual Framework

According to the World Bank (2001), poverty can be defined as the human condition characterised by the sustained or chronic deprivation of resources, capabilities, choices, power, and security necessary for an adequate standard of living, and other civic, cultural, economic, political, and social rights. Extreme poverty refers to people who live on or less than US $1.25 a day; whereas poverty is living on or less than $2 a day. In relative terms, absolute poverty refers to subsistence below minimum, socially acceptable living conditions, usually established based on nutritional requirements and other essential goods. Relative poverty compares the lowest segments of a population with upper segments. Absolute and relative poverty may move in opposite directions in that relative poverty may decline while absolute poverty increases if the gap between upper and lower strata of a population is reduced by a decline in welfare of the former, in which case additional households fall below the absolute poverty line.

Poverty analysis can be approached from objective or subjective perspectives. The objective perspective (or welfare approach) involves normative judgments as to what constitutes poverty and what is required to move people out of their impoverished state. The subjective approach places a premium on peoples' preferences, on how much they value goods and services (or individual utility). This paper uses the objective approach for the conceivable fact that the subjective approach could undervalue and overvalue food consumption when compared to the welfare approach, leading to conflicting results and recommendations as to who are the poor. However, both perspectives bring valuable insights to the measurement and analysis of poverty, neither of which can be said to be right or wrong (Philip and Rayhna 2004).

Two comprehensive definitions of vulnerability are developed by the United Nation International Strategy for Disaster Reduction (UN/ISDR) and the United Nations Development Program (UNDP). Vulnerability may be defined as the "conditions determined by physical, social, economic, and environmental factors and processes, which increase the susceptibility of a community to the impact of hazards" (UN/ISDR 2004, 7). The UNDP defines vulnerability as "a human condition or process resulting from physical, social, economic, and environmental which determine the likelihood and scale of damage from the impact of a given hazard" (UNDP 2004, 11). While there is a consensus on the measures of poverty, most vulnerability measures have recently been developed and most of them have not been adopted. This paper uses the economic approach of measuring vulnerability to poverty as the probability that a household, whether currently poor or not, would find itself poor in the future. That is, the concept of vulnerability is perceived in the income space to express the probability that a household will become consumption poor in the future.

When estimating poverty using monetary measures, we may have a choice between using income or consumption as the indicator of welfare. Most analysts argue that, provided the information on consumption obtained from a household survey is detailed enough, consumption will be a better indicator of poverty measurement than income in terms of various expected problems: consumption is a better outcome indicator than income; may be better measured than income; and may better reflect a household's actual standard of living and ability to meet basic needs. Because income is highly volatile in terms of various shocks and downward biases expected in data collection, consumption is a better proxy to capture welfare.

Poverty is an ex-post measure of a household's well-being. It reflects a current state of deprivation, of lacking the resources or capabilities to satisfy current needs. Vulnerability, on the other hand, may be broadly understood as an ex-ante measure of well-being, reflecting not so much how well off a household currently is, but what its future prospects are. What distinguishes the two is the presence of risk or uncertainty about the future well-being of households. If such risks were absent there would be no distinction between ex-ante (vulnerability) and ex-post (poverty) measures of well-being (Chaudhuri 2003).

Growth and development may or may not be pro-poor. There are two definitions for measuring pro-poor growth— relative and absolute. The relative definition of pro-poor growth compares changes in the incomes of the poor with respect to changes in the incomes of the non-poor. According to this definition, growth is pro-poor when the distributional shifts accompanying growth favour the poor (UN 2000; Kakwani and Pernia 2000; Kraay 2004). Pro-poor growth leads to significant reductions in poverty (UN 2000). Growth is pro-poor if inequality falls (White and Anderson 2001).

In the absolute definition, growth is said to be pro-poor if poor people benefit in absolute terms. According to Ravallion and Chen (2003), the growth process can be said to be pro-poor if it reduces poverty. In this definition the aim is to achieve accelerated poverty reduction through growth and enhanced distributional change. The relative definition of pro-poor growth requires that the income share of the poor increase (World Bank 2005). Pro-poor growth in this case focuses on accelerating the rate of income/consumption growth of the poor and thus the rate of poverty reduction (Ravallion and Chen 2003; DFID 2004).

In this paper, poverty status is determined by the level of households' real consumption per capita in 1994 prices compared to the poverty line of ETB 50 per day. Households with real consumption per capita below ETB 50 per day are considered poor and those above this threshold as non-poor. The determinants of poverty in rural Ethiopia are hypothesised to be idiosyncratic features of households including age, educational level, marital status, primary occupation, social network, livestock holding, and living status of households on the ladder of life. Other covariates include occurrence of drought and regional dummies.

3. Analytical Framework

3.1. Descriptive Methods

The changes in welfare indicators in rural Ethiopia between 2004 and 2009 were analysed by transition rates of households from one welfare status to the other. Accordingly, the transitions in the ladder of life status and poverty status of households in rural Ethiopia were computed. In a panel data, given $y_{it} = v_1$, the probability that $y_{i,t+1} = v_2$ can be estimated by counting transitions, where v_1 and v_2 are ordinal outcomes (such as worse-off, middle level, better-off or poor and non-poor). In interpreting the transition probabilities, the rows reflect the initial values, and the columns reflect the final values. The welfare transition rates are useful methods of data analysis in identifying the percentage of households moving up or down from one status to the other. For instance, the percentage of households falling to or escaping from the poverty trap could be known.

A poverty measure is decomposable if the poverty measure of a group is a weighted average of the poverty measures of the individuals in a group (Foster Greer and Thorbecke 1984). These measures can be expressed as:

$$P_a = \frac{1}{N} \sum_{t=1}^{i=N} \left(\frac{c_{it} - z}{z} \right)^\alpha, \qquad a \geq 0 \qquad (1)$$

Where P_a is the measure of poverty; N is the sample size, c_{it} is real consumption per capita by household i in year t as a proxy measure of welfare, and z is the poverty line. When $\alpha=0$, the resulting measure is the head count index (HCI), or the percentage of the population that is poor. The poverty gap index (PGI) results when $\alpha=1$, and the squared poverty gap index (SPGI) when $\alpha=2$.

The HCI is the measure of incidence of poverty which measures the share of the population whose income or consumption is below the poverty line, that is, the share of the population that cannot afford to buy a basic basket of goods. The PGI, a measure of the depth or intensity of poverty, is defined as the average distance below the poverty line (expressed as a proportion of the poverty line), where the mean is formed over the entire population and counts the non-poor as having zero poverty gap. This provides information regarding how far-off households are from the poverty line. This measure captures the mean aggregate consumption shortfall relative to the poverty line across the whole population. The SPGI is a measure of the severity (or inequality) of poverty and is defined as the mean of the squared proportionate poverty gaps. It takes into account not only the distance separating the poor from the poverty line (the poverty gap), but also the inequality among the poor. That is, a higher weight is placed on those households further away from the poverty line.

3.2. Econometric Methods

To examine the predictability of poverty and vulnerability, standard univariate binary panel models in which the dependent variable represents the choice between the likelihood to be poor and non-poor or vulnerable and not vulnerable are used. The use of panel data and binary response models in this paper are expected to have several advantages, including the evaluation of two successive correlations over two time periods, more efficient estimation attributed to increased degrees of freedom, and reduction of the problems when there is an omitted variable (Bertschek and Lechner 1998; Wooldridge 2002: Greene 2002). The paper tries to extend and augment the earlier works by Dercon and Krishna (1998, 2000), Bigsten et al. (2003), Bigsten and Shimeles (2008), Krishna (2007), and Kitaw and Woldemichael (2008).

A popular model for binary outcomes with panel data, poor or non-poor in this case, is the unobserved effects probit model. The specification of unobserved effects probit model is specified as follows (Maddala 1987; Bertschek and Lechner 1998; Wooldridge 2002; Greene 2012).

$$\Pr\left(y_{it} = 1 \middle| \mathbf{x}_{it}, \alpha_i\right) = \Phi\left(\mathbf{x'}_{it}\, \boldsymbol{\beta} + \alpha_i\right), \ t = 1, \ldots, T \tag{2}$$

$$y_{it} = \begin{cases} 1 \ if \ poor, \ y_{it} > 0 \\ 0 \ otherwise, \ y_{it} \le 0 \end{cases} \tag{3}$$

where $\Pr$ is the probability of a household to be poor, y_{it} is poverty status of household i in year t, $\mathbf{x}_i$ is a vector of explanatory variables ($\mathbf{x}_i$ contains $\mathbf{x}_{it}$ for all t), Φ is the standard normal (probit) distribution function, $\boldsymbol{\beta}_t$ is a vector of parameters, and α_i is the unobserved effect.

Repeated observations on individuals over time and clustered observations in panel data are expected to suffer from correlated observations. The use of generalised estimating equations (GEE) or generalised method of moments (GMM) in a longitudinal data are one of the methods of analysis that account for correlated observations by allowing a possibility of unknown correlation between outcomes. Zeger, Liang and Albert (1988) discuss extensions of generalised linear models for the analysis of longitudinal data by considering two approaches: subject-specific models in which heterogeneity in regression parameters is explicitly modelled; and population-averaged (PA) models in which the aggregate response for the population is the focus of analysis. They used a generalised estimating equation approach to fit both classes of models for discrete and continuous outcomes. When the subject-specific parameters are assumed to follow a Gaussian distribution, simple relationships between the PA and subject-specific parameters are available. In GEE PA estimators, the interest is usually in averaging across the distribution of α_i and consistent estimation of parameters under various assumptions, but the basic model RE is not changed. In the GEE approach to unobserved effects binary response models, the response probabilities are specified conditional only on x_i, the PA model:

$$E(y_{it}|\mathbf{x_{it}}) = E(y_{it}|\mathbf{x_i}),$$
$$for \ all \ t. \tag{4}$$

The simplest linear method used to identify the determinants of consumption dynamics and to predict the expected real consumption per capita is a linear panel data estimator known as random-effects (RE). Accordingly, a household's expected poverty was estimated from the following RE model:

$$\ln c_{it} = \mathbf{x_{it}}\boldsymbol{\beta} + (\alpha_i + u_{it}), \ i = 1,2,...,N. \tag{5}$$

where $\ln c_{it}$ is the log-normalised real consumption per capita of household i in year t,

$\mathbf{x}$ is a vector of explanatory variables determining household real consumption per capita, and $\boldsymbol{\beta}$ is the vector of parameters to be estimated.

Accordingly, vulnerability as expected poverty (V) and its correlates were identified as forwarded by Dutta, Foster and Mishra (2010); Pritchett, Suryahadi and Sumarto (2000); and Philip and Rayhna (2004)

$$V_{it} = \Pr(c_{i,t+1}, = c(\mathbf{x_t}, \boldsymbol{\beta_{t+1}}, \alpha_i, \varepsilon_{it}) \le z|\mathbf{x_i}, \boldsymbol{\beta_t}, \alpha_i, \varepsilon_{it}) \tag{6}$$

where $c_{i,t+1}$ is the household's real consumption per capita at time $t+1$,

z is the poverty line,

α_i and ε_{it}, respectively, are unobservable time-invariant household-level effects and idiosyncratic factors that contribute to differential welfare outcomes, and other notations as explained before.

A household is then considered as vulnerable to poverty if its expected vulnerability is larger than a probability threshold level assumed, p:

$$V_i = \begin{cases} 1 & \text{if } V_i > p \\ 0 & \text{if } V_i \leq 0. \end{cases} \qquad (7)$$

4. Empirical Results

4.1. Description of Variables

Table 3 reports the idiosyncratic features of households and other covariates over time and across households. All the variables used in the analysis were tested for their mean values and proportions between panels (poverty status) and between waves (survey years). Except for household size and the three ladders of life status, mean differences of all other variables between 2004 and 2009 were significant at least at 10 per cent level. Except age and primary occupation, the mean differences for all the other variables across households of different poverty status were significant at one per cent level.

Considerable changes of idiosyncratic features of households and other covariates were observed between 2004 and 2009 and across sample households. The mean difference in real per capita consumption was significant over time and across households of different poverty status. Real per capital consumption was decreased in the period, which is a relevant evidence to verify the negative impact of market and other economic shocks depleting the welfare of households in rural Ethiopia. Educational level was increased in the period, suggesting that less literate households were poor. There was significant change in household size between the poor and the non-poor, which could be attributed to effect of differentiated access to family planning services in rural Ethiopia. However, as expected, the mean family size of poor households was relatively higher as compared to the non-poor. The size of livestock holding was increased between the two periods though the difference in livestock holding of the poor and non-poor households was substantially large. Marital status, farming occupation, and drought occurrence were a bit reduced in the study period. The living status of households was also changed between the poor and the non-poor, leading to escapes from and descents into poverty (see Table 3 for further details).

Table 3. Mean comparison test results between survey years and poverty status

Variables	Survey year			Poverty status		
	2004	2009	t-(z) value	Non-poor	Poor	t-(z) value
Real consumption per capita (ETB)	87.43	59.15	10.37***	107.32	30.60	33.00***
Age	50.54	52.63	-3.44***	51.91	51.38	0.88
Educational level	1.75	2.19	-2.72***	2.09	1.87	1.35*
Household size	5.72	5.70	0.24	5.27	6.23	-9.52***
Livestock holding	2.89	4.89	-10.77***	4.68	3.14	8.23***
Marital status	0.69	0.66	2.04**	0.65	0.70	-2.66***
Primary occupation	0.74	0.71	1.35*	0.72	0.72	0.22
Occurrence of drought	0.59	0.40	9.35***	0.42	0.57	-7.73***
Social network	0.57	0.73	-7.97***	0.72	0.59	6.80***
Ladder of life status:						
Worse-off	0.31	0.32	-0.55	0.25	0.39	-7.74***
Middle level	0.63	0.61	0.71	0.66	0.57	4.49***
Better-off	0.06	0.06	-0.41	0.09	0.03	6.14***
Ethnicity/Regions:						
Tigray	0.09	0.11	-1.63**	0.05	0.16	-9.28***
Oromia	0.22	0.27	-3.25***	0.30	0.18	6.94***
Amhara	0.35	0.31	2.11**	0.42	0.21	11.06***
SNNP	0.34	0.31	1.93**	0.23	0.44	-11.49***

Note: ***, ** and * denote significance levels at 1 per cent, 5 per cent and 10 per cent, respectively. Note also that t-values and z-values are used to test mean difference, respectively, in mean values of continuous and proportion of categorical variables.

SOURCE: Author's computation from data in ERHS.

4.2. Changes in Welfare

4.2.1. Welfare Transition Rates

The transition probabilities of households in rural Ethiopia from one ladder of life to the other are reported in Table 4. The results point out that, every five year, some 48 per cent of the households in the lower ladders of life status remained in the same situation for five years while the majority (50 per cent) had a chance of achieving middle-level ladders of life status. Only two per cent of the household moved up to the top ladders of life, indicating the negligible improvement in their welfare situation. About 24 per cent of the households living in the middle ladders of life moved down to lower ladders of life status while the large majority (69 per cent) remained in the same life status. Households at the middle ladders of life in 2004 which moved up to the higher ladders of life are very few (only 6.9 per cent). Overall, about 31 per cent of the households at the lower ladders of life remained in the same welfare situation while the remaining 63 per cent and six per cent, respectively, moved up to middle-level and top ladders of life.

Table 4. Transition probabilities of households across ladders of life status in rural
    Ethiopia

Status in the ladder of life	Worse-off	Middle level	Better-off
Worse-off	48.04	49.85	2.11
Middle level	24.32	68.78	6.91
Better-off	18.03	65.57	16.39
Total	31.19	62.83	5.98

SOURCE: Author's computation from data in ERHS.

The transition probabilities generally suggest that growth in Ethiopia is pro-poor because considerable welfare transitions were observed at the lower ladders of life. There was very low welfare transition to the top ladders of life which is suggestive of the reduction in relative poverty accompanied by substantially higher number of households moving down and up in the ladders of life.

The transition probabilities of households from one poverty status to the other are reported in Table 5. The results point out that, about 67 per cent of poor households remained in the same poverty status for five years while the remaining 33 per cent could be able to escape out of the poverty. On the other hand, nearly 48 per cent of the households descended into poverty and the remaining majority (52 per cent) remained in the same status. Generally, the period was characterised by descents to and escapes from the poverty trap. About 55.5 per cent of the households remained in the same poverty status while the other 44.5 per cent escaped from poverty. As indicated by the welfare transitions of households, the growth in Ethiopia is pro-poor as indicated by the major poverty dynamics observed in poor households though reducing relative poverty and inequality.

Table 5. Transition probabilities of households between poverty status in rural
    Ethiopia

Poverty status	Poor	Non-poor
Poor	67.3	32.61
Non-poor	48.25	51.75
Total	55.46	44.54

SOURCE: Author's computation from data in ERHS.

4.2.2. Changes in Intensity of Poverty

Table 6 combines and reports the three simple measures of poverty called Foster-Greer-Thorbecke (FGT) decomposable poverty indices: the head count index (HCI), the poverty gap index (PGI), and the squared poverty gap index (SPGI).

Taking the number of poor households falling under the poverty line as a measure of poverty incidence, the number of the poor was increased from 37.5 per cent in 2004 to 52.9 per cent in 2009. About 281 households which were non-poor in 2004 have fallen under the poverty line in 2009. However, the mean poverty gap was substantially reduced from ETB 44.4

in 2004 to ETB 19.6 in 2009. The average distance of real per capita consumption from the poverty line was decreasing. The PGI statistics shows that the depth of poverty was reduced from 88.8 per cent in 2004 to 39.2 per cent in 2009. Severity of poverty was also reduced from 3.6 per cent in 2004 to 0.7 per cent in 2009. The results generally suggest that the depth and severity of poverty were decreasing in rural Ethiopia between 2004 and 2009 even if the number of poor households falling under the poverty trap was increasing. These results are consistent with the welfare transitions computed above in verifying that growth in Ethiopia is pro-poor, contributing to reducing relative poverty and inequality.

Table 6. Incidence, intensity, and severity of poverty in rural Ethiopia

Measures of poverty	Survey year		Changes in poverty measures
	2004	2009	
Head count index (%)	37.5	52.9	15.4
Mean poverty gap (ETB)	44.4	19.6	-24.8
Poverty gap index (%)	88.8	39.2	-49.6
Squared poverty gap (%)	3.56	0.7	-2.86

SOURCE: Author's computation from data in ERHS.

4.3. Determinants of Real Consumption

The factors determining poverty in rural Ethiopia identified by random-effects method are reported in Table 7. All the parameters found to be strongly and significantly affecting real consumption have the expected signs. The variation in real consumption per capita across households and over the years explained by the RE model is about 37.6 per cent between households with overall variation of 25.2 per cent. These results strongly verify the presence of random-effects in the dataset.

The factors determining real consumption per capita in rural Ethiopia are household size, livestock holding, primary occupation, social network, ladders of life, and region. Socially networked households with more livestock holding residing in Amhara, Oromia and SNNP regions consume more compared to their counterparts in Tigray. However, as expected, households with large family size in the lower ladders of life consume less.

Table 7. Random-effects model results of determinants of real consumption in rural Ethiopia

Variable	Coefficient	Standard errors
Age of household head	0.00	0.001
Educational level	0.00	0.004
Household size	-0.09***	0.006
Marital status	-0.04	0.038
Livestock holding	0.01***	0..003
Primary occupation	0.10***	0.036
Social network	0.14***	0.032
Occurrence of drought	-0.02	0.030
Worse-off in the ladder	-0.50***	0.063
Middle level in the ladder	-0.27***	0.058
Oromia	0.06***	0.054
Amhara	0.57***	0.055
SNNP	0.16***	0.052
Constant	4.22***	0.103
Number of observations	2422	
R-squared		
Within	0.030	
Between	0.376	
Overall	0.252	
Wald $\chi^2 (13)$	808.54	

***, ** and * denote significance levels at 1 per cent, 5 per cent and 10 per cent, respectively.

SOURCE: Author's computation from data in ERHS.

4.4. Determinants of Poverty

The results of the panel data estimators are reported in Table 8. The estimation results from both extensions of the estimators are consistent in terms of signs and levels of significance. Out of the hypothesised determinants of poverty dynamics in rural Ethiopia, nine were significant at 1 per cent level. Two variables (marital status and primary occupation) were significant at 10 per cent level of significance.

The major determinants of poverty dynamics contributing to poverty reduction in rural Ethiopia were livestock holding, farming occupation (weakly), social capital, regional state, and the effects of other variables captured by the constant term. It is an important empirical evidence to verify that farming as primary occupation is one means of poverty reduction, which is against the common assertion that farming in Ethiopia is a source of poverty. With different effects in magnitude, regions (not just states) have their own role on poverty reduction. The other variables can be considered as sources of poverty aggravating the likelihood of households to be trapped into poverty. Household size, marital status (weakly) and the lower levels of living status (worse-off and middle-level status) reinforce poverty in rural Ethiopia. The vulnerability of rural households to poverty increases with these variables observed over time.

Table 8. Determinants of poverty dynamics in rural Ethiopia

Variable	RE probit	GEE PA probit
Age of household head	0.000	0.000
Educational level	-0.001	-0.001
Household size	0.135***	0.135***
Marital status	0.126*	0.127*
Livestock holding (TLU)	-0.027***	-0.027***
Primary occupation	-0.140*	-0.139*
Social network	-0.233***	-0.234***
Occurrence of drought	0.028	0.028
Worse-off in the ladder	0.780***	0.779***
Middle level in the ladder	0.464***	0.463***
Oromia	-0.998***	-0.996***
Amhara	-0.865***	-0.864***
SNNP	-0.297***	-0.296***
Constant	-0.508**	-0.507**
Number of observations	2439	2439
Probability (poverty index)	0.458	0.458
Log likelihood	-1441.47	-
Wald χ^2 (13)	-	426.06

***, ** and * denote significance levels at 1 per cent, 5 per cent and 10 per cent, respectively.

SOURCE: Author's computation from data in ERHS.

Note: The likelihood ratio (LR) tests of the correlations between the latent composite errors indicate that the assumption of independent conditionality of the unobserved effects is fulfilled if time dummies are omitted.

The sign of the weak positive effect of marital status on poverty is as expected. The probability of married household heads to be poor increases with their marriage and across time, because household earnings and real consumption (and hence poverty) are likely positively associated with marriage. As expected, households living at the lower ladders of life were relatively poorer. The ability of a household to get an emergency financial access was found to be a good proxy to capture the level of social network a household has. Socially networked households are more likely to be non-poor.

With the exception of the rarely used method of interpreting latent variables, substantively meaningful interpretations are based on predicted probabilities and functions of those probabilities. The predictions from the two models can be demonstrated to verify that they are essentially identical. The hypothesis that the probability of households to fall under the poverty line in rural Ethiopia is 50 per cent was rejected at one per cent level. The test results indicate that the observed probability of households to be poor was less than or equal to 45.8 per cent with a total number of poor households between the two periods to be 1143. The predicted probabilities from the two estimators show almost similar predictions in the sample ranging from 1.8 per cent to 96.7 per cent, with the same mean predicted probability being in the poverty status of 45.8 per cent. During 2004–2009, the likelihood of households to be poor in rural Ethiopia was reduced between.

The estimated marginal and average marginal effects are indicated in Table 9. For a unit change in household size across time and between households, the likelihood of a household to be poor increases by about 5.4 per cent, which is relatively small effect. However, the effort to enhance poverty reduction must consider the negative effect of large family size through relevant policy intervention measures. The same unit change in livestock holding results in a decreasing probability of about 1.1 per cent. This minimal positive effect of livestock holding can be enhanced by promoting livestock production and productivity.

Table 9. Marginal and average marginal effects of determinants of poverty

Variable	Marginal effects	Average marginal effects
Household size	0.054	0.046
Marital status	0.050	0.043
Livestock holding	-0.011	-0.009
Primary occupation	-0.055	-0.047
Social network	0.093	-0.079
Worse-off in the ladder	0.303	0.262
Middle level in the ladder	0.180	0.156
Oromia	-0.358	-0.335
Amhara	-0.323	-0.290
SNNP	-0.116	0.100

SOURCE: Author's computation from data in ERHS.

Note: Only significant estimates are reported. They are more consistent for all versions of the models, and hence interpretation is reported for one of the model results (GEE PA probit).

A discrete change from zero to one (regional change) across time and between individual households in regional states decreases the probability of being poor by about 35.8 per cent in Oromia, 32.3 per cent in Amhara, and 11.6 per cent in SNNP region. This clearly shows that poverty reduction was relatively more in Oromia followed by Amhara and SNNPR. This might be the result of regionally-differentiated poverty reduction efforts or the nature of natural capital (land and agro-ecology and other resources bases) endowed to the regions, or the effect of both. Social network households have could be able to reduce the probability of being poor by about 9.3 per cent. For the same discrete change in marital status, worse-off living status, and middle-level living status, the probability of households to be poor increases, respectively, by about 5.0 per cent, 30.3 per cent, and 18.0 per cent. Households in the lower level of living condition were more vulnerable to poverty.

One of the problems encountered in interpreting probabilities is their nonlinearity: the probabilities do not vary in the same way according to the level of regressors. A better method to summarise the estimated marginal effects is to estimate the average value across the population. A consistent estimator and an asymptotic standard error can be obtained by the delta method (Wooldridge 2002). The estimated average marginal effects are margins at the mean values of all the covariates. As indicated in the last column of the table, all of the average marginal effects are lower than the marginal effects for instantaneous and discrete changes estimated.

4.5. Vulnerability to Poverty

The expected consumption process estimated by alternative linear panel estimators was tested for level of households' vulnerability to poverty (Table 10). Based on the observed and the expected counts of households whose real consumption per capita would be below the poverty threshold (log) at time $t+1$, the estimated vulnerability to poverty was 0.41, which is consistent in both models (RE and PA). This index is lower by about five percentage points than the poverty index estimated in 2004–2006 period (at time t). The results clearly suggest that vulnerability of households to poverty in rural Ethiopia was reduced in the study period.

Table 10. Vulnerability indices estimated from binomial test results

Number of the poor	Estimators of expected consumption	
	GLS RE	GEE PA
Observed counts	1022	1023
Expected counts	1249	1249
Vulnerability index	0.41	0.41

SOURCE: Author's computation from data in ERHS.

Note: The expected consumption process was estimated by employing three extensions of linear panel estimators: generalised least squares RE (GLS RE), between effects, and GEE PA. The binary variables generated from the linear panel estimators could be fitted only for GEE PA probit since the number of zeros from the binary responses at $t+1$ was not sufficient to estimate the other nonlinear panel estimators.

5. Conclusion and Recommendation

This paper analyses the dynamics and determinants of poverty and vulnerability to poverty in rural Ethiopia. The use of the ERHS panel data for the latest two rounds covering a pool of 2495 sample households in the major sedentary farming systems of the country has enabled to consistently estimate the dynamics of poverty and vulnerability and to identify their determinants and correlates, leading to a possibility to narrow the knowledge gap and divergent arguments observed in the last decade. The paper generated new empirical evidence to extend and augment previous studies conducted on the subject.

There were positive welfare changes and transitions indicating the nature of pro-poor growth in Ethiopia. Depth and severity of poverty were substantially reduced, leading to reduction of relative poverty. The dynamics of household poverty was consistently estimated by employing three extensions of nonlinear panel data estimators. The important determinants of poverty dynamics in rural Ethiopia between 2004 and 2009 were household size, livestock holding, primary occupation, ladders of life status, social network, and regional dummies. The predicted probabilities show that the likelihood of households to be poor was 45.8 per cent. Poverty in rural Ethiopia was reduced between 2004 and 2009, indicating that households were escaping from poverty. The estimated marginal effects on poverty dynamics show that there were considerable divergences among regional states in terms of poverty reduction. The estimated vulnerability of households to poverty in rural Ethiopia was 0.41. The vulnerability indices verify that vulnerability of households to poverty in rural Ethiopia was reduced. They were expected to escape from poverty at least in the long run.

The empirical evidence generally substantiates that poverty in rural Ethiopia was high with differentiated spatial and temporal poverty reduction effects. The depth and severity of poverty were markedly different across regions, calling the need for designing differentiated poverty reduction policies suitable to different regions. Vulnerability to poverty was reduced but the speed at which the poor were escaping from poverty was sluggish, which might have led to vulnerability to be poor, even with minor idiosyncratic and covariate shocks.

To bring about accelerated poverty reduction effects by enhancing pro-poor growth in rural Ethiopia, policy makers and other stakeholders need to design relevant policies conditional upon the short-run and long-run dynamics of poverty and vulnerability. The most important policy issues include the following:

1. Regional differences in poverty reduction effects should be optimised by adopting area-specific poverty reduction strategies so that the majority of households generally move to long-run positive welfare effects nationally.

2. The incumbent regime and other stakeholders need to keep the poverty reduction efforts to sustaining income and consumption improvements and to further reduce overall poverty and vulnerability to poverty.

3. Household size, with a national average of 5.7, was consistently identified to be the basic source of poverty in rural Ethiopia, the problem being more serious in Oromia and SNNP regional states, with a regional average of 6.1. This adverse effect on poverty situation should be reversed by long-run and short-run policy interventions,

including family planning and development of households' perception towards family planning.

4. The common assertion by the current regime that farmers engaged in farming as their primary occupation are better-off is not strongly convincing since it was not a correlate of vulnerability to poverty. Smallholder farmers in rural Ethiopia should be supported 'either to move up or to move out'. It is of policy imperative to create employment opportunities in rural areas through income diversification intervention strategies, or find means of labour transfer to other productive sectors of the economy.

5. Economic growth has considerably reduced relative poverty, suggesting that growth was pro-poor in rural Ethiopia. However, there have been differentiated poverty reduction effects among regions as well. Further study is important to empirically identify the sources of regional differences in terms of poverty reduction and omitted idiosyncratic features and covariates in order to design and implement inclusive, sustainable, and proactive area-specific poverty reduction interventions.

References

Awel, Y. M., 2007. Vulnerability and poverty dynamics in rural Ethiopia (*http://www.duo.uio.no/publ/okonomisk/2007/61768/MPhilxThesisxFinal.pdf*, accessed 15/02/2012: 9:25 am).

Bertschek , I. and M. Lechner. 1998. Convenient estimators for the panel probit model. *Journal of Econometrics, 87(2): 329–371.* Bigsten, A. and A. Shimeles. 2008. Poverty transition and persistence in Ethiopia: 1994–2004. *World Development,* Vol. 36, No. 9, pp. 1559–1584.

Bigsten, A., B. Kebede, A. Shimelis, and M. Taddesse. 2003. Growth and poverty reduction in Ethiopia: Evidence from household surveys. *World Development*, 31(1): 87 – 107.

Carter, M., P.D. Little, Tewodaj Mogues, and Workneh Negatu, 2007. Poverty traps and natural disasters in Ethiopia and Honduras. *World Development, 35(5): 835–856.* Elsevier Limited.

Chaudhuri, S., 2003. Assessing vulnerability to poverty: Concepts, empirical methods and illustrative examples. (http://info.worldbank.org/etools/docs/library/97185/Keny_0304/Ke_0304/vulnerability-assessment.pdf, assessed on 26/02/12: 7:14 pm).

Department for International Development (DFID). 2004. What is pro-poor growth and why do we need to know? *Pro-poor growth briefing note 1,* Policy Division. Washington, D.C.: Department for International Development.

Dercon, S. 2004. Growth and shocks: Evidence from rural Ethiopia. *Journal of Development Economics, 74: 309– 329.*

Dercon, S. and J. Hoddinott. 2009. The Ethiopian rural household surveys 1989–2004. *Introduction*. Oxford: Centre for the Study of African Economies.

Dercon, S., and P. Krishna. 2000. Vulnerability, seasonality, and poverty in Ethiopia. *Journal of Development Studies*, 36(6): 25 – 53.

———. 1998. Changes in poverty in rural Ethiopia 1989 – 1995: Measurement, robustness tests, and decomposition. CSAE working paper series WPS 98.7. Centre of the Study of African Economies, Oxford.

Devereux, S. and K. Sharp. 2003. Is poverty really falling in rural Ethiopia? Paper presented at the conference 'Staying Poor: Chronic Poverty and Development Policy', at the University of Manchester, 7 to 9 April 2003.

Dutta I., Foster J. and A. Mishra. 2010. On measuring vulnerability to poverty (http://www.bu.edu/econ/files/2010/08/dp194.pdf), Accessed on 26/02/12).

FDRE (Federal Democratic Republic of Ethiopia). 2004. *Food security program 2004–2009*. Addis Ababa: FDRE.

Foster, J., J. Greer and E. Thorbecke. 1984. A class of decomposable poverty measures. *Econometrica*, 2(81): 761–766. (http://en.wikipedia.org/wiki/Foster_Greer_Thorbecke).

Greene, W. 2002. Convenient estimators for the Panel Probit Model: Further results, (http://archive.nyu.edu/bitstream/2451/26185/3/2-6.pdf.txt).

Gunther, I., and K. Harttgen. 2006. Households' vulnerability to covariate and idiosyncratic shocks. Retrieved from: https://www.ifw-kiel.de/konfer/2006/preg/guenther_harttgen.pdf.

Kakwani, N. and Pernia, E. 2000. What is pro-poor growth? *Asian Development Review 18(1): 1–16*.

Kitaw, M.Y. and A.D. Woldemichael. 2008. *State and dynamics of poverty in Ethiopia. Proceedings of symposium on poverty: Dimensions, dynamics and response options*. InterAfrica Group.

Kraay, A. 2004. When is growth pro-poor? Evidence from a panel of countries. *World Bank Policy Research Working Paper, 3225*.

Krishna, A., 2007. For reducing poverty faster: Target reasons before people. *World Development, Vol. 35, No. 11: 1947–1960*.

Maddala, G.S., 1987. Limited dependent variable models using Panel Data. *The Journal of Human Resources, 22(3): 307–338*.

McKinley, T., 2010. Inclusive growth criteria and indicators: An inclusive growth index for diagnosis of country progress. *Asian Development Bank, Sustainable Development Working Paper Series WPS102049*. Philippines: ADB.

MEDaC (Ministry of Economic Development and Cooperation), 1999. *Poverty situation in Ethiopia*. Addis Ababa: MEDaC, Welfare Monitoring Unit.

MoFED (Ministry of Finance and Economic Development). 2006. Ethiopia: Building on progresses of Plan for Accelerated and Sustained Development to End Poverty (PASDEP). Addis Ababa, Ethiopia.

Naschold, F. 2005. Identifying asset poverty thresholds: New methods with an application to Pakistan and Ethiopia. Paper prepared for presentation at the American Agricultural Economics Association Annual Meeting, Providence, Rhode Island, July 24–27, 2005.

Philip, D. and Md. I. Rayhna. 2004. Vulnerability and poverty: What are the causes and how are they related? (http://www.zef.de/fileadmin/downloads/forum/docprog/Termpapers/2004_3 a_Philip_Rayan.pdf), last accessed on 26/02/12: 4:20 pm.

Pritchett, L., A. Suryahadi, and S. Sumarto. 2000. Quantifying vulnerability to poverty: A proposed measure, with application to Indonesia. *SMERU Working Paper* No.2437, World Bank.

Ravallion, M. and Chen, S. 2003. Measuring pro-poor growth. *Economics Letters, 78 (1): 93–99.*

UN (United Nations). 2000. *A better world for all.* New York, United Nations.

UN/ISDR. 2004. Living with risk: A global review of disaster reduction initiatives. United Nations International Strategy for Disaster Reduction.

UNDP. 2004. *Reducing disaster risk: A challenge for development.* New York: United Nations Development Program.

White, H., and A. Anderson. 2001. Growth vs. Redistribution: Does the pattern of growth matter? *Development Policy Review*, 19(3): 167 – 289.

Wooldridge, J. M. 2002. Econometric analysis of cross-section and panel data. Cambridge: MA, MIT Press.

World Bank. 2005. *Pro-poor growth in the 1990s: Lessons and insights from 14 countries.* Washington, D.C.: The World Bank.

World Bank. 2001. *World Development Indicators 2001.* Washington, D.C.: The World Bank.

Yesuf, M. and R. A. Bluffstone. 2009. Poverty, risk aversion, and path dependence in low-income countries: Experimental evidence from Ethiopia. *American Journal of Economics, 91(4): 1022–1037.*

Zeger, S., K. Liang, and P.S. Albert, 1988. Models for longitudinal Data: A generalized estimating equation approach. *Biometrics, 44(4): 1049–1060.*

CHAPTER FIVE

The Disjuncture between Economic Growth, Poverty Reduction and Social Inclusion in South Africa

Claudious Chikozho

Abstract

Despite realisation of significant economic growth since 1994, the livelihoods of the majority of citizens in South Africa have not been transformed and poverty, unemployment, and inequality have remained 'wicked' challenges. Overall, economic growth in the country has not been sufficiently inclusive and a large proportion of people in various parts of the country still do not enjoy the level of access to basic social and economic services and opportunities that the middle and upper classes in the society take for granted. There has been limited improvement in individual and household welfare, particularly among the social groups (blacks) that were previously disadvantaged by apartheid policies of segregation. As a result, South Africa is still considered one of the most unequal countries in the world. Using both qualitative and quantitative data from published and grey literature, this paper seeks to articulate the main reasons for the disjuncture between economic growth, poverty reduction and social inclusion in South Africa from 1994 to 2014. The paper finds that the post-apartheid state inherited a set of institutions and policies that made up a distributional regime that was originally not intended to be pro-black-poor. Even though the national economic distributional regime was deracialised in the post-apartheid era, this did not transform a distributional regime that revolved around privilege for whites amidst poverty among blacks. It is clear that neither the enfranchisement of the poor, through democratic elections, nor pro-poor rhetoric and interventions crafted in post-apartheid South Africa are sufficient on their own to transform this distributional regime. More systematic efforts at inclusive growth and poverty reduction are required to make the dreams articulated by the government in post-apartheid South Africa real.

Keywords: Poverty, unemployment, social welfare, inclusive growth, transformation

1. Introduction

Since independence, the African development fraternity has been concerned very much with how best to accelerate economic growth on the continent. This focus is not surprising given the number of challenges faced by most of the newly independent states in Africa. Like other African countries that gained independence whilst they were poor, when South Africa overcame apartheid in 1994, it was quite eager to speed up its development. The government articulated the urgent need to provide better livelihoods for its citizens through pro-poor policies and programs and consolidate the independence from apartheid by converting newly won political power into economic progress. Another expressed intention was to quickly address the income and wealth inequalities evident in the society at that time. This would earn social groups that were previously disadvantaged by apartheid policies of segregation the respect and sense of self-dignity that they felt they had been denied in previous decades (see Rapley 2007). Over the years, various development strategies, plans, programs and projects have been implemented in the country to enable the realisation of this vision.

This chapter seeks to articulate the disjuncture between economic growth, poverty reduction and social inclusion in South Africa from 1994 to 2014. The central question addressed in the paper is: *why have the reasonable levels of economic growth witnessed in the country since 1994 not translated into better living standards, lower poverty rates, higher employment rates, and greater social inclusion across the country*? Related questions are: what are the possible ways of sustaining and sharing the benefits of higher national economic performance more broadly in South African society? To what extent is it possible to strive towards a new form of developmental state in South Africa that can promote broad-based and equitable development in the context of an inclusive democracy that enjoys reasonable levels of economic growth? What are the opportunities and constraints evident in this landscape? Answering these questions will enable practitioners and theorists to better understand inclusion-exclusion development discourses and the potential character of sustainable economic growth in Africa.

1.1. Background

Various reviews have concluded that the South African economy has performed relatively well since the demise of apartheid in 1994. Macroeconomic management has been exemplary, with inflation ranging between 3 and 6 per cent and GDP growth averaging a credible 3.3 per cent a year since 1994 (see Bhorat *et al.* 2013). Table 1 presents South Africa's gross domestic product (GDP) and GDP per capita growth rates between the years 1994 and 2012. Despite this significant economic performance, the livelihoods of the majority of the citizens have not been transformed; and poverty, unemployment, and inequality remain 'wicked' challenges. Overall, economic growth in the country has not been sufficiently inclusive and a large proportion of people in various parts of the country still do not enjoy the level of access to basic social and economic services and opportunities that the middle and upper classes in the society take for granted.

There has been limited improvement in individual and household welfare, particularly among the social groups (especially the blacks) that were previously disadvantaged by apartheid policies of segregation. As a result,

South Africa is still considered one of the most unequal countries in the world. Nattrass and Seekings (2001), for instance, point out that South Africa and Brazil hold the undesirable record of having the most unequal distribution of income. For at least two decades, South Africa's Gini coefficient, the most commonly used measure of inequality, has been the highest in the world, increasing from 0.67 in 1994 to about 0.70 from 2008 to 2013 (see World Bank 2011; Finn, Leibbrandt and Ranchhod 2013). This is symptomatic of the massive income disparities that have continued to prevail in the country. Even though a considerable number of blacks have since then enjoyed significant upward mobility and unprecedented prosperity through the Black Economic Empowerment (BEE) program, the wider picture of inclusive growth remains depressing (Table 1).

Table 1. GDP and GDP per capita growth rates, 1994 – 2012

	1994	1996	1998	2000	2002	2004	*2006*	2008	2010	2012	Average 1994 –2012
GDP	3.2	4.3	0.5	4.2	3.6	3.7	0.8	3.6	3.1	2.5	3.2
GDP per capita	1.1	2.1	-1.6	2.1	1.7	2.2	-1.3	2.3	1.9	1.5	1.5

SOURCE: Adapted from Du Plessis and Smit (2006); Finn, Leibbrandt and Oosthuizen (2014)

Education is a critical component of the poverty and inequality challenge in the country. As OECD (2013, 2) points out, skill mismatches represent one aspect of the persistently high unemployment rate in South Africa, especially for the youth. The education system has not been producing the skills needed in the labour market; returns on a high-school certificate, both in terms of finding a job and the earnings premium when employed, are mediocre, while the shortage of skilled workers is reflected in a high premium for university graduates; shortages of learning materials, teachers, support staff and well-trained principals across most of the school system are among the causes of poor outcomes (*Ibid.*). Therefore, if South Africa is to achieve full employment, the quality of basic and vocational education has to be improved.

From the foregoing, one can deduce that while other countries, such as Brazil and India, have seen education gains translate into productivity and employment growth, and large decreases in poverty and inequality, post-apartheid South Africa has not made similar gains. For example, a review by the government of South Africa shows that the poverty rate decreased by 7 percentage points over a 20-year period, from 45 per cent in 1993 to 38 per cent in 2013, for the lower poverty line. When using food poverty level, poverty levels declined by 8 percentage points from 33 per cent to 25 per cent between 1993 and 2013 (see RSA Presidency 2015). It is clear that poverty has declined much more slowly than needed. In addition, most of these gains are often attributable to social policy reforms such as the massive expansion of cash grant transfers rather than transformative economic growth (Finn, Leibbrandt and Oosthuizen 2014). Of equal concern is the fact that inequality has risen further from its very high levels under apartheid (Leibbrandt *et al.* 2010). When a new government came into power in 1994, it was acutely aware of the alarming levels of poverty and inequality in the country. As Finn, Leibbrandt and Oosthuizen (2014) point out, the widespread poverty and extreme inequalities prevalent at the time of the democratic transition represented one of the key areas of policy focus for the first democratic government, as well as one of the sets of outcomes against which its performance has often been judged.

The government of South Africa has since made concerted efforts to assist the poor. From 1994, a wide range of national policies (including Broad-Based Black Economic Empowerment) have allowed some black South Africans to participate meaningfully in the economy. A multi-pronged strategy has also been deployed. This includes land redistribution for accelerated rural development; provision of social grants; incentives for the establishment of small-to-medium businesses; increasing employment opportunities across all sectors; and the eradication of all discriminatory policies and practices inherited from the apartheid regime. Ncube, Shimeles and Verdier-Chouchane (2012) state that to foster inclusion, the government launched the Black Economic Empowerment (BEE) program in order to address the huge racial economic inequality inherited from the apartheid regime. However, only a small segment of the black people in the country has been able to benefit from these interventions in a lasting manner. Poverty and social exclusion have remained widespread and even worsened in some sectors (Seekings 2014). The national development plan finalised in 2012 is intended to transform the South African state into a capable and developmental state able to intervene to correct our historical inequities.... The fact that correction of historical inequities is still on the agenda of South African national development planning, 20 years after independence, suggests that inequality has remained resilient and difficult to address. As a case study, South Africa is quite interesting because it presents the opportunity for scholars to consider the impact of democratisation on inequality, especially given that the pattern and high level of inequality are clearly in part the product of the policies of an undemocratic state in the past (Nattrass and Seekings 2001). The question then is, "how does a new government turn the situation around?"

1.2. The Challenge of Inclusive Growth in South Africa

While the determinants of social inclusion may vary from place to place, in this paper, I am primarily concerned with the concentration of financial resources and wealth in the hands of a few people, which can affect political, social and cultural processes to the detriment of the most vulnerable. As such, I use the term 'inequality' to refer to extreme economic (wealth and income) inequality across different social groups in the society. I also use the term socio-economic exclusion to refer to a situation in which certain social groups (particularly the poor) do not enjoy access to basic goods, services and economic opportunities that the middle and upper income groups enjoy. The widespread prevalence of poverty and inequality in South Africa remains a time-bomb that can discharge at any time in unexpected ways and with highly negative consequences. While it is not officially acknowledged, already the xenophobic attacks that South Africans meted out on foreigners in 2008 and 2015 may be considered as one of the outcomes of having a highly unequal society in which large sections of the population are very poor and excluded from mainstream economic opportunities.

1.3. Methodology

This chapter is the product of a detailed review of the current state-of-the-art literature to create a relatively solid narrative focusing on the dynamics of inclusive growth. In the paper, I use South Africa as a case study that helps in deepening the analysis of inclusive growth trends and the implications of inequality and socio-economic exclusion in society. While a wide search and review of published material that addresses inclusive growth in South Africa was the main focus, other global level studies that present theories associated with the concept were also consulted to strengthen the theoretical base of the paper. Most of the literature used was obtained from general databases, such as the ISI Web of Knowledge, Scopus, JSTOR and EBSCO that contain peer-reviewed journal articles. I also made extensive use of the google scholar search engine to access other relevant publications. This included government documents that directly address South Africa's socio-economic development trajectory.

Due to limitations of time, I purposively selected and reviewed articles that addressed the thematic areas which I believed would sufficiently reflect the various dimensions of inclusive growth in the South African context. These thematic areas are: theories of inclusive growth; economic growth patterns in South Africa since 1994; national income and wealth distribution in South Africa since 1994; poverty and employment levels in South Africa since 1994; social welfare and public service provision; and black economic empowerment and socio-economic transformation in South Africa. All in all, I managed to get 80 articles that had direct relevance to the themes of interest. Most of the articles presented both quantitative assessments of inclusive growth and qualitative narratives to support their arguments. As a result, there was no room to systematically sample data for meta-analyses. Instead, I concentrated on extracting and synthesising information and data that directly addressed the key questions. From the analysis and synthesis, tentative recommendations for addressing the imperatives for inclusive growth in the country begin to emerge.

1.4. Organisation of the Paper

This paper is organised into four main sections. The first section provides an introduction to the subject matter and serves to problematise inclusive growth in the context of South Africa at the national level. It also provides the background to the issue of inclusive growth in South Africa. In essence, the first section defines the problem and sets the main agenda for the paper.

The second section briefly discusses the concept of inclusive growth as it has been conceptualised by various experts at the global level. This is therefore, basically a theory-oriented section designed to place the main issue being studied in its proper context. The third section constitutes the main body of the paper. It presents data and information regarding inclusive growth trends in South Africa. In essence, it presents the case study on which the paper is based. The fourth section is a brief synthesis of the main findings and messages emanating from the paper.

2. Conceptualising Inclusive Growth

In recent decades, inclusive growth has become the main paradigm to use in understanding development processes in the third world. It has also become the strategic recipe to use in attempts at rapid economic growth and national stability.

This is not surprising given the levels of inequality prevailing in various parts of the world. Recent estimates, for instance, indicate that today, there are 16 billionaires in sub-Saharan Africa, alongside the 358 million people living in extreme poverty (Nsehe 2014). Such statistics indicate the absurd levels of wealth that exist alongside extreme levels of poverty on the continent as well as across the globe, with 1 per cent of the population owning 50 per cent of the wealth. They also speak directly to the reason why inclusive growth has gained so much currency over the years. Such statistics also help both theorists and practitioners to better conceptualise and articulate the need for inclusive growth. It is now common cause that income distribution within a country has a significant impact on the life chances of various social groupings in that country (Donaldson 2014).

On their part, social scientists seem to have reached common ground regarding the need for inclusive growth even though there may not be consensus around the exact definition of the concept. They have also identified the key elements constituting inclusive growth. For instance, Lanchovichina and Lundstrom (2009) state that rapid and sustained poverty reduction requires inclusive growth that allows people to contribute to and benefit from economic growth. Fourie (2014) states that internationally, the development of this concept in the past decade sprang from attempts to define a broader concept of economic growth that incorporated equity and the well-being of *all* sections of the population – notably the poor, with poverty being considered either in absolute terms (poverty reduction) or relative terms (the reduction of inequality). Terms such as pro-poor growth, broad-based growth or shared growth signpost these attempts.

One of the most comprehensive and concise definitions of the term is the one provided by the Indian Planning Commission, which defined it as "growth that reduces poverty and creates employment opportunities, access to essential services in health and education, especially for the poor, equality of opportunity, empowerment through education and skill development, environmental sustainability, recognition of women's agency and good governance" (Government of India 2008, 2). In this paper, I adopt the definition by the AfDB (2012) which views inclusive growth as economic growth that results in a wider access to sustainable socio-economic opportunities for a broader number of people, regions or countries, while protecting the vulnerable groups. The AfDB further emphasises that all of this should be done in an environment of fairness, equal justice, and political plurality. Rapid economic growth is often part of the equation in attempts to fully conceptualise inclusive growth but for this growth to be sustainable in the long-run, it should be broad-based across sectors, and inclusive of the larger part of the country's labour force (see Ravallion 2001; OECD 2008). This conceptualisation of inclusive growth implies a direct link between the macro- and micro-determinants of growth. The micro dimension captures the importance of structural transformation for economic diversification and competition, including creative destruction of jobs and firms (Lanchovichina and Lundstrom 2009).

There is already considerable theoretical and empirical evidence to support the assertion that inequality is bad for growth. Naidoo (2013) for instance, carried out an extensive assessment of inclusive growth in developing countries and concluded that in unequal societies, it is much harder to develop the institutions, norms, mores and conventions required for economic growth. In addition, social mobility slows to a crawl in unequal societies. This undermines the incentives for hard work and effort and weakens the human potential of a country. Ostry, Berg, and Tsangardies (2014) used a world income inequality cross-country dataset to examine the links between growth, inequality and redistribution in 153 developed and developing countries. Their findings are consistent with earlier findings which demonstrated that lower inequality is correlated with faster growth in all countries. Moreover, a lower level of inequality contributes to more durable growth and growth episodes are likely to be longer if inequality in a country is lower (Donaldson 2014). It follows that any growth strategy should include elements that address inequality explicitly. Given the extremely high and growing income inequality in South Africa, it makes sense to incorporate a reduction in income inequality as part and parcel of an inclusive growth strategy in the African context (Thorbecke 2014).

3. Inclusive Growth in South Africa: A Historical Narrative

Understanding regarding the meaning and measurement of inclusive growth in the South African context would be incomplete without reference to the legacy of apartheid economic development policies that were deliberately exclusionary and favoured the minority white population over other races in the country. Nattrass and Seekings (2001) state that it is not hard to see how inequality in South Africa was exacerbated by public policies that systematically discriminated on racial grounds, restricting the income-generating opportunities open to the majority of the population. An analytical paper by Ncube, Shimeles and Verdier-Chouchane (2012) states that the historical exclusion of the majority of citizens from sharing the country's wealth and opportunities during the apartheid era created structural rifts that would take decades to mend. In consequence, inequality and chronic poverty persist in the midst of wealth and prosperity. For the successive governments since 1994, the dilemma of ensuring a successful transition without disrupting the social, political and economic fabric is evident (Bhorat, Cassim, and Hirsch 2014). Thus, it is not surprising that the ANC-led government's quest for an inclusive development strategy has remained elusive for more than two decades now. According to Nattrass and Seekings (2001), the available data suggests that the overall level of inequality has changed little with the dismantling of apartheid. Indeed, for a long time, South Africa's Gini coefficient has remained generally stable at a stubbornly high level.

3.1. The Class Character of Poverty and Wealth Distribution in South Africa

Analysts generally agreed that South Africa reflects an increasingly capitalist society, particularly when compared to other middle-income countries that still have a significant small-holding subsistence farming sector (see Gray 2006; Frankel, Smit, B. and Sturzenegger 2007; Ncube, Shimeles and Verdier-Chouchane 2012). However, the social structure is much more diverse and composed of three broad groupings that are not necessarily homogenous. At the top, with incomes well above the national average, is an upper class comprising people with assets or skills that are internationally transferable (Ncube, Shimeles and Verdier-Chouchane 2012). Below them is a large group, with incomes ranging around the median up to above the mean, comprising the urban industrial working class, a range of public sector employees, and some workers in the formal private service sector. The bottom half of society comprises predominantly households that either have no working members at all, or are in the most marginal sectors of the working class (*Ibid.*).

3.2. Employment and Labour

Levels of employment are known to partly determine rates of poverty and inequality in most countries. Keeton (2014) argues that in South Africa, income inequality has hardly changed despite the introduction of social transfers that now reach 16 million poor South Africans partly because the number of jobs created over the past 20 years barely kept pace with growth in the labour force. Consequently, South Africa has one of the highest unemployment rates in the world, at 23.8 per cent in 2014 (OECD 2014), but close to 40 per cent if workers who are now discouraged from looking for jobs are included (see Rodrik 2006; Ncube, Shimeles and Verdier-Chouchane 2012). According to Seeking (2014), poverty in South Africa is driven primarily by unemployment among less-skilled workers, in a context of landlessness. Some working people are poor, but this is generally because the household relies on a single, low income earner (usually in a sector such as agriculture or domestic work) while other adults in the household remain unemployed.

While unemployment has been recognised as a priority for government since 1994, successive ANC-led governments have been spectacularly unsuccessful in reducing it (*Ibid.*). If anything, the unemployment rate has actually increased significantly since the democratic transition, and has particularly affected the young, unskilled and black populations and those living in homelands and in remote and peripheral areas (Ncube, Shimeles and Verdier-Chouchane 2012). Rural unemployment rates tend to be generally higher than urban ones. Rodrik (2006) argues that the reasons for high unemployment rates are rooted in the shrinkage of the non-mineral tradable sector since the early 1990s and the weakness of export-oriented manufacturing which have reduced the demand for unskilled workers. Given the importance of labour income in total household income, unemployment across regions and different socio-economic groups in the country is also strongly correlated with the geographic and socio-economic distribution of income and poverty (Duclos and Verdier-Chouchane 2011). In his 2009 inaugural speech, President Jacob Zuma stated:

> It is my pleasure and honour to highlight the key elements of our program of action. The creation of decent work will be at the centre of our economic policies and will influence our investment attraction and job creation initiatives. In line with our undertakings, we have to forge ahead to promote a more inclusive economy.

The speech reflected the deep-seated structural challenges that the South African economy has been confronted with in a post-apartheid setting. These include jobless growth fuelled mainly by expansion of domestic demand which coexisted with extreme inequality and severe rates of unemployment (RSA Ministry of Economic Development 2011). In 2010, the unemployment rate among the young was close to 40 per cent and inequality during the 2000s was one of the highest in the world where close to 40 per cent of the national income went to the few 10 per cent (Ncube, Shimeles and Verdier-Chouchane 2012). Other estimates also indicate that between 1993 and 2008, for instance, a total of 2.74 million jobs (net) were created, of which 2.5 million were targeted at skilled labour, while unskilled workers lost a total of 770,000 jobs (*Ibid.*). Over the same period, unemployment rates more than doubled from 14 per cent in 1993 to a peak of 29 per cent in 2001, before declining to 23 per cent in 2008. By the time of the world economic crisis in 2010, the unemployment rate had reversed to 25 per cent, using the narrow definition of unemployment (RSA National Treasury 2011). If discouraged workers (those who have stopped looking for work because they do not anticipate finding any) are included in this definition, the figure is substantially higher at about 32 per cent (Seekings 2014).

From a more general level of analysis, the labour market in South Africa has not positively influenced poverty because of the failure to pull individuals from poor households into employment. The unemployment situation worsened between 1993 and 2014, especially for those in the poorest households (see Ncube, Shimeles and Verdier-Chouchane 2012).

According to Leibbrandt, Finn and Woolard (2012), the number of no-worker households has increased by 3 per cent in the last 15 years, thereby significantly increasing the number of households relying on state welfare social assistance programs, especially child grants, as their main form of income. Indeed, the improved aggregate poverty situation is due to increased support from social grants, and not from the labour market (Finn, Leibbrandt and Ranchhod 2013). Even in one-worker households, the poverty incidence remains high. Because of high living costs and the fact that many workers are in low-paid employment, the presence of an employed person in a household is not a guarantee of escaping poverty (*Ibid.*).

The poverty impacts of pervasive unemployment are compounded by a social protection gap that exists for unemployed adults, as social cash grants target people who are not expected to be economically active: children, pensioners, and people with disabilities. This leaves unemployed adults deeply dependent on goodwill transfers from within their communities, placing a large care burden on communities and deepening poverty (Finn, Leibbrandt and Oosthuizen 2014). Leibbrandt *et al.* (2010) go further to show that labour markets play a dominant role in driving inequality. Even though the average share of wage income in total income has remained constant at around 70 per cent over the post-apartheid period, wage income has contributed between 85 per cent and 90 per cent of the total inequality in household income over the years 1993–2008. In contrast, state cash transfers are shown to make up less than 1 per cent of the overall Gini coefficient.

The foregoing suggests that reducing unemployment and creating a better-functioning labour market remains one of the major socio-economic challenges for the government and other key players in South Africa. The South African government explicitly recognises this. Indeed, employment creation has emerged as a top policy priority of the ANC-led government since 1994 even though its success on the ground has been limited. In his 2011 State of the Nation Address, President Zuma declared year 2011 to be the year of job creation and announced the government's intention to spend R9 billion on job creation. The New Growth Path strategy aims to create 5 million jobs by 2020, with 'the creation of decent jobs at the centre of its economic objectives (President Zuma 2011). Nevertheless, there is still lack of solid evidence to show that the government is able to translate this commitment into real change on the ground. Census and sample survey data up to 2014 indicate a clear worsening of income poverty in terms of the absolute numbers of poor people, and probably even the proportion of the population that was poor (see UNDP 2003; Meth and Dias 2004; Finn, Leibbrandt and Ranchhod 2013; Finn, Leibbrandt and Oosthuizen 2014; Bernstein *et al.* 2014; Ncube, Shimeles and Verdier-Chouchane 2012).

3.3. National Economic Growth Policies and the Transformation Agenda

The ANC's economic policy during the 1994 elections was mainly centred on the Reconstruction and Development Programme (RDP). Bernstein *et al.* (2014) states that this was essentially a poverty-alleviation scheme, which, among other things, promised subsidised housing, electricity and other essential services to black people who had been denied these services under apartheid. Most of these policies are still being implemented today. It is however, important to acknowledge that the ANC also abandoned its earlier rhetoric of nationalisation of industries and 'growth through redistribution' in favour of more orthodox policies that are more inclined towards liberalisation (Nattrass 1994). Expansionary economic policies were rejected on the grounds that they would lead to macroeconomic disaster without necessarily benefiting the poor in significant ways.

In 1996, the Ministry of Finance produced the ANC's clearest statement of its orthodox economic policies: a glossy pamphlet, complete with macroeconomic projections, entitled "Growth, Employment and Redistribution" (GEAR) (RSA Government 1996a). GEAR clearly revealed the ANC's growth strategy: deficit reduction was assumed to have positive implications for growth, via its (supposed) positive impact on investor confidence. Such a vision of growth was in stark contrast to the labour union movement's more Keynesian alternative (COSATU 1996). Ncube, Shimeles and Verdier-Chouchane (2012) state that The GEAR strategy focused on macroeconomic stabilisation and trade and financial liberalisation as priorities designed to foster economic growth, increase employment and reduce poverty.

As a consequence, the government reduced fiscal deficits, lowered inflation, maintained exchange rate stability, privatised state assets, cut tax on company profit, decreased barriers to trade and liberalised capital flows. It resembled, in some ways, a structural adjustment programme of the kind promoted under the Washington Consensus (Bernstein *et al.* 2014). Khamfula (2004) points out that fiscal restraint combined with a strategic efficient allocation of resources led to a significantly reduced fiscal deficit. The fiscal deficit has been kept below 3 per cent of GDP over 1998/99 and 2008/09. Public debt levels were below 40 per cent of GDP (Finn, Leibbrandt and Oosthuizen 2014). Overall national economic growth performance has been relatively stable for a long time even though it did not necessarily lead to the creation of jobs in sufficient numbers to reduce unemployment. Figure 1 shows economic growth trends in post-apartheid South Africa.

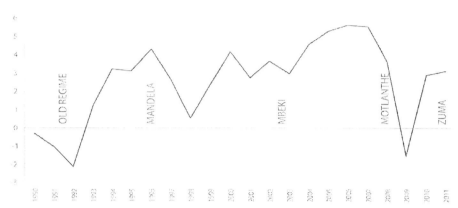

Figure 1. South Africa's Growth, 1990–2011
SOURCE: World Bank (2012a)

In essence, the GEAR strategy has not delivered the promised benefits. Investment and output growth has been disappointing, and employment has declined. This lacklustre performance has been partly due to events beyond the government's control, such as the tight monetary policies of the independent Reserve Bank, and the 'contagion' effects of the Asian and global economic crises (Ncube, Shimeles and Verdier-Chouchane 2012; Bernstein *et al.* 2014). There is mounting evidence that pursuing anti-inflationary policies has undermined growth in the developing world, and the GEAR strategy is probably no exception (see Stiglitz 1998). The assumption that redistribution would come from job creation in a context of reduced public expenditures was not realistic (Ncube, Shimeles and Verdier-Chouchane 2012). Furthermore, by continuing with trade liberalisation in the absence of labour market reforms, the government probably contributed to employment losses. Continued wage growth in the face of falling demand has definitely also contributed to falling employment. The combination of poor growth and pro-union labour legislation has clear effects on distribution in the short-term (see Khamfula 2004; Bhorat *et al.* 2013). In the late 1990s, real wages rose at just over 2.5 per cent per year, whilst employment fell at just under 2.5 per cent per year (Finn, Leibbrandt and Oosthuizen 2014). In essence, the unemployed had not become poorer but at the same time, the number of the poor and unemployed increased significantly as many workers lost their jobs (Bhorat, Cassim and Hirsch 2014).

The combination of rising incomes for those with jobs and falling employment has contributed to greater inequality in the distribution of incomes in society as a whole. If the government is to succeed in reducing poverty, it is necessary to reduce unemployment. The scale of the problem is evident from simulations by Hertz (1998). He estimated that the elimination of unemployment through the creation of 3.8 million low-wage jobs would reduce the number of people in poverty by 43 per cent, and reduce the Gini coefficient by 12 percentage points, that is, a larger reduction than results from redistribution through taxation. Hertz further argued that if the necessary job creation could only be brought about by a reduction in existing wages, then the redistributive impact would be greatly reduced, although there would still be a reduction in absolute poverty. One of the important implications of this is that if these jobs could be created by labour-market reforms that allowed for the creation of new jobs without affecting the existing wage structure, then the redistributive impact would be significant. The government has repeatedly failed to proceed adequately on either front, and hence, has missed an opportunity to make the growth path more redistributive and inclusive (Ncube, Shimeles and Verdier-Chouchane 2012; Finn, Leibbrandt and Oosthuizen 2014). The government's labour market and other economic policies still serve to worsen inequality, undermining the redistributive effects of the national budget.

It is also important to point out that workers' unions in South Africa wield considerable power. Since the advent of democracy in 1994, they have used their institutional and confrontational powers at sectoral and workplace levels to raise real wages, especially for unskilled and lower-paid workers, and to enhance workers' job security (Leibbrandt, Finn, and Woolard 2012). By raising wages and therefore raising the costs of employment, workers incentivise employers to substitute capital-intensive production for labour-intensive production. This entrenches an economic growth path that has little to offer to the huge numbers of less skilled or unemployed workers (Seekings 2014). And yet, in its campaign leading up to the first democratic elections in 1994, the ANC promised '*a better life for all*' by 'attacking poverty and deprivation' as 'the first priority of the democratic government' (see ANC 1994). Through the RDP, the poor were supposed to be empowered to seize economic opportunities 'to develop to their full potential' and 'sustain themselves through productive activity'. In this process, the state would ensure improved access to social security, public education, and other services (*Ibid.*).

In subsequent elections, the ANC and government claimed that they had made progress in reducing poverty. In the 1999 elections for instance, the ANC campaigned around the general theme that South Africa was 'changing' (Lodge 1999). In the 2004 elections, the ANC claimed that it had 'laid the foundation for a better life'. Its election manifesto —entitled '*A people's contract to create work and fight poverty*' — emphasised the creation of 'a more caring society' and a 'radical' reduction in unemployment and poverty (ANC 2004). The following year, a senior ANC member, Cyril Ramaphosa, was quoted as saying that new data showed that South Africans had 'never had it so good'. In 2006, President Mbeki told parliament that 'between 1994 and 2004, the real incomes of the poorest 20 per cent of the population increased by 30 per cent' (Mbeki 2006). In 2009, the ANC claimed to have 'pushed back the frontiers of poverty' (ANC 2009). In late 2012, President Zuma lashed out at reports that income inequality has worsened since 1994 arguing that inequality was actually 'narrowing', whilst poverty in 1994 had been 'worse than what it is now' (see *Cape Times*, 02 November, 2012).

The precise changes in income poverty since 1994 may not be clear but several facts seem quite evident. Firstly, despite the ANC-led government's claims, poverty has remained widespread, with consequences for, *inter alia,* child nutrition, health, and education. Secondly, the proportion of the population living in poverty might have dropped since 1994 but by a very insignificant percentage. Thirdly, and in contradiction to the government's claims, the distribution of income has become more unequal. The rich have benefitted massively from economic growth, while the economic condition of poorer sections of society have hardly improved (see Bhorat, Cassim, and Hirsch 2014). It is becoming increasingly apparent that the basic design of South Africa's public policies affecting both distribution (through the labour market) and redistribution (through education, health care, and social welfare) have experienced only minor changes since the days of apartheid (see Seekings and Nattrass 2005).

3.4. The Black Economic Empowerment Programme
Since coming to power, the ANC government has articulated commitment towards transforming South Africa's racially-skewed society through direct interventions in the economy and various social sectors. Thus, the government launched Black Economic Empowerment (BEE) policies to rectify apartheid inequalities by giving economic opportunities to disadvantaged groups (particularly blacks and women). Bernstein *et al.* (2014) states that BEE was launched in 2000 as official government policy with the Preferential Procurement Framework Act, a law which required the government to favour tenders from black-owned companies. As a policy, BEE envisions the creation and development of new enterprises that produce value-adding goods and services; attract new investment and employment opportunities with the aim of redistributing wealth by transforming the ownership of companies; and eliminating the racial divide (Ncube, Shimeles and Verdier-Chouchane 2012).

The fundamental pillars of company transformation include: ownership, management control, employment equity, skills development, preferential procurement, and enterprise development. A company's BEE status is determined by a scorecard that quantifies performance based on predetermined weights assigned to the seven pillars (Gqubule 2006). In 2003, further BEE legislation was promulgated to promote sector-specific 'charters', each of which called for a specified number of BEE deals to be concluded (Turok 2008). For instance, the Minerals and Petroleum Development Resources Act of 2004 backed up these laws by requiring mining houses to become BEE compliant if they wanted to renew their mining licences (see Hirsch 2005). In essence, the launch of the BEE strategies and policies was one of the first steps towards attempts at ensuring inclusive growth in South Africa.

From 2003, BEE has been renamed Broad-Based Black Economic Empowerment. Indeed, the 2001 report of the BEE Commission pointed out that the BEE needed to be broadened and made more inclusive (Bernstein *et al.* 2014). In February 2007, the government tried to spread the benefits of BEE more widely through the establishment of Codes of Good Practice that allow companies to use a wider range of business practices, including affirmative action and employee share ownership schemes, in order to earn BEE points. BEE compliance is now being strongly transmitted through value-chains because the BEE status of suppliers affects the BEE status of contractors. The process has brought black-owned and black -led firms into the economy more quickly than might have been the case (*Ibid.*).

In 1994, corporations in South Africa had started appointing black non-executive directors and sold part of their businesses to black empowerment groups. Financial institutions provided funding for black people without capital to go into business (Hirsch 2005). Andrews (2008) argues that the outcomes of the BEE program have been mitigated. BEE beneficiaries were a small closed group, especially because the BEE structures were protected by elites. Therefore, a second generation empowerment program was more meaningful. All along the years, BEE has changed from white businesses' efforts to increase black acquisition in SMEs to a process with specific measures aimed at increasing black equity and participation at all levels of the society (see Ncube, Shimeles and Verdier-Chouchane 2012).

At the inception stage, BEE gained political support because it was largely believed that it would ensure reduction in potential for civil strife as more people from the disadvantaged groups actively participated and benefited from economic development processes. This was also expected to eventually produce a relatively non-racial 'growth coalition' necessary for sustainable capitalist development that would build investor confidence in the country (Bräutigam, Rakner, and Taylor 2002). Correspondingly, BEE is described as 'a coherent socio-economic process that brings about significant increases in the number of black people that manage, own and control the country's economy and a way of reducing income inequalities' (Sartorius and Botha 2008). BEE has led to a gradual increase in the black middle class, while ownership of capital on the Johannesburg Stock Exchange has, as at 2008, grown to 4 per cent due to direct intervention through BEE industry charters, and legislative measures (*Ibid.*). Seekings (2014) states that at the extreme end, Patrice Motsepe — born in 1962 and without inherited wealth — became the wealthiest South African, with a fortune of approximately US$3 billion (although probably still lagging behind the expatriate Rupert and Oppenheimer families).

The BEE policy has had its fair share of critics. Several of these critics claim that the lack of a coherent definition of BEE measures distorts beneficiary groups and as a result, has only served to enrich the politically connected elite. For instance, Bernstein *et al.* (2014) argues that only a very small number of the black political and economic elite have benefitted (in some cases again and again) from these arrangements, and the process is often said to promote corrupt relationships between business and government. In addition, BEE policies have led to the practice of large businesses hiring well-placed members of the ANC in order to secure good standing with the new government and to reposition themselves in the post-apartheid society. Share ownership deals ensued, and a few ANC members quickly became very rich. The critics also believe that in its original form, BEE remains largely patrimonial and a strong instrument for accumulating patronage (see Engdahl and Hauki 2001; Boshoff and Mazibuko 2003).

There are other theorists who claim that BEE measures could impede foreign investment and contribute to widening the premium on foreign ownership of firms (see Jackson, Alessandri and Black 2005; Southall 2005). While foreign firms are exempt from the BEE ownership provision, they are expected to comply with other elements, including preferential procurement of inputs from locally-owned companies. However, Mebratie and Bedi (2011) show that after accounting for firm level fixed effects, foreign firms were not more productive than domestically-owned firms in South Africa. In other words, since foreign direct investment is considered to disproportionately favour more productive firms, and since there are no productivity premiums to foreign ownership, compliance with BEE procurement measures are not bound to favour foreign firms vis-à-vis domestic firms.

There are also other experts who have done detailed assessments of the impact of BEE on poverty, equality and wealth distribution. Visagie (2013) carried out such an assessment from a quantitative perspective and established that the relative growth in the size of the social classes in South Africa has certainly become pertinent. Partly due to the BEE policies, the affluent middle class grew in size by an additional 2.7 million people, from 7.7 million in 1993 to 10.4 million in 2008. At the same time, the number of people in the upper class more than trebled during the same period and its share of the population more than doubled to 2.8 per cent. In the lower classes, the number of people also grew; importantly, the number of people in the lowest income class grew mostly slowly – thus, its share of the total population declined (*Ibid.*). Table 2 depicts shifts in class size from 1993 to 2008.

When one takes into account the racial composition of the middle and upper classes, an interesting picture also emerges. Estimates show that the number of middle-class Black Africans more than doubled between 1993 and 2008; whereas the number of whites in the middle class actually shrunk by nearly a third. In the upper class, the number of Africans grew from 19, 000 to 257, 000 in 15 years; hence, the story of the strong growth of the black middle and upper classes (Visagie 2013).

Table 2 . Shifts in class size, from 1993 to 2008

	Lower class income/month		Middle class income/month	Upper class income per month	Total
	Below poverty line (<R550)	Above poverty line (R515 – R1399)	R1400 – R10000	>R10000	
1993(share %)	22.7(56.9)	9.1(22.7)	7.7(19.3)	0.4(1.1)	39.9(100
2000(share %)	24.6(56.0)	9.8(22.4)	8.7(19.8)	0.8(1.9)	44.0(100
2008(share %)	25.1(51.7)	11.8(24.2)	10.4(21.3)	1.3(2.8)	48.7(100

SOURCE: Adapted from Visagie (2013)

3.5. Social Welfare and Public Services

In 1994, the ANC promised to provide improved access to social security, public education, and other social services. In 1996, the country's new constitution guaranteed socio-economic rights, subject to available resources (RSA Government 1996b). Seekings (2014) states that democracy might not have brought lasting economic benefits to poor South Africans in terms of the distribution of market incomes, but it has brought considerable benefits in terms of redistribution through the fiscus. Through social welfare programs, the government has made a concerted effort to assist the poor. Burger (2014) states that South Africa has an extensive social welfare system that comprises a variety of social grants and cash transfers, including child grants. It reaches over 16 million out of a population of 52 million people and this expenditure constitutes 3.4 per cent of GDP (RSA National Treasury 2014). The value of cash transfers and public expenditure on services, such as healthcare and housing, almost doubled, in real terms, between 1995 and 2006. Public expenditure has also become better targeted at the poor (Bernstein *et al.* 2014). By 2006, the poorest 40 per cent of the population received 50 per cent of all social spending, including both the estimated value of services as well as cash transfers. Almost 49 per cent of spending on school education accrued, at least nominally, to the poorest 40 per cent of the population, as did 57 per cent of spending on public clinics and 43 per cent of spending on public hospitals *(Ibid.)*.

Cash transfers were even better targeted on the poor, with 70 per cent of old-age pensions, 62 per cent of child support grants, and 59 per cent of disability grants going to the poorest 40 per cent of the population (Ncube, Shimeles and Verdier-Chouchane 2012). Some social spending was not well targeted on the poor: only an estimated 24 per cent of public expenditure on housing accrued to the poor, and the poor benefited from only 5 per cent of public expenditure on universities (Leibbrandt, Finn and Woolard 2012; Finn, Leibbrandt and Oosthuizen 2014). Partly as a result of the way the government has tackled poverty (i.e. by focusing on cash transfers and the delivery of housing, electricity, water, sanitation and access to healthcare and education), there has been a particularly dramatic fall in what is called 'multi-dimensional poverty' since 1993 (Bernstein *et al.* 2014). Despite these efforts, poverty has remained entrenched. Its effects have been exacerbated by high levels of HIV, which have shortened life expectancy, while malnutrition and hunger remain persistent, particularly among children. Secondly, while the proportion of the population living in poverty has dropped, the actual number of people living in poverty may have increased as the population has also grown (*Ibid.*). While social assistance programmes have redistributed income to the poor and helped bring poverty levels down from 53 per cent to 44 per cent of the population, they have not changed the nature of poverty in South Africa (Ncube, Shimeles and Verdier-Chouchane 2012).

Broadly speaking, poor South Africans have not moved beyond getting a survivalist grant to accessing the opportunities that will allow them to permanently leave behind the circumstances that hold them in poverty (Gray 2006). In addition, rather than supplementing existing incomes, public cash transfers have mostly become substitutes for the private cash transfers (remittances) that poor households used to receive from their relatives who were working as miners or as urban migrants. Apart from some lump-sum transfers for important events, such as funerals and weddings, regular private cash transfers have all but dried up, mostly as a result of the job losses in low-income sectors, such as agriculture, mining and textiles (Bernstein *et al.* 2014). The degree of reliance on the state's cash transfers seems to have increased enormously since 1994. Almost one in every two South African households receives a means-tested grant (*Ibid.*).

Although the more important weakness of the anti-poverty programme has been the government's failure to promote job-intensive growth or effective schooling for the poor, poverty is also perpetuated by the very low proportion of South Africans who are self-employed or who operate in the informal sector. In 2008, the informal sector employed only 26 per cent of the workforce (Finn, Leibbrandt and Oosthuizen 2014). According to Gray (2006), social security has become the only poverty alleviation measure within the development welfare system. Indeed, in the post-1994 period, the right to social security and assistance has been secured for all people in need (Bernstein *et al.* 2014). The White Paper for Social Welfare, published in 1997, introduced the concept of 'developmental social welfare', which means that both social and economic development are interdependent and mutually reinforced.

Most analyses of changes in income poverty levels in the 2000s point to the big effects of the expansion of social grants (Seekings 2014). Between 1994 and 2009, real expenditure on social assistance more than doubled. This was also a period of sustained economic growth; so the rising expenditure was more modest in relation to GDP, rising from 2 per cent to 3.5 per cent. The number of individual beneficiaries rose more than five-fold (Finn, Leibbrandt and Oosthuizen 2014). A detailed analyses by Pauw and Ncube (2007) shows that not only has the share of social grant expenditure in GDP increased significantly since the first democratic election, but the number of recipients of social grants has increased substantially. In 1996/1997 for instance, social grant transfers accounted for about 2.5 per cent of GDP, and by 2005/2006 this share had increased to more than 3 per cent. In turn, the number of beneficiaries increased from approximately 3 million in 1997 to 9.4 million in 2005, an average annual growth rate of more than 15 per cent. By the end of the 2010/2011 fiscal year, almost 13.4 million individuals had received a social grant (Bhorat *et al.* 2013). This constitutes an aggregate growth rate of almost 365 per cent in the total number of grant recipients between 1997 and 2011. With more than one in four South Africans — and almost one in every two South African households — now receiving means-tested grants, it is not surprising that social assistance programmes make a major dent on income poverty (Ncube, Shimeles and Verdier-Chouchane 2012).

A detailed analysis of the sources of income of different income deciles shows that by 2008, the poor deciles were relying overwhelmingly on social grants; whereas around 1994, remittances were playing a very important role (Leibbrandt, Finn and Woolard 2012). Therefore, the expansion of public cash transfers has been concurrent with the decline in remittances. The available evidence also shows that the record of redistribution through social welfare in South Africa is remarkable, and probably without parallel in countries across the global south. A key question though is whether the massive social welfare programs are sustainable in the long-run. Burger (2014) argues that the transfer welfare state is likely to be fiscally unsustainable in the long-run, while the dominance of social transfers does little to lift the poor out of dependency and into skilled and better-paying jobs. In this paper, I agree with Finn, Leibbrandt and Oosthuizen's (2014) view that it is most unfortunate that the expansion of government social grants has not been complemented by a reduction in the unemployment rate. As Leibbrandt *et al.* (2010) points out, the labour market is certainly by far one of the most important factors to consider when decomposing poverty and inclusive growth.

Despite the massive social welfare programs, Lorenz curves developed by Leibbrandt *et al.* (2010) suggest a high level of inequality. The richest 20 per cent of people earn about 70 per cent of the total income, and the second richest about 20 per cent of total income. Thus, the poorest 60 per cent together only earn about 10 per cent of the total income in the population. This is approximately true regardless of which dataset is being used, and is exceptionally low by international standards. The big picture conclusion is that inequality has remained mostly stable and stubbornly high over the post-apartheid era, even in the face of high levels of expenditure on social welfare (see Van der Berg 2011).

3.6. Gender Imbalances

In most analysis of inclusive growth in South Africa, an often forgotten component is the gender dimension of the challenge. An assessment by the *Mail and Guardian* of 24/04/2015 is quite revealing in this regard. For instance, they quote a gender expert (Laura Grant) as stating that South Africa's gender wage gap is among the world's worst. Men get the lion's share of income, with women earning a third less on average than men. For example, in 2013, the average taxable income for women was about R16, 000 per month while men earned an average of about R21, 000 per month. This puts South Africa at the top end of the global gender wage gap. The findings of this assessment are consistent with the ILO's (2014) analysis of 83 countries which reveals that, globally, women in paid work earn on average between 10 per cent and 30 per cent less than men. Research by the ITUC (2014) also puts the global gender wage gap at an average of 22.4 per cent and South Africa's at 33.5 per cent.

The South African Revenue Services tax statistics comprise 5.2 million taxpayers who were assessed in the 2013 tax year. In the lower income brackets, the earnings of men to women is fairly even. The bulk (37 per cent of the women and 30 per cent of the men) earned in the R12, 500 and R25, 000 a month taxable income bracket. But, it's in the higher income brackets (from about R40, 000 a month upwards) that the gender wage gap really starts to become too glaring. Only 4.6 per cent of women earn more than R500, 000 a year, but nearly 11 per cent of men do (*Mail and Guardian* 24/04/2015). Men also outnumbered women three to one in the five highest salary brackets. Among the taxpayers who earn R1 million a year or more, men outnumbered women by five to one. At R2 million a year or more, it became seven to one and, in the top income bracket, R5 million a year or more, there were 10 men to every woman (*Ibid.*).

The World Bank's gender and development unit argues that such glaring gender gaps at the top of the wage earning spectrum are easily explained by what is known as '*gender sorting*' (see World Bank 2013). This refers to a situation in which women are concentrated in less-productive jobs and run enterprises in less-productive sectors with fewer opportunities for business scale-up or career advancement (*Ibid.*). The available evidence suggests that this is the case for South Africa where women hold only 3.6 per cent of chief executive positions, 5.5 per cent of chair person positions, and 21.4 per cent of executive management positions (Business Women's Association of South Africa's Women in Leadership Census 2012). The Institute of Race Relations' South Africa Survey 2014–2015 shows that 30 per cent of managers and slightly more than 40 per cent of professionals are women, but the largest numbers of women are employed as clerks, in sales and service, and as elementary (or low-skilled) and domestic workers.

At the risk of belabouring the point, it suffices to point out that there are also visible and invisible elements that contribute to the marginalisation of working women, related to an institutional culture within a largely male-dominated environment. These relate to internal company policies and practice, access to skills training, and a sense that men are taken more seriously than women in decision-making. This situation is even harder for black women. It also has a direct bearing on the extent to which women are embraced or excluded by economic growth policies. While jobs can bring gains for women, their families and communities, gender disparities persist in South Africa such that women remain largely marginalised from socio-economic development processes. This is a key dimension to be taken into account when analysing inclusive growth challenges and processes.

3.7. Land Redistribution

While it is not the major focus of this study, land redistribution remains a hotly contested socio-economic and political issue in South Africa. Bernstein *et al.* (2014) states that a set of more gradually implemented policies aimed to change the racial composition of ownership in South Africa, and in particular the ownership of land was introduced by the new government. However, the land reform process has been criticised for its slowness in implementation. More than 20 years after democracy, most of the farmland in South Africa is still owned by the white population. For example, by March 2009, only 5.3 million of the 24.6 million hectares targeted had been transferred through land redistribution (Kleinbooi 2010). The target of transferring 30 per cent of land from white land owners to blacks has proved resilient and as of 2008, only 4 per cent of the target had been achieved (Hall 2009). This scenario is unlikely to have changed much by 2014. This raises serious doubts regarding the extent to which the target can be achieved. The process has also had very limited impact in reducing poverty or promoting sustainable development. New legislation was proposed in 2011 to replace the willing-seller-willing-buyer model which is mainly blamed for slowing down the implementation process (see UNECA 2012).

Slowness in implementing land and agrarian reforms implies that the country's rural economy is still characterised by deep-seated inequalities, with many households trapped in a vicious cycle of poverty (Kleinbooi 2010). Food insecurity, malnutrition and unemployment remain ongoing challenges and many rural households continue to depend on government hand-outs for survival (Cousins 2005). One of the more critical elements in sustaining food production is to improve the living conditions of rural communities by assisting small farmers' to access land and water and enhance their agricultural productivity. Therefore, the land and water reform question, as it is posed academically in South Africa, remains at the cutting edge of the development and inequality debate.

The land reforms have not only been criticised for slowness in implementation but also for being beset by challenges related to the production performance of the redistributed farms. Typically, poor performance of the 'new' farms has mainly been associated with a range of factors, including poor maintenance of irrigation infrastructure and equipment; high energy costs where pumping of water is involved; lack of institutional support in terms of access to credit; marketing and draught power; lack of extension services and farmer training; local conflicts; and weak local organisation (see Bembridge 2000; Reardon *et al.* 1999). The foregoing discussion suggests that although necessary, land reforms in South Africa will only be effective if embedded within a broader programme to restructure the agrarian rural economy and ensure more inclusive growth. In this paper, I emphasise the importance of analysing and articulating the key factors that constrain or enhance the reform process, productivity of the 'new' farmers who benefited from the reform process, and broader processes of rural economic transformation. It is important to now re-open the theoretical space for debating the agenda for a new rural economy in South Africa and to empirically explore the emerging nuances of inclusive growth strategies in the country.

4. Discussion and Conclusion

The evidence provided in this paper indicates that the post-apartheid state inherited a set of institutions and policies that made up a distributional regime that was originally not intended to be pro-black-poor. The distributional regime was deracialised in the post-apartheid era but this did not and probably could not transform a distributional regime that revolved around privilege for whites amidst poverty among blacks. It is clear that neither the enfranchisement of the poor, through democratic elections, nor pro-poor rhetoric and interventions crafted in post-apartheid South Africa was sufficient to transform this distributional regime. The politics of distribution and re-distribution primarily through employment and wages, and to some extent, land reform contrasts with the politics of redistribution through the fiscus, including both cash transfers and 'in kind' benefits from public education, health care, and other services. In the former case, organised labour exerts an effective veto over pro-poor reforms of labour market policies. The available evidence also shows that during the first fifteen years after 1994, the poverty headcount rate (i.e. the proportion of people living in poverty) and the poverty gap (the aggregate gap between incomes and the poverty line, as a proportion of total income in society) probably declined, especially if a higher poverty line is used, but the absolute number of people living in poverty seems to have risen.

In essence, poverty may have declined somewhat, and indeed, the social welfare system has reduced the non-monetary levels of poverty and social exclusion. However, poverty and socio-economic exclusion clearly remain very pressing concerns in a country in which most of the poor have become so dependent on the public social welfare system instead of working to uplift themselves out of poverty. Relative to other middle income countries, South Africa has a high poverty rate, especially considering its GDP per capita levels. Poverty is probably also very high relative to the overall level of development since South Africa's level of income inequality is high and actually rising all the time since 1994. Overall, South Africa has remained an exceptionally unequal society in terms of both class and race.

When Thabo Mbeki described South Africa as a 'two-nation' society in 1998, with 'one of these nations being white, relatively prosperous, regardless of gender or geographic dispersion...and the second and larger nation being black and poor, it seems safe to assume that very few people were surprised. Even though a considerable number of blacks have since then enjoyed significant upward mobility and unprecedented prosperity, the wider picture of inclusive growth remains depressing (see Finn, Leibbrandt and Ranchhod 2013). Some Black African people may have enjoyed rapid upward mobility (through BEE), but they have generally done so from semi-privileged starting points, while the poor have very few opportunities. Children growing up in poor homes, especially in poor and rural neighbourhoods, are much more likely to be disadvantaged in terms of nutrition and health, access to proper education, completing school, connections in the labour market, and knowledge of how to find jobs or otherwise earn a living. Poverty thus reproduces poverty. In short, a large majority of South Africans have not experienced substantial improvements in their income level and access to opportunities since the end of apartheid. Therefore, income poverty persists and any attempts to address the challenge have to take this into consideration.

It is now clear that in South Africa, the state plays a major role in shaping both the overall growth path of the economy and specific markets, especially the labour market, with profound implications for distribution and redistribution. The diverse roles played by the state in shaping 'who gets what, when, and how' can be understood as constituting a distributional regime that has profound implications for efforts at inclusive growth. Clearly, the post-apartheid growth path was good for employers and for those workers who kept their jobs. Those workers who lost their jobs and did not find new employment and the chronically unemployed can now be counted among those who were badly affected. This outcome is especially undesirable in terms of poverty because of the declining links between well-paid workers in formal employment and the marginalised and unemployed.

The end of apartheid might have been accompanied by more radical changes in public policy, perhaps in populist, pro-poor directions. The constraints on populism (or other forms of radical policy transformation) need to be understood. The bottom line is that distribution has been shaped by the struggles between a powerful labour movement enjoying strong ties with the ruling party, and employers in a globalised context. The poor have not only been left out of this struggle, but have actually been disadvantaged by the compromises over distribution made by capital, labour, and the state. The poor have benefitted a lot from social welfare redistribution, including through social grants, subsidised health care, housing, and, to a more limited extent, public education and municipal service delivery. However, this has not lifted them out of poverty and the roots of dependency on the state continue to run deep. Theorists are also beginning to question the sustainability of the massive social welfare programs.

4.1. Conclusion

The discussions and supporting data presented in this chapter show that the disjuncture between economic growth, poverty reduction and social inclusion in South Africa is very real and various components and sub-components of that disjuncture have to be addressed urgently. Poverty, inequality and social exclusion in the country certainly have historical and structural causes that are deeply entrenched and also closely intertwined with issues of unemployment and an education system that is still too weak to reverse the gap. This makes the challenge much more complex and difficult to deal with. Addressing the issue will require a more integrated and multi-pronged approach. Since 1994, the Government has been implementing various policies and programmes, especially fiscal policies, to address the challenge.

While poverty has fallen since 1994, the decrease has been far less significant than anticipated. Massively expanding social grants are certainly unsustainable in the long-run and have been accompanied by a rise in inequality, particularly among black South Africans. To become more inclusive and to further entrench democracy, South Africa needs much faster and more labour-intensive growth. It is important to acknowledge that under democracy, South Africa has realised a number of national socio-economic achievements. For example, it remains a politically stable country that has generated new economic opportunities, reduced poverty to some degree and produced some inspiring innovations. However, if South Africa is to become a truly inclusive society, it needs to generate higher rates of growth, sustained for a long period. The process of growth has to also address the needs of poorer social groups in the society.

The evidence presented in the paper also shows that race and gender continue to remain overwhelming determinants of the poverty profile in South Africa. Trends in inequality suggest that one of the world's most unequal societies has quite possibly become the most unequal. It is also evident that income inequality between racial groups is driving this overall increase. In terms of assessing the impact of social grants on poverty and inequality, the analysis shows that poor households' access to grant income has increased considerably. However, this is not necessarily cause for celebration. Several analysts recommend less dependence on social grants and an increase in employment levels as a more sustainable option. Some analysts also believe that the attempt to transform the racial patterns of ownership of the means of production through direct government intervention schemes, such as BEE, has created racialised and increasingly clientelistic relations between business and the state. This does not address inclusive growth priorities. Rather, it tends to benefit only a few elites.

It seems the road to poverty reduction and inclusive growth remains a long one for South Africa even though the government has tried out various options in the past. However, this is a vicious cycle that can be broken through appropriate policies and institutions designed to attack poverty directly. While rapid economic growth seems a basic foundation for poverty reduction, it can never be assumed that it will automatically translate into inclusive growth on its own. There is always need for the government to deliberately and actively make growth inclusive. This suggests that it would be a gross mistake to focus on national economic growth and assume that inequality will take care of itself, not only because inequality may be ethically undesirable but also because the resulting growth may be low and unsustainable. Therefore, redistribution should be thought of as part of the broader basket of solutions and national tools for promoting faster growth, and not just a desirable outcome to be sought through a redistributive growth path.

References

African Development Bank (AfDB). 2012. *African Economic Outlook 2012*. Addis Ababa: AfDB.

African National Congress (ANC). 1994. *The Reconstruction and Development Programme*. Johannesburg: ANC.

African National Congress. 2009. *Election Manifesto: Working Together We Can Do More*. Johannesburg: ANC.

————. 2004. *Election Manifesto: A People's Contract to Create Work and Fight Poverty'*. Johannesburg: ANC.

Andrews, M. 2008. Is black economic empowerment a South African growth catalyst? (Or could it be?). *Faculty Research Working Papers Series, RWP08-033*, June 2008, John F. Kennedy School of Government, Harvard University.

Bembridge, T. J. 2000. Guidelines for rehabilitation of small-scale farmer irrigation schemes in South Africa. *WRC Report No. 891/1/00*, Pretoria.

Bernstein, A., De Kadt, J., Marius Roodt, M. and Stefan Schirmer, S. 2014. South Africa and the pursuit of inclusive growth. CDE Country Report 2014, Johannesburg.

Bhorat, H., Cassim, A. and Hirsch, A. 2014. Policy co-ordination and growth traps in a middle-income country setting: The case of South Africa. *UNU Wider Working Paper 2014/155*.

Bhorat, H., Goga, S., Van der Westhuizen, C. and Tseng, and others. 2013. South Africa: Labour market and social welfare outcomes in the context of the crisis. *In:* Barbosa, A. and Cacciamali, M. (Eds.) *The "dynamic south", economic development and inclusive growth: The challenges ahead.* São Paulo: CEBRAP.

Boshoff, C. and Mazibuko, N. E. 2003. Employee perceptions of share ownership schemes: An empirical study. *South African Journal of Business Management, 31,* February 2013.

Bräutigam, D., Rakner, L. and Taylor, S. 2002. Business associations and growth coalitions in Sub-Saharan Africa. *Journal of Modern African Studies, 40(4),* pp. 519–547.

Burger, P. 2014. *How suitable is a 'developmental state' to tackle unemployment, inequality and Poverty in South Africa?* Accessed 28/06/2015 from: www.econ3x3.org .

Business Women's Association of South Africa. 2012. *Women in Leadership Census, 2012.* Johannesburg: BWASA.

Cape Times Newspaper, 02 November, 2012

Cousins, B. 2005. Agrarian reform and the 'two economies': Transforming South Africa's countryside. *In*: Hall, R. and Ntsebeza, L. (Eds.) *The land question in South Africa: The challenge of transformation and redistribution.* Programme for Land and Agrarian Studies, University of the Western Cape.

COSATU. 1996. *Social equity and job creation.* Accessed 22nd May 2015 from: http://www.cosatu.org.za.

Donaldson, A. 2014. *Redistribution is part of the toolkit to promote growth.* URL: www.econ3x3.org. Accessed 26th May 2015.

Duclos, J-Y. and Verdier-Chouchane, A. 2011. Analyzing pro-poor growth in Southern Africa: Lessons from Mauritius and South Africa. *African Development Review, 23(2),* pp. 121–146.

Du Plessis, S. and Smit, B. 2006. Economic growth in South Africa Since 1994. *University of Stellenbosch Economic Working Papers: 1/2006.*

Engdahl, C. and Hauki, H. 2001. Black Economic Empowerment: An introduction for Non-South African businesses. Master's Degree Thesis, Department of Law, Gothenburg University, Gothenburg.

Finn, A., Leibbrandt, M. and Ranchhod, V. 2013. Post-apartheid poverty and inequality trends. *In:* R. Kanbur (Ed.). *The Oxford Companion to the Economics of South Africa.* Oxford: Oxford University Press.

Finn, A., Leibbrandt, M., and Oosthuizen, M. 2014. Poverty, inequality, and prices in post-apartheid South Africa. *UNU WIDER Working Paper 2014/127,* Helsinki.

Fourie, F. 2014. How inclusive is economic growth in South Africa? Accessed on 28th May 2015 from: www.econ3x3.org.

Frankel, J., Smit, B. and Sturzenegger, F. 2007. South Africa: Macroeconomic challenges after a decade of success. *Havard University School of Government Working Paper Series, RWP07–021,* April 2007.

Government of India. 2008. *Eleventh five-year plan (2007–2012).* New Delhi: Government of India Planning Commission.

Gray, M. 2006. The progress of social development in South Africa. *International Journal of Social Welfare 2006, 15 (Suppl. 1)*, pp. 53–64.

Gqubule, D. 2006. *Making mistakes, righting wrongs: Insights into Black Economic Empowerment.* Johannesburg: Jonathan Ball.

Hall, R. 2009. *Another countryside? Policy options for land and agrarian reform in South Africa.* PLAAS, University of the Western Cape.

Hertz, T. 1998. The relationship between poverty, inequality and unemployment in South Africa. *SANER Working Paper No. 9*, Cape Town.

Hirsch, A. 2005. *Season of hope: Economic reform under Mandela and Mbeki.* Pietermaritzburg: University of KwaZulu-Natal Press.

International Labour Organization (ILO). 2014. *World of Work Report 2014: Developing with jobs.* Geneva: ILO.

International Trade Union Confederation (ITUC). 2014. *Global Rights Index: The world's worst countries for workers.* Geneva: ITUC.

Jackson, W. E., Alessandri, T. M. and Black, S. S. 2005. The price of corporate social responsibility: The case of Black Economic Empowerment transactions in South Africa. *Federal Reserve Bank of Atlanta Working Paper, 2005–29*, Georgia.

Keeton, G. 2014. Inequality in South Africa. *Journal of the Helen Suzman Foundation, Issue 74*, Nov. 2014.

Khamfula, Y. 2004. *Macroeconomic policies, shocks and economic growth in South Africa.* New Delhi: Global Development Network.

Kleinbooi, K. 2010. *Review of land reform in Southern Africa.* PLAAS, University of the Western Cape.

Lanchovichina E. and Lundstrom S. 2009. Inclusive growth analytics: Framework and application. *World Bank Policy Research Working Paper 4851.* Washington, D.C.: World Bank.

Leibbrandt, M., Woolard, I., Finn, A. and Argent, J. 2010. Trends in South African income distribution and poverty since the fall of apartheid. *OECD Social, Employment and Migration Working Papers 101.* Paris: OECD.

Leibbrandt, M., Finn, A. and Woolard, I. 2012. Post-apartheid changes in South African inequality. *In:* Gornick, J. and M. Jäntti (Eds.), *Income inequality: Economic disparities and the middle class in affluent countries.* Palo Alto, CA: Stanford University Press.

Lodge, T. 1999. *Consolidating democracy: South Africa's second popular election.* Johannesburg: Wits University Press.

Mail and Guardian Newspaper. 24th April 2015.

Mbeki, T. 2006. Address of the President of South Africa, Thabo Mbeki, at a Joint Sitting of the Houses of Parliament on the Occasion of the 10th Anniversary of the Adoption of the Constitution of the Republic of South Africa. Cape Town, May 8, 2006.

Mebratie, A.D. and Bedi, A. S. 2011. Foreign direct investment, Black Economic Empowerment and labour productivity in South Africa. *IZA Discussion Papers 6048.* Institute for the Study of Labour.

Meth, C., and Dias, R. 2004. Increases in poverty in South Africa, 1999–2002. *Development Southern Africa, 21, 1,* pp59–85.

Naidoo, K. 2013. *Reducing Inequality to Promote Growth: A Proposed Policy Package.* Accessed 28th May 2015 from: www.econ3x3.org.

Pauw, K., and L. Ncube. 2007. The impact of growth and redistribution on poverty and inequality in South Africa. *DPRU Working Paper 07/126*, Cape Town: Development Policy Research Unit.

President Zuma, J. 2011. *State of the Nation Address.* Pretoria: The RSA Presidency.

President Zuma, J. 2009. *Inaugural Speech 2009*. Pretoria: The RSA Presidency.

Nattrass, N. 1994. Politics and economics in ANC economic policy. *African Affairs, 93:* pp. 343–59.

Nattrass, N. and Seekings, J. 2001. Democracy and distribution in highly unequal economies: The case of South Africa. *Journal of Modern African Studies, Vol. 39, No. 3 (Sep., 2001),* pp. 471–498.

Ncube, M., Shimeles, A. and Verdier-Chouchane, A. 2012. South Africa's quest for inclusive development. *AfDB Working Paper No. 150.* May 2012, Tunis.

Nsehe, M. 2014. 'The African Billionaires 2014'. Accessed on 20th April 2015 from:

http://forbes.com/sites/mfonobongnsehe/2014/03/04/the-africanbillionaires-2014.

Organisation for Economic Co-operation and Development (OECD). 2014. *Going for growth: Avoiding the low-growth trap*. Paris: OECD Publishing.

———. 2013. *OECD economic surveys: South Africa 2013*. Paris: OECD Publishing.

Ostry, J., Berg, A., and Tsangardies, C. 2014. Redistribution, inequality and growth. *IMF Staff Discussion Note*, Washington D.C.

Rapley, J. 2007. *Understanding development: Theory and practice in the third world.* Boulder: Lynne Rienner Publishers.

Ravallion, M. 2001. Growth, inequality and poverty: Looking beyond averages. *World Development, 29(11),* pp. 1803–1815.

Reardon, T., Barrett, C., Kelly, V. and Savadogo, K. 1999. Policy reforms and sustainable agricultural intensification in Africa. *Development Policy Review, Vol. 17 (1999),* pp. 375–395.

Republic of South Africa (RSA). l996a. *Growth, Employment and Redistribution Programme.* Pretoria: RSA Government.

Republic of South Africa (RSA). l996b. *Constitution of the Republic of South Africa, Act 108 of 1996.* Pretoria: RSA Government.

RSA Ministry of Economic Development. 2011. The New Growth Path: The Framework, Republic of South Africa. Accessed from 20/04/2015: http://www.economic.gov.za/publications/new-growth-path-series.

RSA National Treasury of South Africa. 2011. *Securing inclusive growth.* Pretoria: RSA National Treasury.

Republic of South Africa. 2012. *National Development Plan Vision 2030.* Pretoria: RSA Government.

RSA National Planning Commission. 2012. National development plan vision 2030. Pretoria, Government of South Africa.

Republic of South Africa Presidency. 2015. *Twenty year review of South Africa, 1994 – 2014.* Pretoria: RSA Government.

Rodrik, D. 2006. Understanding South Africa's economic puzzles. *Economics of Transition,* 16(4), pp. 769–797.

Sartorius, K. and Botha, G. 2008. Black Economic Empowerment ownership initiatives: A Johannesburg Stock Exchange perspective. *Development Southern Africa, 25 (4),* pp. 437–453.

Seekings, J. 2014. South Africa: Democracy, poverty and inclusive growth since 1994. *Centre for Development and Enterprise Working Paper.* Johannesburg.

Seekings, J. and Nattrass, N. 2005. *Class, race and inequality in South Africa.* New Haven: Yale University Press.

Southall, R. 2005. Black Empowerment and corporate capital. *In:* Daniel, J. Southall, R. and Lutchman, J. (Eds.). *The State of the Nation: South Africa 2004–2005.* Cape Town: HSRC Press.

Stiglitz, J. E. 1998. Towards a new paradigm for development: Strategies, policies, and processes. Presentation made as the 1998 Prebisch Lecture at UNCTAD, Geneva, October 1998.

Thorbecke, E. 2014. The structural anatomy and institutional architecture of inclusive growth in Sub-Saharan Africa. *UNU WIDER Working Paper 2014/041.* Helsinki.

Turok, B. 2008. *From the Freedom Charter to Polokwane: The evolution of ANC economic policy.* Cape Town: New Agenda Publishers.

United Nations Development Programme (UNDP). 2003. *Human Development Report 2003 - Millennium Development Goals: A compact among nations to end human poverty.* New York: UNDP.

United Nations Economic Commission for Africa (UNECA). 2012. *Unleashing Africa's potential as a pole of global growth: Economic report on Africa 2012.* Addis Ababa: UNECA.

Van der Berg, S. 2011. Current poverty and income distribution in the context of South African history. *Economic History of Developing Regions, 26(1),* pp. 120–40.

Visagie J. 2013. *Is the middle class becoming better off? Two perspectives.* Econ3x3. 15 July 2013. Accessed 29th May 2015 from: www.econ3x3.org/article/middle-class-becoming-better-two-perspectives.

World Bank. 2013. *Gender at work: A companion to the 2013 World Development Report.* Washington, D.C.: World Bank.
———. 2012b. *World Development Indicators 2012.* Washington, D.C.: World Bank.

———. 2012a. *South Africa economic update: Focus on inequality of opportunity.* Washington, D.C.: World Bank

———.2011. *South Africa Economic Update: Focus on savings, investment, and inclusive growth.* Washington DC: World Bank.

CHAPTER SIX

Social Policies for Inclusive and Sustainable Development: A Comparison of Social Health Protection Systems in Uganda and Thailand

Julius Omona

Abstract

This is a comparative study on the social health protection systems of Thailand and Uganda. The motivation is premised on the social health protection extremes of the two countries — Thailand is renowned for having achieved universal coverage but Uganda has not. Thus, the study undertook to compare the two countries by answering the question: Why has Thailand managed to provide universal coverage to all its citizens while Uganda has not? The specific questions to answer are thus: What are the current health programmes and coverage for each country? How do the social health protection programmes exclude others in the process of achieving the social security objective of universal coverage? How is the social health protection system financed in each country? What are the institutional and legal frameworks for universal health coverage for each country? What are the impacts of the current social health protection on the population and the economy? The study was guided by the comprehensive outcome framework of social protection by Sen (2009), and Fine and Leopold's (1993) public sector system of provision (PSSOP). This was a desk review that relied on qualitative and quantitative evidence and presentation. The findings are that Thailand achieved universal coverage after it introduced the universal coverage scheme (UCS) in 2001. Political commitment, in particular, played a major role in achieving this. Consequently, Thailand now has one of the best health indicators in the world and the sector is sustainable. In contrast, despite good laws, Uganda does not have a universal scheme. The national health insurance scheme is still in draft form — largely due to limited political will. Accordingly, Uganda's health indicators are among the worst in the world as it is viewed as unsustainable. It is recommended that Uganda implements a universal scheme, as a matter of urgency, and learns from the experience of Thailand. Thailand also needs to address some of the lingering challenges which are currently discrediting her achievements in this sector.

Keywords: Social health protection, exclusiveness, sustainability, Thailand, Uganda.

1. Introduction to the Study

This introductory section covers the background, research questions, methodology and organisation of the paper.

1.1 Background

The World Health Organisation (WHO) World Health Assembly of 2005 and WHO World Health Report of 2010 called for all health systems to move towards universal coverage — defined as access to adequate health care for all, at an affordable price (Wang and Pielemeier 2012; Rabovskja 2012). The affordability of health care is a key issue in most countries. In high-income countries, increasing costs, financial constraints of public budgets and economic considerations regarding international competiveness have all made social health protection reform a political priority. In many high, middle and low-income countries, providing affordable health care is high on the development agenda, given the large number of people lacking sufficient financial means to access health services; worldwide, millions of people are pushed into poverty every year by the need to pay for health care (International Labour Organisation [ILO] 2008).

Why focus on social health protection (SHP)? This is because it is an important tool for overcoming the vicious circle of poverty and ill health, and can contribute to sustainable development. Good health promotes economic growth (Sachs 2002; Gyimah-Brempong and Wilson 2004; Bloom *et al.* 2004). According to estimates by the WHO Macroeconomic Commission on Health, a 10 per cent increase in life expectancy leads to an additional increase of between 0.3 and 0.4 percentage points in the annual per capita income. As a result, a typical high-income country with an average life expectancy of 77 years has a 1.6 per cent higher annual growth rate, in comparison to a typical low-income country with an average life expectancy of 48 years. Extending social health protection also means moving towards enhanced risk-pooling of financial resources within a society. Empirical evidence supports the hypothesis that the degree of risk-sharing within a country's health financing system impacts positively on the attainment of overall health system goals, namely fair financing and the level of health and of responsiveness of their distribution across the respective population (Carrin *et al.* 2001). Studies from Kenya, Senegal and South Africa show that where patient fees exist, the insured use more outpatient services than the non-insured (Scheil-Adlung *et al.* 2007). Another important issue is that social health protection reduces, to a certain extent, a household's financial loss (Scheil-Adlung *et al.* 2007). A study on social health protection in Vietnam not only confirmed these findings but also found that a reduction of out-of-pocket (OOP) payments leads to a higher than average increase in consumption. This is consistent with the hypothesis that households tend to considerably hold back consumption when faced with the risk of high OOP expenditures (Wagstaff and Pradhan 2005). Hörmansdörfer (2009) specifically states that social health protection facilitates pro-poor growth and poverty reduction through some of the following channels:

a) It helps to improve the health status of people. Social protection removes barriers related to high illness-related costs that prevent people from seeking health services.

b) It prevents impoverishing health-care expenditures. It does this by preventing patients from paying substantial user charges or co-payment in a manner that can cause economic ruin for families.

c) It substitutes inefficient health-related risk-coping mechanisms, especially in developing countries, such as selling productive assets, cutting down expenditures on other basic necessities, such as food and clothing, and taking children away from school.

d) It promotes social stability and social cohesion since it is based on grounds such as solidarity and equity. In this way, it strengthens the bonds of cooperation and reciprocity, thus enhancing social stability and social cohesion.

e) It contributes to empowerment since the schemes provide participatory decision-making structures which strengthen the voice of the poor, and may improve the responsiveness and quality of health services.

Uganda and Thailand are among the low-income countries making or implementing health policies to enable their citizens to have inclusive and sustainable health services. Thailand reached near-universal health coverage as far back as 2002, shortly after the launch of the universal coverage scheme (UCS). It has succeeded in extending social health protection to all, even while experiencing economic recession. It has developed what is now a comprehensive social health protection system that articulates schemes for all employment statuses (ILO 2014). In contrast, Uganda's health care system still falls far short of reaching the WHO goals. The government is the main provider of health services amidst many challenges. Some of the health services provided by private providers, which are contributory, benefit only those in formal employment. Community-based health schemes are also member-based and are hampered by limited coverage at national level (Wang and Pielemeier 2012). This paper thus compares the social health care contexts of the two countries, with the aim of enabling Uganda to draw lessons from the good policy practices of Thailand.

1.2. Research Questions/Problem

The key question is: Why has Thailand managed to provide social health protection to all its citizens while Uganda has not? The specific questions to answer are as follows: What are the current health programmes and coverage for each country? How do the social health protection programmes exclude others in the process of achieving the social security objective of universal coverage? How is the social health protection system financed in each country? What are the institutional and legal frameworks for universal health coverage (UHC) for each country? What are the impacts of the current SHP on the population and the economy?

1.3. Methodology

The research adopted a comparative research design, with the purposes of exploring and describing the issues related to the SHP systems of Uganda and Thailand. It is a quantitative and predominantly qualitative research study, based on literature from WHO, ILO and United Nationals Children's Fund [UNICEF] regional health reports from the East Africa Community and the Association of Southeast Asian Nations (ASEAN), and country-specific health reports, policies, policy briefs, journal articles, and conference papers, amongst other sources. Content and thematic analysis, on the basis of the research questions, constituted the basis of data analysis, synthesis and presentation. It is hoped that this method has generated sufficient research data useful for informing health policies, generally in the contexts of developing countries, and specifically in Uganda and Thailand. The research also provides baseline data for further qualitative and quantitative research on this topical subject.

1.4 Organisation of the Paper

The paper is organised into four parts. The first part, which is the introductory section, includes the background to the problem, the questions addressed by the paper, the methodology, and the organisation of the paper. The second part deals with the theoretical/conceptual framework and literature review. This section contains the major theories and constructs relating to the study, which have guided the entire paper. The third part contains the synthesis of findings — both qualitative and quantitative from secondary sources, and the discussion thereof. The last part consists of the conclusion and recommendations.

2. Theoretical and Conceptual Frameworks and Literature Review

This section covers the theoretical framework, the key concepts guiding the paper and the literature review with respect to the conceptual issues.

2.1 Theoretical Framework

Two theories underpin this paper on SHP. The first is the comprehensive outcome framework for social protection by Sen (2009). This theory describes a state of affairs that can be rich and incorporates processes of choice, and not only narrowly defined ultimate results. According to this approach, the content of outcomes can also be seen, including all the agency information that may be relevant as well as all the personal and impersonal relations that may be seen as important in resolving the problem at hand. Hence, the theory focuses on the deontological emphasis of actions (actions' adherence to normative rules), the functioning or relations between outcomes and institutional complementarily. In the current study, the outcomes are presented as impacts, and the intuitional complementarily is identified through the range and qualities of institutions involved in determining health policy and systems development, including the challenges thereof. The second set of theories is Fine and Leopold's (1993) public sector system of provision (PSSOP), which examines the chain of provision for production, distribution and consumption. With respect to health, consumption of health care is connected to the changing pattern of production and distribution of health care systems. Common methods of production and distribution are the public, private commercial, community-based and informal; and using different combinations of the four health care models: Bismarck, Biveridge, National Health Insurance (NHI), and OOP. These theories, or versions of the same, have been widely applied by WHO (2002, 2008), UNICEF (2012) and ILO (2008).

According to UNICEF (2012), SHP falls within the overall social protection system of public and private policies and programmes, aimed at eliminating the economic and social vulnerabilities of all persons in order to ensure their equitable right to a decent standard of living. UNICEF(2012) contends that social protection generally comprises four core components that address the specific social and economic vulnerabilities related to poverty and deprivation: social transfers to protect and prevent individuals and households from economic shocks while supporting the accumulation of human and financial assets; programmes to ensure access to services and overcome social barriers to access at the community, household and individual levels; social support and case services to identify and respond to social vulnerability and deprivation; and legislation and policy reform to remove inequalities in access and address issues of discrimination and exclusion.

Theoretically, there are three basic principles that are required to remove vulnerabilities. The first is inclusive social protection, combined with the second — the progressive realisation of universal coverage. An inclusive social protection approach recognises the diverse and overlapping vulnerabilities faced by at-risk populations. Progressive realisation acknowledges that countries vary in current protection systems, coverage and gaps, and require a context-appropriate approach to achieve universal converge. These two principles are embedded in the socio-legal and institutional framework of the country through the promotion of the third precept — national ownership and context specificity (UNICEF 2012). The three tiers work together to progress towards UHC. The first is a base tier of protection delivered through free services for all citizens, such as childhood vaccinations, regarded as goods of high public merit (WHO 2002). The second tier generally comprises government-led and centrally managed SHP mechanisms, including NHI schemes. The third tier comprises diverse private and specialised insurance schemes to cover those seeking more depth and breadth of coverage. This tier includes occupational and accident insurance, specialised coverage for the military and private sector plans (UNICEF 2012). The third tier primarily responds to market demand generated by wealthier households working in the formal and civil sectors (UNICEF 2012). It can be noted that the first tier tends to be government-sponsored and free to all citizens, while the third tier is accessible primarily to the wealthy, which means there are some obstacles to some of these schemes as well as social exclusion. The dominant force at each tier also determines the nature of financing of the health care system.

Theoretically, for any health system to achieve UHC, progress towards universal coverage should be made along three dimensions (WHO 2008): breadth of coverage; depth of coverage; and heights of coverage. Breadth of coverage refers to the proportion of the population that enjoys SHP. Depth of coverage refers to the essential health services necessary to address people's health needs effectively, which are covered through benefits. Height of coverage refers to the portion of health care costs covered through pooling and pre-payment mechanisms. These can all be achieved by eliminating three categories of barriers: inability to enrol in schemes; inability to use the scheme when enrolled; and barriers to receiving appropriate and quality care (ILO 2008).

2.2 Conceptual Framework

The key concepts applied in this study are SHP, UHC, and inclusive social policy and sustainability. The guiding questions of the study are framed within these concepts. According to WHO resolution 58.33 of 2005 and the World Health Report of 2010 (2), UHC stands for the goal of ensuring that all people have access to the health services they need without the risk of financial ruin (East Africa Community 2014; Rabovskaja 2012). The idea of UHC requires that every individual has access to the required quality and quantity of health care services without imposing financial risk on the people who seek such services. Ensuring access to these needed services by every individual implies equity in access to health care. In this case, access to health care services should not be determined by financial ability but need. Those with high income need to subsidise the poorest while those with good health ought to subsidise those with poor health. This is what is considered to be cross-subsidisation within the broad concept of SHP and UHC. The World Health Organisation defines UHC as the desired outcome of health system performance, whereby all people who need health services (promotion, prevention, treatment, rehabilitation, and palliation) receive them without undue financial hardship (East Africa Community 2014). Universal health coverage has two interrelated components: full spectrum of good quality essential health services according to need; and protection from financial hardship, including possible impoverishment, due to OOP payments for health services. Both components should benefit the entire population. According to the international terminology in use, there is some variation (and at times confusion) concerning the difference between UHC and SHP. The current trend in the international debate points towards the similarities between UHC and SHP, with some newer publications (WHO Action Plan 3) even suggesting possible interchangeable use. However, strictly speaking, the term UHC does not include the idea of compensating income loss during illness in the sense of SHP (such as ILO definition 4), which in turn does not necessarily include universality (East Africa Community 2014). In this study, therefore, in spite of the variance in their focus, SHP and UHC are interchangeably applied, given the fact that both aim at ensuring equitable access to essential quality health services at affordable prices.

Social exclusion is a widely used term today, but not necessarily a clear-cut concept (Williams *et al.* 2014). It can varyingly be considered as a condition/status or as a multidimensional and dynamic process. When viewed as a condition/status, it is seen as an outcome where individuals or groups are excluded, as they are unable to fully participate in society as a result of their social identity (gender, religion and race) or social location (remote areas, segregated territories and low-paid jobs). Alternatively, social exclusion can be viewed as a multidimensional and dynamic process, whereby social interactions and organisational/institutional barriers hamper individuals from attaining a decent livelihood, hinder a country from attaining a sufficient level of human development and hamper a state from offering equal citizenship to its citizens. Social exclusion therefore generates, sustains and reproduces poverty, enhances inequalities, and restricts social, political and economic participation for some marginalised individuals or groups, and prevents them from accessing institutional sites of power or engaging with powerful organisations. Research done in the health sector has established that causes of and risk factors for exclusion from effective coverage manifest across four dimensions of power relationships that constitute the continuum from inclusion to exclusion: economic, political, social, and cultural (Popay *et al.* 2008). Key characteristics of each dimension are described below:

a) The social dimension is constituted by proximal relationships of support and solidarity, such as friendship, kinship, family, clan, neighbour, community, and social movements that generate a sense of belonging within social systems. Along this dimension, social bonds are strengthened or weakened.

b) The political dimension is constituted by power dynamics in relationships which generate unequal patterns of both formal rights embedded in legislation, constitutions, policies and practices, and the conditions in which rights are exercised, including access to safe water, sanitation, shelter, transport, and power, as well as services such as health care, education and social protection. Along this dimension, there is unequal distribution of opportunities to participate in public life, to express desires and interests, to have interests taken into account, and to have access to services.

c) The economic dimension is constituted by access to and distribution of the material resources necessary to sustain life such as income, employment, housing, land working conditions, and livelihoods.

d) The cultural dimension is constituted by the extent to which diverse values, norms and ways of living are accepted and respected. At one extreme along this dimension, diversity is accepted in all its richness; at the other, there are extreme situations of stigma and discrimination.

Given the complex, multidimensional, dynamic nature of social exclusion, risk factors or drivers of social exclusion in each dimension interact and are more often mutually reinforcing in their impact on social exclusion (Williams *et al.* 2014).

Social protection (SP) refers to an inclusive system of public and private policies and programmes   aimed at preventing, reducing and eliminating economic and social vulnerabilities related to poverty and deprivation (Devereux and Sabates-Wheeler 2004). Sustainable development is a concept coined by the International Union for the Conservation of Nature (IUCN) Report of 1980 and is defined as "... development that meets the needs of the present without compromising the ability of future generations to meet their own needs" (WCED 1987, 3). In the context of this paper, sustainable development refers to meeting the health needs of the current population in a manner that is long-lasting and beneficial to all.

2.3 Literature Review

Many developing countries have tried or are attempting to achieve UHC for their populations through inclusive health policies for sustainable development. It is crucial to review these experiences in the light of the research questions.

2.3.1 Current Health Policies/Programmes and Coverage

Burundi is one of the countries making fast strides towards achieving UHC. It is doing this through multiple programmes, all supported by the government (East African Community 2014). They include free care, CAM (*Carte d'Assistance Médicale*), MFP (*Mutuelle de la Fonction Publique*) and private insurance, including community-based health insurance (CBHI). Free care was created in 2006 and targets all pregnant women and children less than five years. So far, the coverage is 22 per cent of the population. *Carte d'Assistance Médicale* was first introduced in 1984 but revised in 2012. It targets two-thirds of the population, which consists of all people living below the poverty line. So far, the population covered is 31 per cent (East Africa Community 2014). *Mutuelle de la Fonction Publique* was created in 1980. It targets between 11 and 13 per cent of the population. These are public servants who constitute about 1 to 1.2 million. So far, 10 per cent of these have been covered (East African Community 2014). The last programme is private insurance which was created in the 1990s and, in the case of CBHI, in 2008. It targets 2 per cent of the population, which comprises those in formal employment. So far, 2 per cent of the population have been covered. Though the coverage under these programmes looks impressive, there are still lingering issues that need to be tackled. For instance, it is widely acknowledged that the SP systems in

Burundi are fragmented. The lack of consistency of the current SHP schemes creates a counterproductive system which is fragmented, with limited coordination and also reflects duplications and gaps (East African Community 2014). Other countries, such as China, Ghana, Rwanda, and Vietnam, are equally operating multiple SHPs with impressive degrees of coverage (UNICEF 2012). Though still faced with some challenges, countries such as the Philippines, Brazil and Costa Rica have made progress over the years with multiples programmes and are nearing universal coverage (Hörmansdörfer 2009). In this paper, the focus is on the programmes and coverage for Thailand and Uganda.

2.3.2 How Do Some People Get Excluded in the Process of Achieving Social Security Objectives?

Literature is rife with avenues through which people get excluded from receiving or having access to health services. One set of exclusions arises when people are unable to enrol in schemes, largely caused by unrealistic eligibility criteria such as birth registration, overly restrictive citizenship requirements, outdated and inaccurate poverty indices, or insufficient funding of administrative mechanisms to provide equitable enrolment opportunities (UNICEF 2012). The second source of exclusion is the inability to use the scheme when enrolled. This could be due to barriers related to non-portability of schemes and insufficient coverage of OOP costs, such as transport, co-payments and unofficial or informal fees (UNICEF 2012). The third set of exclusions arises when potential beneficiaries are unable to obtain appropriate and quality services. In many cases, care may be inappropriate to the needs of each person, especially those in high-vulnerability groups such as children, women or families facing other forms of discrimination. Such avenues of exclusion have been evident in SHP systems of countries such as Brazil and Costa Rica, which are continuously working to improve on their schemes towards achieving universal coverage (Hörmansdörfer 2009). This paper has explored the terrain of exclusion for Thailand and Uganda.

2.3.3 Financing of Social Health Protection System

Different countries have financed their health care systems differently, depending on their socioeconomic, political and ideological orientations. For instance, in Ghana, the government is using multiple sources of funding to finance the NHI scheme such as a 2.5 per cent deduction from workers' social security contribution, a 2.5 per cent sales tax (value added tax) for health insurance, government budgetary allocation, donations, and investment from accruals to the NHI fund (East Africa Community 2014). The health care financing sources in Kenya are as follows (GoK 2010, 2012): The public sector contributed 25 per cent of the funds in 2011/2012. The private sector, including employers and private insurers, contributed the largest proportion of funds, up to 43 per cent in 2011/2012. Private health spending contributes the largest share of health care financing in Kenya. Donors' contributions to this sector have also been increasing over the years. For instance, the proportion of funds originating from donors has increased from 31 per cent in 2001/2002 to 35 per cent in 2009/2010. What is clear from the preceding analyses is that funding of the SHP system requires huge financial investment, and this demands a concerted effort from both the private and public sectors.

2.3.4 Institutional Framework to Support Health Care Systems

Many countries that are implementing SHP policies are aligning them to some national and international health care framework. For instance, the framework for social protection in Tanzania is constructed with the guidance of a number of international conventions that the country has signed (McIntyre *et al.* 2008; Mdee 2009; Mtei and Mulligan 2007). Among these are the Universal Declaration of Human Rights 1948; the International Convention on Economic, Social and Cultural Rights 1966; the African (Banjul) Charter on Human and Peoples' Rights 1981; and the ILO Social Security framework. Other domestic laws within which health care services are crafted are the national constitution; the National Social Security Fund Act No. 28/1997; the Public Service Retirement Benefits Act No. 2 of 1999; the Insurance Act No. 10 of 2009; and many others under various stages of discussion and promulgation. Like Tanzania, Rwanda's SHP is also aligned with the international conventions. Besides, there are local institutional frameworks that govern SP programmes. Rwanda has many laws regarding the legal aspect of SHP. These include the constitution of 2003; the SP policy of 2005; SP for survivors of the 1994 genocide against Tutsi; and child protection rights, amongst others (East Africa Community 2014). Thailand and Uganda have also aligned their SHP policies to the same international conventions, since both are members of the United Nations (UN). They only differ in their national and regional legislation and regulations by virtue of the differences between them, in terms of geographical context and ideological orientation.

2.3.5 Impacts of Social Health Protection

Reports abound of countries that have implemented SHP schemes with a positive impact on the health of the population and the economy. Countries such as Vietnam and China fall in this category (Basaza, O'Connell and Chapčáková 2013). The introduction of an NHI scheme in Ghana, in 2004, saw a unique mix of social insurance and mutual health organisational principles that is driven by strong political commitment and a pro-poor focus, and has led to improved health outcomes for the population (Hörmansdörfer 2009). Similarly, in Tanzania, the government initiated schemes, such as the National Health Insurance Fund (NHIF) for public sector employees and the Voluntary Community Health Funds (VCHF) for informal sector workers and poor households at local level, which are being successfully supplemented by private health insurance and micro-insurance schemes run by churches, informal sector groups and cooperatives, with positive health outcomes for the population (Hörmansdörfer 2009). South Korea is a prominent example of the successful introduction of SHI. After the adoption of the Health Insurance Act in 1963, it took the entire population of South Korea only 26 years to be covered by the SHI in 1989. Part of the high economic growth that the country has experienced since then is attributed to health care programmes (Hörmansdörfer 2009). The impressive coverage of SHP in Rwanda, which has made it a role model in the region in this regard, has not only contributed to its fast economic growth and development in the region, but also to its quick recovery during the post-genocide period (East Africa Community 2014). In countries such as Bangladesh, India, Mali and Nigeria, however, many remote and rural populations are unable to use benefits to which they are entitled — thus ideally not benefiting from such schemes (UNICEF 2012).

In conclusion, inasmuch as many countries have achieved universal and near UHC with impressive impacts, there are a number of lingering issues that need to be tackled. For instance, in Kenya, the SHP coverage by 2007 was still only 25 per cent of the population, despite being the first country in Africa to introduce compulsory health insurance in 1966 (ILO 2008). The low coverage has been attributed to institutions being too weak to support health care services. Similarly, in Senegal, the coverage by 2007 was only 11.7 per cent (ILO 2008). The key challenge here is how to extend the coverage to the informal economy (ILO 2008). In India, where the coverage was only 5.7 per cent by 2007, much of the challenge remains owing to the fact that only 1 per cent of the gross national product (GNP) is spent on health care (Gupta 2007). Even in Indonesia, where the coverage is 54.6 per cent, the challenges remains owing to financial constraints and the poor management of private sector schemes (ILO 2008). This paper reviews the SHP contexts of Thailand and Uganda, identifies lingering issues and offers recommendations accordingly.

3. Results of the Documentary Review on the Two Countries

3.1 Country Profiles

Uganda, located in East Africa, was a British colony from 1894 until it gained its independence in 1962. Uganda has a population of 34.9 million (Government of Uganda [GoU] 2014). It has a land size of 241, 038 square kilometres, slightly smaller than the state of Oregon, USA, and the geographical coordinates are 1 00 N, 32 00 E. Only 27.94 per cent of the land is arable, with 9.11 per cent under permanent crops. The other 62.95 per cent of the country comprises urban areas, mountains, roads, and water bodies. Its gross domestic product [GDP] (purchasing power parity-PPP) is $54.37 billion,[1] while the GDP growth rate was 5.6 per cent and the GDP per capita was $550 in 2012 (Basaza, O'Connell and Chapčáková 2013). The major religions are Christianity and Islam. The motto is "For God and my Country". The type of government is a republic. In terms of human development, the 2013 report ranked Uganda as 161st out of 182, making it one of the poorest countries, with a human development index of 0.456 (UNDP 2013). The proportion of the population employed in the informal sector in 2012 was 54.5 per cent and 14.7 per cent was urbanised (GoU 2012a). Over the 2000 to 2010 period, Uganda experienced an annual average economic growth of 7 per cent (GoU 2012b). Nevertheless, an estimated 24.5 per cent of the population was living below the $1 per day poverty line, and more households became impoverished as a result of health expenditure on a daily basis. Despite significant progress towards the Millennium Development Goals (MDGs), it was deemed unlikely that MDG 4 (child survival) and MDG 5 (maternal health) would be met (UNDP 2010). A lack of financial access to health services, the resultant poor health, and the high disease burden of the poor have been identified as drivers of poverty in Uganda (Basaza, O'Connell and Chapčáková 2013). This demonstrates the urgency of minimising financial barriers to health services, hence the justification for this paper.

A unified Thai kingdom was established in the mid-fourteenth century. Thailand, formerly known as Siam, is the only Southeast Asian country never to have been colonised by Western powers. It has a land size of 513,000 square kilometres and a population of 67,741,401. Thailand has only two dominant ethnic groups − the Thai (95.9 per cent) and the Burmese (2 per cent), with the rest constituting about 2.2 per cent. The GDP (PPP) is $ 1,054.999 billion, the GDP is $ 397.475 billion and the GDP per capita is $ 5,771. The motto is "Nation, Religions, King". The type of government is a unitary constitutional monarchy (World Fact Book 2013).[2] Buddhism is the professed faith of 94.6 per cent of the population. Islam is embraced by 4.6 per cent, while the rest of the population practise Christianity, Hinduism and other religions (ILO 2007). In terms of human development, the 2013 Human Development Report ranked Thailand 89th, with a human development index of 0.7222 (United Nations Development Programme [UNDP] 2013). The economy is sufficiently healthy to support SP policies. There is sufficient health care, increasing productivity from better human capital and sufficient income security for every age group − children, working age adults and the elderly (Sakunphanit 2014). Despite huge differences in socioeconomic, political, geographical and historical factors, Uganda has some lessons to learn from Thailand's SHP experience.

3.2 Current Health Programmes, Social Exclusion and Coverage

Health services constitute the SP programmes being provided to Uganda for fighting vulnerability. Like in many countries, the SP is organised in three layers that include non-contributory, compulsory and complementary social security (ILO 2006). The government of Uganda is the main provider of health services which are administered by the Ministry of Health. Currently, health protection is minimal in all three dimensions: height, depth and breadth. Community-based health insurance schemes were first created in 1995. Most of these schemes operate in the southern part of the country and in private not-for-profit facilities. The social exclusion comes about because the services offered are only those available at the contracted facilities and exclude referrals and portability. Besides, in those areas where CBHI exist, the poor are not subsidised, hence the premium is still considered expensive. Accordingly, where such schemes operate, they cover only between 5 and 10 per cent of the population. They are micro-schemes and the total enrolment in the country is 140,000 people (Basaza, Criel and Van der Stuyft 2007). There are also other informal community health insurers, such as funeral groups, which also lend money for health care and transportation of the sick. These are localised, small-scale and voluntary. Furthermore, there is family assistance whereby family members contribute money for health care for the sick. Like all small homogenous entities, they are unable to diversify risk across the population and are susceptible to adverse selection (Mwesigye and Pearson 1997; Masiko 1998).

Private commercial insurance schemes cover only an additional 1 per cent of the population and are mainly limited to in-house private health maintenance plans of a few large firms in addition to some third-party insurance schemes (Basaza, O'Connell and Chapčáková 2013). The first scheme in this category is African Air Rescue, which started in 1994. The majority are employer-based schemes and 75 per cent of these schemes have their own facilities, with the remaining schemes being run by insurance companies. These schemes target private formal sector workers and their dependants. Very few members join as individual families. Just like the CBHI, private commercial health insurance schemes (PCHIS) do not cover immunisation and treatment for HIV or tuberculosis because these services are supposed to be provided free by government programmes (East Africa Community 2014). Accordingly, those seeking treatment for such diseases usually do not receive treatment.

Government health facilities provide free health care. These free services began when the government abolished user fees in government facilities in 2001, except the private wings in hospitals (East Africa Community 2014). Free care is also accessed in the health care facilities of the uniformed services, such as the military, prisons and police, by members of the forces and their dependants. However, despite the free care, some segments of the population do not believe in free care and under-the-table payments do take place (Orem and Zikusooka 2010), which excludes other people from utilising this scheme. Government subsidies and donations to private providers constitute another scheme in the health sector that offers SP, and this source accounts for 30 per cent of the health services in Uganda (GoU 2013). Through this source, the government provides subsidies through public-private partnerships, which account for about 10 to 20 per cent of their operational costs. This has enabled private not-for-profit providers (PNFPS) to lower user fees. Under this scheme, the private not-for-profit providers receive government subsidies in the spirit of providing free public health services such as immunisation. The major shortcoming of this arrangement is that the not-for-profit providers are limited in their coverage. Most are located in the urban centres, thus excluding particularly the most vulnerable rural inhabitants from accessing such a service.

The proposed NHI scheme is being spearheaded by the Ministry of Health and will initially target coverage for people in formal employment. The scheme will require both the employee and the employer to each contribute 4 per cent of the employee's salary with no co-payments. The scheme will begin with 10 per cent of the national population (formally employed and their dependants) and later expand to cover the entire population (Orem and Zikusooka 2010). The informal sector will be required to pay a prescribed premium, which has not yet been decided. Though the scheme is supposed to be run under an autonomous organisation, there is currently lack of capacity in the Ministry of Health to design the scheme, amongst other challenges (East Africa Community 2014).

In view of the above, it is widely acknowledged in the region that Uganda has made the least effort to create nationally owned SHP systems. The implementation of the NHI scheme is taking too long. Consequently, Uganda is worse off in terms of SHP safety nets compared to all other nations in the region (East Africa Community 2014). Generally, for the entire population, coverage under SHP is less than 1 per cent. The SHP system in Uganda is categorised as having limited coverage, poor quality of care and is characterised by under-the-table payments (East Africa Community 2014).

Thailand reached near-universal coverage in 2002, shortly after the launch of the UCS in 2001 (ILO 2014). The goal of the UCS is to equally extend quality health care to all citizens, according to their needs, regardless of their socioeconomic status, which underlies the fact that a universalistic approach was chosen rather than a targeted one. The country chose to implement a purchaser-provider split. Some of the key outcomes of this approach are: Thai people disburse 13.7 per cent of total health care expenditure from their own pocket; the government spends $93.1 per person per year on health; up to 99.4 per cent of births are attended by skilled health staff; and maternal mortality ratio is 48 per 100,000 live births.

Generally, SHP in Thailand is clearly categorised into two (Paitoonpong *et al.* 2010). Firstly, the contributory transfer programmes consist of statutory social insurance, an occupational security system and voluntary social protection. The statutory social insurance consists of a social insurance or social security scheme (SSS) and unemployment insurance. The occupational security system consists of government pension fund and pensions for employees of state enterprises. Voluntary social protection consists of a provident fund, retirement mutual fund (RMF) and private insurance. Secondly, the non-contributory transfer programme (health care and social assistance) consists of the universal health care (30 baht)[3] programme and the old age living allowance.

The broad categories above are covered under the following specific health schemes: Civil Servant Medical Benefit Scheme (CSMBS), created in 1963 and targeting civil servants, retired civil servants and their dependants. The coverage rate was 16 per cent by 2008 (ILO 2014). Another scheme is the compulsory social security scheme (SSS), created in 1990. This covers private sector workers and their dependants, and by 2008, the coverage was 7 per cent. The major scheme is the UCS, created in 2001. It covers the rest of the population that do not fall in the above two categories. The coverage by 2008 was 75 per cent. All three schemes are thought to offer comprehensive coverage, except in special cases for organ transplants, plastic surgery and infertility treatment. As of today, the coverage stands as follows: 78 per cent under UCS, 7 per cent under the SSS for private workers and 15 per cent for CSMBS (Sakunphanit 2014); these are reflected in the breadth, height and depth. However, though coverage is now universal, there are issues of exclusion. For instance, ethnic minorities and stateless people are excluded because they lack identity cards (IDs)[4] or exclusion may arise from lack of information; there is also the issue of geographical imbalances — poor availability of health care in some communities and lack of indemnity for HIV. Furthermore, it has been reported that migrant workers are excluded from SSS because of non-declaration by employers (Schmitt 2014).

3.3 Financing of SHP Systems

Financing of the SHP in Uganda is carried out by the government, private providers, households and donors (Basaza, O'Connell and Chapčáková 2013). In 2001, Uganda pledged to increase national spending on health to at least 15 per cent of the national budget, in line with the Abuja Declaration at the summit of African heads of state (Barya 2011). Since then, government health expenditure as a percentage of total government expenditure has remained under 10 per cent. It was 7 per cent in 2010. The total health expenditure (THE) per capita in 2010 was 52 per cent, which was 9 per cent of nominal GDP. The government health expenditure was 22 per cent of THE, which was $11.2 per capita per annum. Household expenditure on health was 42 per cent of THE, and the balance of 36 per cent came from donors and NGOs. Additionally, in 2010, household OOP spending on health per capita was $22. In terms of financing sources as a percentage of THE, private spending provides 49 per cent, donors and NGOs 36 per cent and government 15 per cent (GoU 2013).

In Uganda, despite user fees being waived from primary health care (PHC) services, indirect costs (such as payment for transportation to clinics), informal fees (such as illegal payments demanded by providers for free services) and unofficial fees (such as requiring patients to purchase medicines that are no longer in stock) [UNICEF 2012] are negative methods of financing the health sector which instead act as barriers to receiving health care. Overall, health sector financing in Uganda is both project-oriented and vertically-oriented, with low investments in overall system improvement. The incidence of catastrophic health expenditure among the poor steadily increased from 1996 to 2006 despite the abolition of user fees, which was partly due to the greater use of private providers by the poor (East African Community 2014). Another factor was medicines frequently being unavailable in public facilities, obliging patients to pay higher prices to acquire medicines at private pharmacies (Basaza, O'Connell and Chapčáková 2013; Orem and Zikusooka 2010). The government allocates an average 7.4 per cent of the budget to the sector. Other than revenue collected through taxation and budget support, there is no other resource-pooling mechanism at national level. The private commercial health insurance schemes are obliged by the insurance regulatory authority (IRA) to reinsure the collected premiums and to have reserves. At CBHI level, the schemes lack a pooling mechanism except for the save-for-health supported schemes in greater Bushenyi and Luwero districts that have district pool and district representatives (East African Community 2014).

In Thailand, the national-care financing system has the following coverage: The social security scheme (SSS) provides coverage to private formal economy workers. By 2006, 7.4 million cardholders were eligible for health care benefits under the scheme. There is also the non-contributory civil servants' medical benefit scheme (CSMBS), covering about 7 million eligible people (some 3 million civil servants as well as about 4 million eligible dependants — children, spouses and parents by 2006). The UCS, which is the largest scheme, benefits two categories of people — the people who are exempted from payment of the 30 baht ($ 0.75) per episode and almost an equal number who must make a co-payment of 30 baht at the point of service. There is also voluntary private health insurance, which covered some 5 million people by 2007. Lastly, there is a self-payer/non-covered group (people in remote areas — about 3 million) (ILO 2008). As of 2006, the overall insurance coverage in Thailand accounted for 97.8 per cent of the population. Of this figure, 75.3 per cent consisted of universal coverage and 22.5 per cent fell under the SSS and CSMBS.

By 2013, financing sources and methods were as follows: Under the universal coverage scheme, the 30 baht co-payment for services was still in place, though this could be waived by the director of the facility where care was received. This scheme is also funded under the global budget for inpatient care (donor) as well as capitation for outpatient care and prevention. The average cost was roughly $88 per capita by 2011 (ILO 2014). The main funding sources are non-contributory and general taxes. For the compulsory social security scheme, the financing method is risk-adjusted capitation for inpatient and outpatient services. The cost was roughly $69 per capita by 2011. The funding sources are contributory and payroll tax as well as tripartite contributions (ILO 2014). The CSMBS financial method involves a fee-for-service for outpatient services and diagnosis-related group (DRG)[5] services for inpatients. The cost was roughly $440 per capita by 2011. The funding sources are non-contributor and general taxes (ILO 2014). Table 1 shows the UCS budget per capita from 2002 to 2012.

Table 1. Trend in the UCS budget per capita, 2002-2012

Year	UCS budget per capita Baht	US ($)	Baht (2007 price)
2002	1,201	27.9	1,407
2003	1,201	28.9	1,381
2004	1,308	32.5	1,464
2005	1,396	34.7	1,495
2006	1,718	45.3	1,757
2007	1,983	57.4	1,983
2008	2,194	65.8	2,082
2009	2,298	66.9	2,199
2010	2,497	78.7	2,312
2011	2,693	88.3	2,405
2012	2,895	93.1	2,408

SOURCE: National Health Security Office (NHSO) (2012).

Table 1 shows a general progress in the UCS budgets over the years. It can be concluded that both Uganda and Thailand are using, to varying degrees, a mixed or hybrid approach to financing and eligibility, comprising Bismarck, Beveridge, NHI, and OOP models. However, considering all sources of and commitment to funding the health care system, Thailand has a more comprehensive and effective financing system than Uganda.

3.4. Legal and Institutional Framework and Actors Involved in Health Care Policies

From the regulatory perspective, Uganda is the only East African country that does not have a national insurance scheme, although there is a draft bill under scrutiny before implementation. The following constitute the international, regional and national legal documents and frameworks for SHP in Uganda (East Africa Community 2014):

• The 1995 Constitution of the Republic of Uganda, as amended, states, "the state shall take all practical measures to ensure the provision of basic medical services to the population". It does not, however, provide health as a right to all citizens (Government of Uganda [GoU] 1995, 18).

• Universal Declaration of Human Rights, 1948: Uganda is a signatory to this framework which guarantees everyone the right to social security in the event of unemployment, sickness, disability, widowhood, old age or other lack of livelihood in circumstances beyond a person's control.

• The International Convention on Economic, Social and Cultural Rights, 1966. This obliges the government to put in place measures to ensure access to social security, including social insurance, for everyone.

• The Convention on the Rights of Persons with Disabilities, 2006. This obliges the government to provide access to SP to persons with disabilities.

- The UN Convention on the Rights of the Child, 1989. This compels the government to help children who are poor and in need, either directly or through their guardians.

- The Livingstone Call to Action, 2006. This obliges African States to put in place costed plans for the implementation of direct income support programmes.

- The African Union Social Policy Framework, 2008. Uganda is also a signatory to this framework which calls on member governments to recognise that SP is a state obligation, with provisions in national legislation (GoU 2013).

- Insurance (Amendment) Act 2011. This put in place the IRA of Uganda. The country does not have a specific health insurance act. This act provides for the regulation of private commercial health insurance schemes. These are health management organisations (which in Uganda are known as health membership organisations) and insurance companies which provide health insurance as one of the schemes. This act provides for the regulation of any other premium-receiving institution, including CBHI schemes.

- The 2011 to 2016 presidential manifesto of Uganda's ruling party, the National Resistance Movement (NRM), which includes the development of a health insurance scheme as one of the work programmes in the health sector.

- The futuristic country planning framework, Vision 2040, which provides for universal health insurance as one of the pillars of development into a middle and upper-income state.

- The National Development Plan, 2010/2011 to 2014/2015, which is a five-year country planning framework that provides for national health insurance and aims at universal coverage and SHP.

- The 2010 National Health Policy, which stipulates the promotion of sustainable alternative health financing mechanisms.

- The Health Sector Strategic and Investment Plan of 2010/2011 to 2014/2015, which identifies social health insurance and community health insurance as financing mechanisms for this plan.

At the moment, the country does not have a specific health protection policy (East African Community 2014; Basaza, O'Connell and Chapčáková 2013). The health sector is in the process of drafting a health sector financing strategy that will include broader aspects of SHP and health-care reforms.

The drafts laws, bills and regulations, and key policies under consideration are as follows:

- The Health Insurance Bill: This is the only draft currently being considered. It provides for the establishment of an NHI scheme with provisions for a SHI scheme for formal sector workers (in government and in the private sector). The bill has not progressed much since 2006. There is limited political support for SHP (Basaza, O'Connell and Chapčáková 2013).

- Regulations for private commercial schemes and CBHI: The IRA is in the process of developing regulatory instruments and guidelines for PCHIS and CBHIs. Currently, all the CBHIs in Uganda are registered with the Registrar of Companies, the nongovernmental organisations (NGOs) board and with districts as community-based organisations (CBOs).

- The draft National Social Protection Policy Framework for Uganda 2013: The Ministry of Gender, Labour and Social Development is in the process of drafting a comprehensive SP policy, upon which social health protection shall be anchored.

- The draft Health Sector Financing Strategy: The health sector is in the process of drafting a Health Sector Financing Strategy that will include broader aspects of SHP and health care reforms.

- The COMESA Treaty[6] to which Uganda is a signatory: Article 16 states: "[e]very individual shall have the right to enjoy the best attainable state of physical and mental health; parties to the present Charter shall take the necessary measures to protect the health of their people and to ensure that they receive medical attention when they are sick". The draft protocol on East Africa Community Regional Cooperation and Health, Chapter IV, article 7 provides for the East Africa Community partner states to commit to attain UHC. The formulation, implementation and management of health-related policies and programmes fall under the docket of the Ministry of Health.

Like Uganda, and being a member of the UN, Thailand is also a signatory to international laws and regulations such as the Universal Declaration of Human Rights, 1948; the International Convention on Economic, Social and Cultural Rights, 1966; and the UN Convention on the Rights of the Child, 1989. All these provide the framework for crafting Uganda's SHP policies and programmes.

The 1973 Thai constitution was the turning point. It emphasised that health services for the poor should be provided free of charge. The 1977 constitution (revised) was even more emphatic on the issue of health, stating that health should be considered as an entitlement of Thai citizens and equal access to basic health services should be guaranteed (ILO 2007). The Social Security Act 1990, which established the Social Security Fund and its administrative body, the Social Security Office, covered the health needs of workers. The UCS is only one public health protection scheme, which provides health care coverage to all citizens who are not covered by any other public health protection scheme. The National Health Security ACT B.E. 2545 (2002) is the legal basis for the UCS. The Ministry of Public Health (MOPH) is responsible for formulating, implementing and managing all health-related policies and programmes. In the same ministry, an autonomous body, the National Health Security Office (NHSO), was created under the National Health Security Board [NHSB] (United Nations Research Institute for Social Development [UNRISD] 2014). According to the law, the board is authorised to prescribe the types and limits of health service for UCS. The NHSB also appoints the NHSO secretary-general, who is in charge of NHSO operations. Under the law, the NHSO is responsible for the registration of beneficiaries and service providers, and administers the fund and pays claims according to the regulations set out by the NHSB (UNRISD 2014).

3.5. Impacts of Universalisation

The NHI scheme in Uganda, which is the equivalent of the Thailand UCS, is still in draft form. Consequently, the health sector terrain is characterised by an inequitable burden of health care spending. For instance, the incidence of catastrophic health care expenditure among the poor steadily increased from 1996 to 2006 despite the abolition of user fees, which was partly due to the greater use of private providers by the poor. Current protection is minimal, with community health insurance (CHI) schemes being accessible to between 5 and 10 per cent of the population in the few areas where such schemes operate (Basaza *et al.* 2007). There is co-payment for both inpatient and outpatient care, which is up to 20 per cent of the health care bill. The scheme targets the rural poor who have some income to pay the premium. Those who cannot afford to pay the premium, such as women, children and the elderly, are excluded. The schemes lack a mechanism for enrolling the indigent, who form 24.5 per cent of the population (Basaza *et al.* 2007). Private commercial health insurance schemes cover only an additional 1 per cent of the population and are mainly limited to the in-house private health maintenance plans of a few large firms in addition to some third-party insurance companies (Basaza *et al.* 2009). It should also be noted that both community-based health insurance and private commercial insurance schemes do not cover immunisation and treatment for HIV or tuberculosis because they are provided free by vertical government programmes. However, it should not be forgotten that government facilities are faced by the following challenges: poor quality care; stock outs of medicine; understaffing; poor infrastructure; and inadequate funding. All these challenges impact negatively on Ugandans. Some of the 2011 health indicators for Uganda bear testimony to this scenario: The under-five mortality rate (per 1,000 live births) was 90; the infant mortality ratio (per 1,000 live births) was 54; the maternal mortality ratio (per 100,000 births) was 352; and the contraceptive prevalence rate was 30 per cent (GoU 2012b). Other health indicators are: 72 per cent of the population have physical access, within 5 kilometres, to any health facility; 40 per cent of child deliveries occur in health facilities; disease prevalence is 43 per cent; malaria accounts for 52 per cent of morbidity; and 70 per cent of mortality is attributed to preventable conditions (GoU 2012b). Table 2 further illustrates some of the alarming health indicators in Uganda compared to other countries.

Table 2. Estimated access deficit in Uganda compared to other developing countries

Country	Estimated access deficit Staff-related (in % of pop.)	Birth-related (in % of live births)
Burukina Faso	85	43
China	34	17
Columbia	40	9
Ghana	66	53
Peru	42	29
Philippines	29	40
Uganda	78	61

SOURCE: ILO (2008).

According to the table, in China, the estimated staff-related access deficit indicates that 34 per cent of the population has no access to health services — and this figure rises to 40 per cent in Columbia. This is comparable to a staff-related access deficit of 42 per cent in Peru. In terms of birth-related deficit, this is 61 per cent in Uganda and 53 per cent in Ghana. On average, Uganda is the worse off, considering the countries and the estimated parameters. It should, therefore, be noted that, in the absence of effective SHP and in the face of soaring OOP health costs, the development of an equitable, sustainable health financing mechanism for the NHI is seen as a key strategy.

In Thailand, where there is UCS, the impacts are far and wide. The implementation of the UCS has had a positive outcome for health care access and health care utilisation. For instance, the utilisation rate rose after implementation, with outpatient visits per person increasing from 2.45 to 3.23, and inpatient admissions per person increasing from 0.094 to 0.114 (UNRISD 2014). A recent study to evaluate the impact of UCS on health care utilisation and access, using a quasi-experimental method, found that UCS reduced the probability of foregoing formal health care when ill by 11 per cent, and increased the opportunity of inpatient admissions by 18 per cent, with the greatest effect of outpatient care access being on the poor and rural populations (Limwattananon *et al.* 2013).

The implementation of the UCS also has an impact on protection against health spending shocks. A number of studies found that the incidence of catastrophic health spending from health payments decreased after the introduction of UCS (Somkotra and Lagrada 2009; Limwattananon *et al.* 2007; Health Insurance System Research Office [HISRO] 2012). The findings show that after UCS in 2002, the proportion of households with catastrophic health spending declined compared with the period before

UCS — from 6 per cent in 1996 to 3 per cent in 2008. The reduction occurred in almost all economic groups, with a higher reduction being registered among the UCS members in the poorest quartile group, from 6.8 per cent to 2.8 per cent, while the members in the richest group also dropped from 6.1 per cent to 3.7 per cent. An analysis by HISRO in 2012 estimated that from 2003 to 2008, more than 100,000 households were prevented from impoverishment, owing to OOP health care spending (HISRO 2012).

The UCS also has an impact on population health. Data from the world development indicators showed a continuously declining trend of neonatal, infant, child and adult mortality after the introduction of UCS (UNRISD 2014). Though it is difficult to solely attribute these changes to the impact of UCS, given its declining trend prior to UCS and the potential effect of many contextual factors, recent evidence from a team of US economists using a quasi-experimental analytical approach showed that the introduction of UCS has created a significant reduction in their infant mortality, after controlling for other factors (Gruber *et al.* 2014).

The other impact, which looks more indirect, is that the introduction of UCS has changed the perception of the public regarding health care as a citizen's right. Before this, health care was mainly an individual or family responsibility, unless they were covered by health insurance provided through their employer (CSMB) or SSS or unless they purchased private insurance. Now, everyone feels that they have a right to quality health care and there is public-felt ownership of the programme, hence people are more likely to express their opinions regarding how health care should be provided. Many civic groups were formed to support UHC, and in particular UCS, and these have been vocal in shaping the health policy directions of UCS (HISRO 2012). Publicly provided health care is no longer a social assistance programme operated and controlled by the government, but it is one component of a publicly financed health care scheme to ensure the right to health care for everyone (UNRISD 2014).

The introduction of the UCS has also witnessed increased emphasis on system accountability. A number of systems and programmes have been implemented to monitor and improve public accountability of NHSO (and UCS) and health care providers. For instance, there are five representatives from civil societies on the NHSB. The NHSB also has an external monitoring system to evaluate its performance every year in relation to a number of key performance indicators. The results are then reported to the NHBS for system improvement (NHSO 2012).

The introduction of the UCS has also led to increased financial autonomy of the public hospitals, thus allowing many health providers to better respond to the demand for health care of their population. The purchaser-provider split and strategic purchasing of health care services were key components of the health sector reform in 2002. The financial system in the public health care sector shifted from inputs-based financing to a more decentralised financial management system based on outcome-based payments. The financial authority previously controlled by the MOPH was transferred to the NHSO. Hospitals that are UCS contracting partners receive funding based on the number of registered members and clinical care episodes provided. They can then use their revenues from UCS for hospital operations and maintenance. Some hospitals, with more funding under the new payment system, are enabled to improve their health care infrastructure to expand health care services. This would not have been easily achieved in the previous top-down budgetary system, where the process required many steps of approval. Most public hospitals with staff shortages, due to a zero-growth policy in the public sector, can hire more staff as hospital employees to ease the workload (UNRISD 2014).

With the introduction of UCS, a new culture and mechanisms to promote the use of evidence for healthy policy decisions emerged. This attests to the emergence of health information and research system development that had never been witnessed before. To carry out strategic purchasing, for instance, UCS requires an extensive information system for beneficiary registration; benefits decision; health care process and output monitoring and evaluation; and health care payments. These, for instance, made it necessary for all Thai citizens to have an identity card (ID) card with a unique ID number, which is also used for their house registration. The HISRO conducts research and development on health financing and health service system development (UNRISD 2014).

3.6 Discussion

The discussions are handled thematically by country, on the basis of the objectives that guided this paper.

Compared to Thailand, Uganda still has a long way to go in its attempt to universalise its SHP. The only health programmes that are active are the free services offered in government facilities, government subsidies to private health providers, community-based health insurance schemes and private commercial health insurance schemes, all of which have limited coverage and have excluded many deserving members of the population. In a country where the absolute poverty level is as high as 24.5 per cent (GoU 2012b), it is particularly risky to surrender the health care of the majority of the population to the private sector or to private individuals (OOP).

Despite the many and good international, regional and national frameworks that are supportive of the development of comprehensive SHP, Uganda is the only East African country without a UHC scheme (East Africa Community 2014; Basaza *et al.* 2013). Besides this, the country neither has a specific health protection policy nor a social health insurance agenda. There is no specific health insurance act. The only current framework hinges on the Insurance (Amendment) Act 2011, which put in place the IRA (East Africa Community 2014). Besides the lapses in the legal framework, Uganda also does not have an autonomous body, akin to

Thailand's NHSO, Health Insurance System Research Office and NHSB (UNRISD 2014). In an economy where the welfare of the people is treated as a right, such institutions are necessary for systems improvement, monitoring and accountability.

All the foregoing point to the fact that there is limited political support to social health insurance and the passing of the NHI Bill would be one of the indicators of government commitment. Such a lack of political commitment in the entire health sector is seen also in the meagre budget allocated to the health sector. Such a meagre budget has been responsible for the poor quality of health infrastructure services in public hospitals. To help improve the quality of the health care delivery system, the government, in 2010, borrowed 26 million dollars[7] from the World Bank and purchased medical equipment, which was delivered to 230 health facilities across the country (Karugaba 2015). However, audit reports in 2014 found that most of this equipment was lying idle and some of it was sub-standard and could not be used (Karugaba 2015). It is, therefore, not surprising that under such circumstances, the catastrophic expenses rose between 2001 and 2010 respectively (Basaza *et al.* 2013; Orem and Zikusooka 2010). In a bizarre case of provision of political support to another country, instead of its medical sector, the Ugandan government recently entered into a private arrangement with the Trinidad and Tobago government, involving the transfer of 283 of its medical personnel to the service of the latter. This is happening at a time when Uganda has a doctor to patient ratio of 1:24,725, against a WHO recommendation of 1:1,000; and a nurse to patient ratio of 1:11,000 against a recommendation of 1:500 (Kateera 2015). In comparison, Trinidad and Tobago has 10 times as many doctors, three times as many nurses, 22 times the per capita health spending, and 32 times the per capita GDP and universal health insurance! Furthermore, Trinidad and Tobago has a population of 1.3 million compared to 37 million Ugandans. Only 42 per cent of expectant Ugandan mothers, compared to 98 per cent of Trinidadians, have access to skilled maternal health services. Ugandan mothers are four times more likely to die during childbirth. Three times as many Ugandan children die before the age of five and life expectancy is 58.65 years (Asedri 2015; Musisi 2015; Kateera 2015). Instead of Uganda drawing some lessons of good practice of universal health care from Trinidad and Tobago, which is really a 'developed country' by Uganda's standards, the politicians decided to do the unthinkable! What can be more bizarre than this? Hopefully, the government will yield to the public outcry and reverse the decision.

The poorly developed SHP has had a deplorable impact on the population, with attendant poor quality health indicators (GoU 2012b). This means that Uganda's SHP is not facilitating pro-poor growth and poverty reduction (Hörmansdörfer 2009). This scenario is captured in the 2013 Human Development Report, which rightly places Uganda in 161st position out of 182, making it one of the poorest nations in the world. In terms of health care services, WHO ranks Uganda 186th out of 191 countries in health care provision (Okeya 2015). Fighting poverty, increasing productivity and investments, and registering sustainable growth and development cannot, in any way, be achieved with such a national health status. However, Uganda should not lose hope. The strong legal and regulatory foundation should be fully exploited. The discovery of oil in the Albertine region that is projected to earn the country $2 billion per year (Omona 2012) when full production begins in 2017, with political commitment, should be able to provide adequate and reliable financial impetus to finance critical sectors of the economy, including the health sector. Besides, the ongoing national ID registration and the 2014 national census should be used to provide data for proper planning of the health sector.

Compared to Uganda, the SHP system in Thailand is commendable. It is an undisputed fact that Thailand has achieved universal coverage, a state desired by many countries. With 47 million (75 per cent of the population) covered under the UCS, and the remaining 25 per cent covered under the other CSMB scheme and SSS (UNRISD 2014), universal coverage is self-evident. Though these multiple approaches look simple, it should be borne in mind that the policy initiatives and reforms regarding health schemes dates back to 1975. It has been a long journey. The Asian crisis of 1997 was a major starting point for a review and reform in general of SP. Many SP schemes were upgraded, strengthened or introduced in line with the International Monetary Fund (IMF), the World Bank and Asian Development Bank conditionality that crisis-affected countries declare, in a letter of intent, a set of policies that give due consideration to the social impacts of the crisis (Paitoonpong *et al.* 2010).

Perhaps the greatest asset in the development of the SHP system has been political commitment. This has been attested over the years by the favourable health sector financing. It is widely acknowledged that the health financing reform accompanying the establishment of UCS also created significant impacts on the health care financing functions and health system arrangements (UNRISD 2014). The government allocates 4.5 per cent of GDP, representing 14.5 per cent of its budget on health (ILO 2014). This has been reflected in annual increments of the UCS budget per capita, since 2002 (NHSO 2012). Political commitment has also been reflected in the creation of a sustainable and robust legal and institutional framework for the operation of SHP schemes. The creation of the UCS in 2001 was the turning point. In 2002, the newly elected Thai government passed the National Health Security Act, one of the nine priorities for reform highlighted during the campaign and a response that was long demanded by civil society (ILO 2014). With such political commitment, within just a few years, Thailand succeeded in extending SHP to all, even while experiencing economic recession. It was also able to embed the reform process in law, thereby developing what is now a comprehensive SHP system, articulating schemes for all employment statuses. Besides, the country was able to finance the UCS or '30 baht scheme' through the reallocation of spending (mainly defence, transport and communication, and social services) and fiscal space extension [increased value added tax [VAT] and taxes on luxury goods, alcohol and tobacco products] (ILO 2014). Most governments, especially the dictatorial ones in developing countries, find it particularly hard to reallocate funds from defence to finance a soft sector such as health.

As part of its political commitment, Thailand has developed a robust institutional framework for achieving SHP. It has a fully funded MOPH, which has become one of the main contractors of the NHSO. The NHSO channels the funds to the contracted providers, using several active purchasing mechanisms, with capitation and DRGs as the main payment methods. In addition, the NHSO also supports and collaborates with the HISRO, an independent, non-profit research agency created after UCS to conduct research on health financing and health services system development. Besides, there is the National Health Security Board (NHSB) which, among others, is in charge of revising the benefits package and making recommendations on the adoption of new drugs and technologies. With such institutions in place, the health care system in Thailand is more sustainable than Uganda's, with comprehensive health care outcomes. China, Ghana, Rwanda, and Vietnam are all good examples of how political will greatly expanded SP programmes (UNICEF 2012).

However, despite the above achievements, health care in Thailand still has some lingering questions that need attention. Equity, quality and efficiency are still a challenge to the system (ILO 2007; Schmitt 2014). It has been observed that Thailand still retains a fragmented health insurance system and single-fund management is not politically feasible at the moment. Fragmented SHP schemes are very likely to be inequitable and not likely to work in the interests of the poor. This is borne out by the different government subsidies for different schemes. There is, for instance, inequity in access to antiretroviral therapy (ART) under the CSBMS and universal coverage (Schmitt 2014), and the packages for informal workers are unattractive. Quality of care provision at the health centres and district hospitals in rural areas is still different from that in urban areas, where there is greater use of higher-level hospitals. Primary health care and an appropriate referral system are a key strategy for overall systems efficacy and better quality. Unfortunately, implementation has been much more difficult. There was no real primary health care system in Thailand before the universal coverage era. Thai people were familiar with the freedom of choice in visits to any health facilities and could directly contact specialists. Creating a new look of primary health care centres, establishment of some public primary health care centres staffed with full-time physicians and increasing competency of health personnel at primary health care centres have been ongoing. This effort has, however, only been successful in terms of an increase in the proportion of people visiting the health centres (ILO 2007).

The assessment of the entire health care system has also revealed a number of gaps (Schmitt 2014). A considerable number of migrant workers, who represent 5 per cent of the labour force, are not covered under any scheme. In some cases, employers collect the contributions for SSS, but do not register such workers. The issue of stigma/confidentiality for those suffering from HIV/AIDS is crucial. There is also no portability between schemes. Even though the benefits package is rather comprehensive, UCS benefits are restricted to using health care services only from a specific health care provider network (UNRISD 2014). Some categories of workers, such as domestic workers, are also excluded. The UCS package also contains a negative list that identifies health conditions or clinical interventions that are excluded (Jongudomsuk *et al.* 2012). Such a list of excluded services can have serious consequences for the poor. It is also noted that the majority of Thai people cannot afford to pay a contribution/premium to obtain enough income security and, besides, the current fiscal space of government is insufficient to cover every citizen (Sakunphanit 2014).

4. Conclusion and Recommendations

4.1 Conclusion

This paper examined the SP and UHC for Uganda and Thailand within the theoretical framework stated by Sen (2009), and Fine and Leopold (1993). The two countries were selected because of the levels of their SP and universal coverage status — Thailand has reached universal coverage while Uganda has not. It can be concluded that the paper achieved its objectives. It established that both countries are using multiple models, such as Bismarck, Beveridge, NHI, and OOP, in different combinations in order to deliver social health care protection to their citizens. The public and private sectors are used in varying proportion in the provision of health care services. It can also be concluded that in trying to achieve the social security objectives, the programmes for both countries are excluding some portions of their populations. The portions of the populations being excluded are usually the most vulnerable — the poor, women, children or predominantly foreigners, in the case of Thailand. This social exclusion is more pronounced in Uganda, where the NHI policy is in draft form. Thai's introduction of UCS in 2001 was the turning point in its health care provision.

The findings reveal that the level of SHP in both countries is dependent on political commitment, which is more visible in Thailand. This is attested by the favourable budgets that have been passed progressively, since 2002, to finance activities in the health sector. The progressive but favourable budgets have been made possible through the reallocation of funds from otherwise sensitive ministries such as that of defence. Besides this, there has been unwavering political support in Thailand for creating viable institutions to support the delivery of SHP services. Such institutions include the MOPH, the NHSO and the NHSB, which are all operationalised by supportive laws. All these developments have made Thailand's SHP more inclusive and sustainable, compared to Uganda's.

The impacts of such commitment are both evident on the Thai people and the health care system itself. The access and utilisation rate of health care services has increased more than ever before with the introduction of the UCS. The positive impacts on the population's health are seen in the declining trends in mortalities. There has also been a marked decline in catastrophic health spending in all economic groups, thanks to the comprehensive health care system. Together with this, it has been found that people's perceptions of health care provision has changed — people now view health care as a right, unlike before the introduction of UCS when health care was predominantly considered to be the responsibility of individuals and families. The creation of robust institutions in the Thai health sector has also ushered in the era of system accountability and increased the financial autonomy of public hospitals, thus allowing health facilities to better respond to the health demands of the population. This, together with the emergence of health information and research systems development, has enhanced health policy decision-making based on evidence. The lesson that can be learnt from Thailand is that the SHP can be built on political commitment, good governance and stewardship.

Despite the impressive achievements, the Thai health system still has some lingering issues. The issues of equity, quality and efficacy are visible. Thailand still runs a fragmented SHP system that is largely inequitable. The quality of health care delivery at the health centres in the rural and urban areas is not at par. Though Thailand boasts universal coverage, there are pockets of people excluded from the systems, in the categories of migrant workers and domestic servants. As an aspect of segregation, too, the UCS package contains a list of health conditions and clinical interventions that are excluded from coverage. These exclusive cases mainly affect the poor and the underprivileged. The scheme is also accused of rigidity — lack of portability between schemes, by restricting beneficiaries to receiving treatment/attention only under the scheme for which they have registered.

In Uganda, the provision of health services is dominated by the government and administered by the Ministry of Health. Despite the supportive legal and institutional frameworks at international, regional and national levels, there is still no health insurance policy, hence no NHI akin to the UCS of Thailand. The NHI is still in draft form but, even then, it is planned only to begin with a small proportion of the national population (the formerly employed and their dependants) and will consist of contributions from both the employer and employee, but without co-payment. Other current SHP programmes are community-based health care, private commercial insurance schemes and informal sector schemes, which all provide inadequate coverage. Thus, a big proportion of the population is not covered by the current SHP system.

Uganda is known in the entire East Africa region to have made the least effort to create a nationally owned SHP system. In fact, it is renowned for having the worst SHP safety net in the region. Even the little that is being provided is reputed to be of poor quality and is plagued by under-the-table payments. The informal sector, reputed for poor quality and being unreliable, still constitutes a formidable source of health care in Uganda. Many of the woes of the health sector are blamed on lack of political commitment. The lack of commitment is reflected by the limited budget accorded to the health sector, which is a sharp contrast to the scenario in Thailand. A greater proportion of the funding of the SHP comes from private spending, which favours the rich more than the poor. It is no wonder, then, that the incidence of catastrophic spending has been high over the years. This situation has not been made any better by the low investment in overall system improvement, compared to what happens in Thailand.

Consequently, the impacts of weak political commitment on the health sector are evident — an unsustainable health sector and unsustainable national development. Health indicators, such as mortality and morbidity rates, are among the highest in Africa, together with weak systems development. It is no surprise, therefore, that WHO places Uganda among the worst-performing nations in health care provision. Consequently, the SHP falls short of facilitating pro-poor growth and poverty reduction. Uganda's human development index, which places it among the poorest countries in the world, should only be expected, therefore. Nonetheless, all cannot be lost. With the revenue expected to be earned from oil and the current efforts to issue a national ID to every citizen, the health sector can be revamped, if there is sufficient political commitment.

This paper is limited by the fact that it relied only on desk reviews, thus missing the human aspects that would have emerged if other methods such as focus group discussions, questionnaires and key informant interviews were included. However, the paper makes significant policy and theoretical contributions to the ongoing SHP debate. In terms of policy development, the paper highlights key reforms that Uganda needs to learn from Thailand and undertake, in order to improve its SHP system and delivery. Indeed, other developing countries that have not attained universal coverage can equally learn from the experience of Thailand. The paper also observes that although universal coverage has been attained in Thailand, there are still lingering issues that need to be tackled if a comprehensive, inclusive and sustainable package is to be delivered to its citizens. In addition, the paper demystifies the fallacy that lesson-drawing of good practice is only possible in a North-to-South relationship, by proving that a South-to-South alignment is a possibility in this globalising world. Theoretically, the paper confirms that the theoretical frameworks for SHP, as espoused by Sen [2009] (comprehensive outcomes) and Fine and Leopold [1993] (PSSOP), and widely but variously applied by WHO, UNICEF and ILO, are indeed realistic and universal frameworks for analysing this sector, specifically when applied within the contexts of the four health care models — Bismarck, Beveridge, NHI, and OOP.

4.2 Recommendations

4.2.1 Uganda

- Uganda should note that UHC is achievable, but it is a process. Like Thailand, it should put policies in place to remove financial, social and other barriers to individuals' access to the health care services that they are entitled to receive.

- Uganda should build on the strengths of the existent favourable legal and institutional framework, and continually aim at improving the health sector by meticulously learning from the successes and challenges of Thailand.

- Uganda needs to urgently implement its NHI scheme. This is crucial in covering the proportion of the population that is not covered under the existing health care services. The scheme could be revisited to cover all other citizens not currently covered under any programme, instead of planning to start with 10 per cent of the working population.

- Besides implementing the proposed NHI scheme, Uganda needs to create autonomous institutions similar to the NHSO and the NHBS in Thailand, to foster systems development, accountability and effectiveness in the health sector. One aspect of systems development could take the form of the compilation of reliable health data, and the starting point could be the current national ID registration process that has just been concluded.

- Uganda should learn from Thailand that indeed, sustainable SHP is built on political commitment, good governance and stewardship. Irrational decisions such as the plan to send health care workers to Trinidad and Tobago should be shelved.

- Uganda should learn that owing to the crucial importance of SHP for sustainable poverty reduction, this programme should be supported at all costs, including soliciting donor support for the sector. Health care programmes should be prioritised when the time is ripe for allocating the expected revenue from oil.

4.2.2. Thailand

Thailand needs to acknowledge the lingering issues affecting the health sector and address them head-on. In particular, it should:

- Through appropriate programmes, eliminate barriers to access and utilisation for the underprivileged such as the immigrants and domestic workers.

- Fight social exclusion by incorporating some of the diseases that are currently on the negative list for support under the UCS.

- Fight poverty through appropriate strategies to put money in the hands of the Thai people, hence enable them to effectively pay for their health care services;
- Ensure that programmes are portable to clients.

Notes

[1] All '$' refers to US dollars.

[2] World Fact Book is a Central Intelligence Agency (CIA) managed data source that is reliable and globally recognised. It collects data on all countries on all parameters —economic, sociocultural and political. Retrieved April 2, 2015 from https://www.cia.gov/library/publications/the-world-factbook/geos/th.html

[3] This was a scheme introduced in 2001, in Thailand, with the aim of achieving full population coverage in health care. The scheme is also known as the '30 baht' scheme — baht is the Thai currency. The 30 baht is, therefore, the co-payment that beneficiaries must make at the point of service (ILO 2008). By 2014, the '30 baht' was equivalent to $ 0.38 (UNRISD 2014).

[4] To access health services under the UCS, every Thai is issued with an ID. The NHSO worked with the Bureau of Registration and Administration, and the Department of Provincial Administration, to improve the Ministry of Interior's vital registration system and birth registry to better capture the Thai population. All Thai citizens are required to have an ID and a unique ID number, which is also used for their house registration. The national ID number is used for health insurance or a social protection purpose. The UCS has also adopted the national ID card as its membership card, so all individual-level information is linked to the unique ID numbers (UNRISD 2014).

[5] Diagnosis-related group. The adjusted DRG for outpatients is <2 and for inpatients it is ≥2 (ILO 2014).

[6] COMESA refers to the Common Market for Eastern and Southern Africa. It is a 21-member country group, spanning from Libya to Swaziland, formed in December 1994 to facilitate trade among member states. It is also considering a common visa scheme to boost tourism amongst member countries. Retrieved on   April   13,   2015, fromhttp://www.comesa.int/attachments/article/28/COMESA_Treaty.pdf

[7] Equivalent to 60 billion Uganda shillings at shillings 2,300 per dollar in 2010. Retrieved on December 31, 2010, from

http://www.bou.or.ug/bou/collateral/interbank-forms/2010/Dec10.html   on 21/04/2015.

References

Asedri, V. 2015. Export of health workers to Trinidad and Tobago is unpatriotic. *Daily Monitor*, April 3, p. 11. Kampala, Uganda.

Basaza, R. K., O'Connell, T. S. and Chapčáková, I. 2013. Players and processes behind the national health insurance scheme: A case study of Uganda. *BMC Health Services Research*, 13: 357.

Basaza, R. K., Pariyo, G. and Criel, B. 2009. What are the emerging features of community health insurance schemes in East Africa? *Risk Management and Health Policy*, 2: 47–53.

Bloom, D. E., Canning, D. and Sevilla, J. 2004. *The effects of health on economic growth: A production function approach.* Washington, D.C.: World Bank.

Carrin, G., Zeramdini, R., Musgrove, P. Poullier, J. and Valentine, N. 2001. The impact of the degree of risk-sharing in health financing on health system attainment. *In*: *Health financing for poor people,* edited by A. S. Preker and G. Carrin, 397-416. Washington D.C.: World Bank.

Devereux, S. and Sabates-Wheeler, R. 2004. Transformative social protection. *IDS Working Paper*. Sussex, United Kingdom.

East African Community. 2014. Situational analysis and feasibility for harmonisation of social health protection systems towards health coverage in East African Community partner states. Arusha, Tanzania.

Fine, B. and Leopold, E. 1993. *The world of consumption*. London: Routledge.

Government of Kenya (GoK). 2010. *Strategic review of national hospital insurance fund.* Nairobi, Kenya.

———. 2012. *Kenya social protection review.* Nairobi, Kenya.

Government of Uganda (GoU). 1995. The Constitution of the Republic of Uganda; Statutory Instrument 354/1995; (Amendment) Act 13/2000, Act 11/2005, Act 21/2005; Section xx. Entebbe: Government Printers.

———. 2012a. *2012 Statistical abstract.* Uganda Bureau of Statistics. Kampala, Uganda.

———. 2012b. *Uganda poverty status report 2012.* Kampala, Uganda.

———. 2013. *The national social protection policy framework for Uganda. Second draft.* Ministry of Gender, Labour and Social Development. Kampala, Uganda.

———. 2014. *National population and housing census. Provisional results.* Ministry of Finance and Planning. Kampala, Uganda.

Gruber, J., Hendren, N. and Townsend, R. M. 2014. The great equalizer: Health care access and infant mortality in Thailand. *American Economic Journal: Applied Economics*, 6 no. 1: 91–107.

Gupta, I. 2007. Health coverage for all: Strategies and choices for India. *In: Extending social health protection: Developing countries experiences,* edited by J. Holst and A. Brandrup-Lukanow, 111–120. Eschborn, Germany: GTZ.

Gyimah-Brempong, K. and Wilson, M. 2004. Health human capital and economic growth in Sub-Saharan Africa and OECD countries. *The Quarterly Review of Economics and Finance*, 44 no. 2: 296–320.

Health Insurance System Research Office (HISRO). 2012. *Thailand's universal coverage scheme: Achievements and challenges.* HISRO. Nonthaburi, Thailand.

Hörmansdörfer, C. 2009. Health and social protection. *In: Promoting pro-poor growth: Social protection*, 145–153. Washington, D.C.: Organisation for Economic Cooperation and Development (OECD).

International Labour Organisation (ILO). 2006. Social protection: Building social protection floors and comprehensive social security system. Retrieved April 1, 2015, from http://www.social-protection.org/gimi//guess/Uganda

———. 2007. *Thailand: Universal health care coverage through pluralistic approaches.* ILO sub-regional office for East Asia.

———. 2008. *Social health protection: An ILO strategy towards universal access to health care.* Geneva: ILO.

———. 2014. *Social protection in action: Innovative experiences. Thailand's universal health coverage.* ILO Special Report, March.

Jongudomsuk, P., Limwattananon, S., Prakongsai, P., Srithamrongsawat, S., Pachanee, K., Mohara, A., Patcharanarumol, W. and Tangcharoensathien, V. 2012. Evidence-based health financing reform in Thailand. *In The economics of public health care reform in advanced and emerging economies,* edited by D. Coady, B. Clements and S. Gupta, 307–326. Washington, D.C.: International Monetary Fund.

Karugaba, M. 2015. Equipment worth Sh60 billion lying idle in hospitals – Auditor-General's Report. *Sunday Vision*, April 11, p. 6. Kampala, Uganda.

Kateera, J. M. 2015. Medical staff export: A crime against humanity. *Sunday Monitor,* April 12, p. 15. Kampala, Uganda.

Limwattananon, S., Tangcharoensathien, V. and Prakongsaib, P. 2007. Catastrophic and poverty impacts of health payments: Results from national household surveys in Thailand. *Bulletin of the World Health Organisation*, 85 no. 8: 600–606.

Limwattananon, S., Neelsen, S., O'Donnell, O. A., Prakongsai, P., Tangcharoensathien, V., van Doorslaer, E. and Vongmongkol, V. 2013. Universal coverage on a budget: Impacts on health care utilisation and out-of-pocket expenditures in Thailand. *CESifo Working Paper No. 4262*, May. Munich, Germany.

Masiko, A.1998. Community-based health financing: The Kisiizi experience: Can it be sustained? A dissertation submitted for the award of Masters of Arts degree, Leeds University, United Kingdom.

McIntyre, D., Garshong, B., Mtei, G., Meheus, F., Thiede, M., Akazili, J., Ally, M., Aikins, M., Mulligan, J. A. and Goudge, J. 2008. Beyond fragmentation and towards universal coverage: Insights from Ghana, South Africa and the United Republic of Tanzania. *Bulletin of World Health Organisation,* 86 no. 11: 871–876.

Mdee, I. 2009. Challenges and opportunities of community-based health funds (CBHF) in the emerging social health insurance policy environment in East Africa. National Health Insurance Fund Act No. 8 of 1999, Tanzania.

Mtei, G., and Mulligan, J. A. 2007. Community health fund in Tanzania: A literature review. Ifakara Health Institute. Dar es Salaam, Tanzania.

Musisi, F. 2015. Who will save Uganda's limping health system? *Saturday Monitor*, April 4, p. 21. Kampala, Uganda.

Mwesigye, F. and Pearson, M. 1997. Kisiizi hospital health society: Pioneering rural social health insurance. *Uganda Ministry of Health Journal*, 1 no. 4: 60–64.

National Health Security Office (NHSO). 2012. *National Health Security Office annual report.* Bangkok, Thailand: NHSO.

Okeya, M. 2015. Norway envoy decries poor health services. *Daily Monitor*, March 31, p. 16. Kampala, Uganda.

Omona, J. 2012. Funding higher education in Uganda: Modalities, challenges and opportunities in the twenty-first century. *Makerere Journal of Higher Education*, 4 no. 1: 11–44.

Orem, J. and Zikusooka, C. 2010. Health financing reform in Uganda: How equitable is the proposed national health insurance scheme? *International Journal of Equity in Health*, 9: 23.

Paitoonpong, S., Chawla, A. and Akkarakul, N. 2010. Social protection in Thailand: Current state and challenges. In *Social protection in East Asia: Current state and challenges,* edited by M. G. Asher, S. Oum and F. Parulian, 265–291. ERIA Research Project Report 2009-9. Jakarta, Indonesia: ERIA.

Popay, J., Escorel, S., Hernández, M., Johnston, H., Mathieson, J. and Rispel, L. 2008. Understanding and tackling social exclusion. Final report to the WHO Commission on the Social Determinants of Health from the Social Exclusion Knowledge Network. Social Exclusion Knowledge Network.

Rabovskaja, V. 2012. Universal health coverage: Reflections from a development perspective. *Deutsche Gesellschaft für Internationale Zusammenarbeit,* October. Issue No. 14.

Sachs, J. D. 2002. Macroeconomics and health: Investing in health for economic development. Report of the Commission on Macroeconomics and Health. Geneva: WHO.

Sakunphanit, T. 2014. Social protection assessment: Thailand context. International Conference on Strengthening Social Protection for ASEAN community, July 8-9, Centara Grand at Central Plaza Ladprao, Bangkok, Thailand.

Scheil-Adlung, X., Asfaw, A., Booysen, F., Lamiraud, K., Reynaud, E., Juetting, J., Xu, K., Chatterji, S., Evans, D., James, C. and Muchiri, S. 2007. Impact of social health protection on access to health care, health expenditure and impoverishment. A comparative analysis of three African countries. In *Health financing in the developing world: Supporting countries' search for viable systems,* edited by G. Carrin, 151–175. Brussels, Belgium: University Press Antwerp.

Schmitt, V. 2014. Social security and social protection in Thailand: Results of the assessment based national dialogue. Paper presented at a national dialogue, March 13, Bangkok, Thailand.

Sen, A. 2009. *The idea of justice.* Cambridge: Harvard University Press.

Somkotra, T. and Lagrada, L. P. 2009. Which households are at risk of catastrophic health spending: Experience in Thailand after universal coverage. *Health Affairs,* 28 no. 3: 467–478.

United Nations Development Programme (UNDP). 2013. *Human development report 2013.* NY: UNDP.

―――. 2010. *Millennium development goals report for Uganda 2010.* NY: UNDP.

United Nations Children's Fund (UNICEF). 2012. National health insurance in Asia and Africa: Advancing equitable social health protection to achieve universal health coverage. A report funded by Rockefeller Foundation.

United Nations Research Institute for Social Development (UNRISD). 2014. *The impacts of universalisation: A case study on Thailand's social protection and universal health coverage.* Geneva, Switzerland.

Wagstaff, A. and Pradhan, M. 2005. Health insurance impacts on health and non-medical consumption in a developing country. *Working Paper Series* 3565. Washington, D.C.: World Bank.

Wang, H. and Pielemeier, N. 2012. Community-based health insurance: An evolutionary approach to achieving universal coverage in low income countries. *Journal of Life Sciences,* 6 no. 3: 320–329.

World Commission on Environment and Development (WCED). 1987. *Our common future.* London: Macmillan.

World Health Organisation (WHO). 2008. *The world health report 2008 - primary health care (now more than ever).* Geneva: WHO.

―――. 2002. Global public goods for health: Report of Working Group 2 of the Commission on Macroeconomics and Health. Geneva: WHO.

Williams, G., Mladovsky, P., Dkhimi, F., Soors, W. and Parmar, D. 2014. Social exclusion and social health protection in low and middle income countries: An introduction. *In: Studies in health services organisation and policy,* edited by B. Criel, V. De Brouwere, W.V. Damme and B. Marchal, 32: 1–13.

CHAPTER SEVEN

Productivity and Informality in Rwanda: Evidence from the Food Processing Sector

Johnson B. Rukundo

Abstract

The objective of this paper is to understand productivity in the informal food processing sector in Rwanda. It highlights the determinants of the informal sector, with a special focus on Rwanda. Data was collected from all five provinces in Rwanda, with a sample of 200 informal food processing enterprises. Results from a Probit Model indicates that gender, initiative to formalisation, experience, age of a firm, cost prices, and sale prices, explain productivity in the informal sector. Results show that if gender, tax on income, government's initiatives for formalisation, and cost prices change from zero to one, the probability for outcome informality taking value one decreases respectively by 32.8 per cent, 57.3 per cent, 47.3 per cent, and 41 per cent, other variables held constant. The informal sector is a last resort for the poor to make a living in a developing country like Rwanda; any discouragement of the production of these firms is likely to generate high unemployment, poverty and income inequality.

Keywords: Productivity, informal sector, food processing, Probit Model, informal firms.

1. Introduction

This chapter examines the factors influencing informal employment in Rwanda, and in particular, the impact of informal employment on productivity. The non-farm informal sector plays an important role in most African economies, accounting for a large share of gross domestic product (GDP) as well as employment. In developing countries, key sectors are totally or partially informal, notably commerce, agriculture, transportation, handicrafts, and much of manufacturing (Taymaz 2009). Although the informal sector is regarded by many researchers and policymakers as an income-generating arena that developing countries need, there is also evidence that shows that informal firms are less productive, employ unskilled labour, do not pay taxes on income, and pay lower wages. The continuing growth of the informal sector increases a burden on formally established firms. There is also a belief that firms are resorting to employing a greater number of informal employees when difficult external factors, such as low levels of economic activity, fluctuations in demand, low productivity, and restrictive labour legislation confront them (Benjamin and Mbaye 2012). Despite the extensive literature on the drivers that contribute to the persistence of firms in the informal sector, the importance of individual drivers to the growth of the informal sector continues to be a debated issue. Firms operating informally are less regulated and pay no taxes than firms that operate formally. Distortions arise in the presence of a large informal sector that constrains the structure of the labour market and inhibits the quality of employment.

In Rwanda, despite government efforts to formalise the informal sector, evidence indicates that its importance in the economy has changed greatly. There has been growth in the formal sector, and the percentage level of the formal private sector that contributes to GDP increased from 21 per cent to 24 per cent (NISR 2013). Abbott and Rwirahira (2011) state that the government of Rwanda's Vision 2020 explicitly promotes private sector development and recognises the informal sector as a key part of the economy. This is closely linked to the fact that informality has important implications for productivity, economic growth and inequality of income. A drive from the informal sector to a formal sector allows firms to effectively plan for their future investments and expand their business activities. In addition, formalisation would increase domestic revenues. In Rwanda, the informal sector refers to establishments that are not registered with the revenue authority body to pay local or national taxes and do not maintain regular operational accounts (NISR 2014). The informal sector in Rwanda continues to expand due to stagnant job creation in the formal sector, high levels of unemployment and a potentially economically active labour force, which is increasingly looking for informal employment.

This study also contributes to the literature on the relationship between informality and productivity. A large body of literature shows that there is a strong negative correlation between informality and productivity of firms in developing countries. This chapter begins with a review of the literature on productivity in the informal sector, regulation and governance of informal firms, and the contributions of employees in the informal sector, specifically in food processing. Section 3 describes the data and methodology used in the study, while Section 4 presents estimates of the extent of productivity in informal food processing firms in Rwanda. The final section presents the conclusion and some policy implications.

2. Literature Review

2.1. Informality

Informal economic activities include any market-based legal production of goods and services, deliberately hidden from authorities to avoid taxation or costly regulation, and also working or hiring labour without an employment contract. There is a large body of literature on the determinants of informality (Kucera and Xenogiani 2009; Perry *et al.* 2007; Schneider and Enste 2000) as well as a growing body of literature on how various notions of governance and social norms shape economic development and other aspects of society. Most such studies, however, focus on economic growth as an outcome of interest (Glaeser *et al.* 2004; Hall and Jones 1999). Empirical cross-country evidence by Johnson *et al.* (1998) and Friedman *et al.* (2000) suggests that the unofficial economy tends to be larger, not where taxes are higher, but in countries where the regulatory burden is higher, corruption is more widespread and where the rule of law is weaker. Loayza *et al.* (2006), for a sample of about 70 countries, found that the level of business regulation is on its own correlated positively with informality, but when the quality of governance interacts with the level of regulation, regulation is negatively related with informality. While the use of various indicators of quality of governance has been questioned (Langbein and Knack 2010), it is probably fair to conclude from the above studies that it is not only the design of formal rules and regulations that determines the size of the informal sector, but also the manner in which they are implemented and obeyed.

Loayza *et al.* (2010) analysed a broader set of determinants of informality for a sample of about 85 countries and found that informality is negatively related with law and order, business regulatory freedom, and with schooling achievement. Restricting the focus to Latin America, "policy and institutional variables related to the quality of the state are the most important factors explaining the differences in informality" (Loayza *et al.* 2010, 179). Torgler and Schneider (2007) add tax morale to the set of explanatory factors for cross-country variation in informality. Various indicators of good governance relate negatively to the size of the shadow economy, but also the willingness of citizens to pay taxes is related negatively with the size of the shadow economy. While the use of various indicators of quality of governance has been questioned (Langbein and Knack 2010), it is probably fair to conclude from the above studies that it is not only the design of formal rules and regulations that determines the size of the informal sector, but also the manner in which they are implemented and obeyed. Diego and Kimie (2012) identify three main lenses through which informality can be studied: Firms, workers and untaxed activities. They also define important determinants of informality, namely age, gender, and education; and their work does not ignore other determinants such as marital status, strata and occupation.

2.2. Informal Employment

This study uses the term 'informal employment' to refer to those employees (wage workers, self-employed and entrepreneurs) who are not registered in any social security organisation. The 'informal firm' is defined as a firm that employs informal employees, while the 'informal sector' is defined as a set of informal firms. The informal sector is highly heterogeneous. Fields' (1990) work characterises informal employment as 'easy-entry' and 'upper-tier'. Clusters formulated by Fields are compatible with those advanced by Martin *et al.* (2009) work that distinguishes between low productive informal firms and highly productive informal firms. This work exhibits dramatic heterogeneity within sectors, and even within sub-sectors in terms of productivity.

The concept of informal employment is considered to be relevant not only for developing countries but also for developed countries, many of which the concept of informal sector is of limited relevance. Informal employment is understood to include all remunerative work, both self-employment and wage employment that is not recognised, regulated, or protected by existing legal or regulatory frameworks as well as non-remunerative work undertaken in an income-producing enterprise. In recent decades, developing countries have experienced a steady and substantial increase in the proportion of workers that have been characterised by the informal employment status. It is evident that informal employment in almost all countries is over 50 per cent. Some economists estimate informal employment on the basis of the differences between household labour survey statistics and employment figures provided by enterprises. In other words, informal employment refers to the part of employment that is not recorded because enterprises do not report it to evade insurance and tax or for other reasons (Cai and Wang 2004).

2.3. Informality and Productivity

Substantial literature shows that there is a strong negative correlation between informality and productivity of firms in developing countries. Steel and Snodgrass (2008) attribute the productivity differential to unequal access to public services. However, one of the most cited stylised fact associated with informality is the productivity differential between informal and formal firms. Gelb *et al.* (2009) compare the productivity of informal firms and formal firms, using surveys on the investment climate for a number of countries of Southern Africa and Eastern Africa. Their results confirm that formal sector firms are, on average, more productive than informal firms. A recent comprehensive study on informality shows that the difference in labour productivity between firms that operate informally and formally is about 30, on average, for several Latin American and Caribbean countries (Perry *et al.* 2007, 173).

One of the main factors that may lead to a productivity gap between formal and informal firms is the lack of access to markets and services by informal firms (Djankov *et al.* 2003). Informal firms may not benefit from key public goods, enforcement of property rights and contracts. This could increase their transaction costs due to inefficient contractual relations — a part of informal firms' resources will be wasted due to inefficient institutional mechanisms under which informal firms are forced to operate. The lack of access to credit provided by state or private-owned banks may have a detrimental impact on productivity because of two reasons. Firstly, capital constrained informal firms will scale down their capacity and operate below the efficient scale of production. Secondly, high cost of capital or limited outside financing will force informal firms to substitute low skill labour for physical capital (Amaral and Quintin 2006). Thus, informal firms are likely to have lower capital intensity and lower labour productivity than formal firms.

A usual suspect of productivity differentials is the existence of economies of scale. The negative correlation between the extent of informality and firm size is one of the robust stylised facts on informality: informal firms are usually small. If economies of scale are relevant, at least among very small firms, and if informality is widespread among small firms, then a productivity gap will arise between average informal and formal firms (Perry *et al.* 2007). Although the 'economies of scale' argument is frequently adopted by policymakers, there is no robust empirical evidence on the degree of economies of scale. Moreover, even if the production function exhibits economies of scale, any productivity difference between informal and informal firms will disappear once it is conditioned to size. In addition to economies of scale, productivity differentials could arise not because of intrinsic characteristics of informal and formal firms, but because of self-selection of more productive (more educated) workers and entrepreneurs into the formal sector.

2.4. The Non-Farm Informal Sector in Rwanda

The non-farm informal sector is a major employing sector in Rwanda and contributes to a significant proportion of economic activity. The informal sector accounts for 64 per cent of the output in industry in Rwanda. However, being informally employed does not automatically mean being poor, having low productivity or being excluded from services and social security. In Rwanda, as in many parts of the world, the informal economy also includes small-scale entrepreneurs who are not poor and have a large capacity for innovation as well as a large potential to grow. An estimated 1.25 million Rwandans were employed in the informal sector in 2010/2011, an increase of 6 percentage points over 2005/2005 (NISR 2013). While employment rose in both the informal and formal sectors, the increase was much larger in the informal sector. Although the prevalence of formal enterprises in the country is as low as nearly 7 per cent, it absorbs a high proportion of working people (NISR 2014). Many firms and individuals in Rwanda are engaged in informal employment and it is less likely that they would transform from informal to formal employment (Abbott 2010).

The employment size is about 42.6 per cent in the formal sector, whereas the rest hold jobs in the informal sector. The results reveal that while the vast majority of working people in informal enterprises are concentrated in only two economic activities (46.7 per cent in wholesale and retail trade, and 31.7 per cent in accommodation and food service activities), the distribution of formal enterprises' employment over economic activity does not suffer from similar acute inclination. Rather, employment is distributed over a wider range of economic activities. During the three-year period, the formal sector achieved a higher growth rate (43.7 per cent) compared to the informal sector [24.8 per cent] (NISR 2014).

According to the enterprise survey of 2014, informal sector enterprises have achieved remarkable growth. In addition to mining and quarrying, for which the highest increase rate was found, other sectors such as service activities (51.7 per cent), construction (35.3 per cent), and accommodation and food services (34.2 per cent) have also registered growth. The growth level of the remaining growing economic activities fluctuates between 16.1 per cent for manufacturing and 22.4 per cent for administrative and support services activities. Among the economic activities of the informal sector that have experienced a drastic decline between 2011 and 2014, the following are notable: electricity, gas, steam, and air conditioning supply (100 per cent); finance and insurance activities (100 per cent); real estate activities (90 per cent); and water supply, sewage, waste management, and remediation activities (89.7 per cent).

The decrease rate of the remaining declining economic activities in the informal sector ranges from 2.9 per cent for human health and social work activities, to 23 per cent for information and communication activities. Based on the literature, this chapter provides answers to the following questions: What factors influence productivity in the informal food processing sector? In particular, how much impact does low productivity have on informal firms and employment?

3. Data and Variable Description

The study used descriptive survey design. A sample of 200 informal firms actively engaged in the informal food processing sector were selected, using a multi-stage sampling technique. Data was collected across all provinces of Rwanda (East, North, West, and South) and Kigali City. In each province, two districts were randomly selected as well as two sectors, to obtain the required sample. A list of food processing enterprises was obtained at each district, and out of the total firms a sample of 40 informal firms was selected at district level in two sectors. A questionnaire was developed to capture information from the food processing firms and trained field research assistants were engaged to assist in the exercise. In order to access the food processing firms, research authorisation was acquired from the Directorate of Research, University of Rwanda. Field assistants underwent a two-day training so as to comprehensively understand the content of the questionnaire. A questionnaire developed in English was not translated and enumerators used the local language to explain the questions to interviewees. Data collected from all the 200 respondents in food processing enterprises was entered into a statistical package for social sciences (SPSS) programme. Subsequently, the data was edited and used to analyse the productivity and informality of food processing firms in Rwanda. The main reason for focusing this study on food processing was due to the fact that it is the second informal economic activity in Rwanda.

In order to analyse employment and productivity in Rwanda, and to understand the dynamics, constraints and potential of the informal sector, the study employed an exploratory data and Probit Model analysis. Exploratory data analysis is a an important tool for checking assumptions, conducting preliminary selection of appropriate models, determining relationships among the explanatory variables, and assessing the direction and rough size of relationship between explanatory and outcome variables. Probit analysis was used as an appropriate model for qualitative data since it is an important tool used to analyse many kinds of binary response experiments in a wide variety of fields. Probit analysis is a specialised regression model of binomial response variable. Linear Probit Model imposes linear structure to capture the dependency of outcomes on covariate (explained variable on independent variable) as a simple function, particularly when there are several explanatory variables. By doing so, it allows for the identification of model parameters and also provides the significance probability of parameters (P-value) to conclude on covariates that significantly explain the outcome informality.

3.1. Model and Variable Description

The chapter proposes an eight-variable Linear Probit Model (LPM) for productivity, and a six variable model for employment, with the outcome variable being informality and covariates employment and production factors. For the outcome, a binary variable was created for informality (1) and formality (0). First, employment factors are used to capture the effect of employment on informality: education level, age of the owner of the business enterprise, number of years of experience before starting a business, and the wages to employees. Due to the lack of capacity-building policies for quality employment in the informal sector, the turnover of employees is not important in the informal sector and informality does not place much emphasis on the quality of products.

Secondly, the study used production factors to capture variability in the production process. To capture the effect of informality on natural completion distortion, the study used categorical variables: sale prices, cost prices and quality of product in comparison with main domestic competitors. Both sale and cost prices were restricted to higher (1), average/about the same (2) and lower (3). To explain the effect of enforcement quality on informality, producers' knowledge on the government's initiatives was used to formalise the informal sector. Due to data limitations, both variables were restricted to government initiatives that are known (1) and initiatives that are not known (0). The expected results were that lower prices predominate in the informal sector, which implies that sale of products in the informal sector is rapid. Furthermore, the gender effect is used as a proxy for the employment environment with female (1) and male (0). To achieve this, the study generates coefficients in β and tests their significance to explain the outcome variable and subsequently generate marginal probability effects and test if each of these marginal probability effects equals zero.

The LPM presentation is:

$$Y_i = \beta_1 + \beta_2 x_{i2} + \ldots + \beta_k x_{ik} + \varepsilon_i \text{ where } Y_i \in \{0, 1\} \tag{1}$$

The main interest is in the importance of each covariate in explaining the outcome. Therefore, the reduced-form Probability Model based on the LPM is:

$$Y_i = \beta X_i + \varepsilon_i, \text{ and } Y_i = \text{Informality}_i \in \{0, 1\} \tag{2}$$

where X_i is a set of employment and production factors as described above, of column vector matrix elements that capture the contemporaneous interaction across the outcome and ε_i denotes the error terms which should be independent and normally distributed. The coefficients in β are unknown and the recursive structure of the LPM is achieved by assuming that not all variables of interest will respond to the variability in the model.

4. Empirical Results and Analysis

4.1. Exploratory Data Analysis

Figure 1 shows the levels of education for respondents in the food processing sector. Statistics shows that the majority of respondents (employers) in the informal food processing sector possess low levels of education. From the literature, this finding implies that education level is inversely correlated with informality and formalisation is well understood by employers with a high level of education. The highest fraction of employers owning informal firms have secondary education (45 per cent), while 21 per cent have primary education.

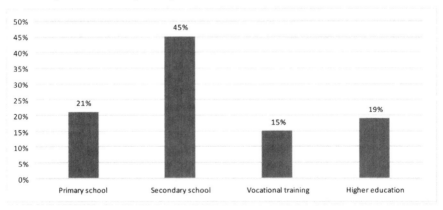

Figure 1. Education Level of Firm Owners

SOURCE: Generated from fieldwork data (2013).

This further confirms a negative correlation between education and informality. The lower the level of education an individual holds, the more the chances of being absorbed into the informal sector, and this has an impact on the level of wages earned. The study found the same results for Rwanda. Individuals absorbed in the informal sector have primary, secondary and vocational training.

As can be observed from Figure 2, the starting point of business, especially for employers operating informally, shows that the most predominant way of starting business is by the individual alone (67 per cent) and starting business as a family (16 per cent). Both ways of starting business explain the presence of informal wage labour, self-employed, paid and casual work in Rwanda's informal sector. Paid and/or unpaid domestic workers include mostly family members. However, in cases where family members are unpaid workers, it is likely to have an impact on productivity in the informal sector. Where individuals access incomes and have their own savings, it is always easy to establish a business alone. This signifies that the large number of informal establishments are started by individuals, others by families, and to some extent with business partners who have access to finances, with sufficient collateral or enough savings. In each case, the question remains as to whether there could be possibilities of expansion of the establishment that may increase output.

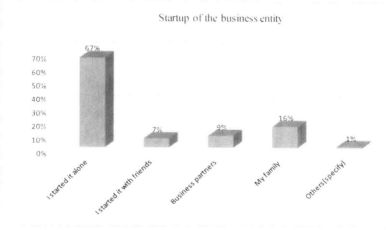

Figure 2. Startup of the Informal Business Entity
SOURCE: Generated from fieldwork data (2013).

When compiling productivity and profit, informal employers do not take into account the time and work of unpaid family workers in the business. Apart from the low productivity in informal firms due to low investments by individuals, associated with low incomes, informal business establishments are challenged by the quality of their produce as they face competition from formally established firms (see Figure 3). The most important reason as to why individuals opt to operate informally is due to lack of sufficient capital. Limited capital reduces expansion and limits individuals to operating on a small scale. Secondly, owners of informal establishments believe that taxes contribute to their decision to operate informally.

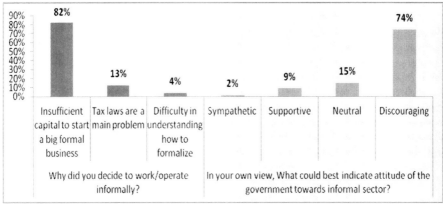

Figure 3. Reasons for Operating Informally

SOURCE: Generated from fieldwork data (2013).

In Rwanda, any establishment that is not registered with the Rwanda Revenue Authority for national taxes is classified as informal. Informal firm owners believe that taxes involved in operating a business are high, while a few (4 per cent) of the respondents stated that it is difficult to formalise their businesses entities. Limited access to credit is also a characteristic of informality. Bank credit is largely an option only for the formal sector, while most small enterprises are confined to informal loans from friends, relatives, family, and tontines. Although informal firm owners agree (74 per cent) that the government does not give much support to the informal sector, they have no opportunity to formalise as long as they do not access credit and lack sufficient capital. The elaboration of the results on reasons for operating informally are indicated in Figure 3 above.

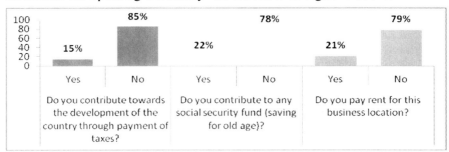

Figure 4. Contributions from the Informal Sector

SOURCE: Generated from fieldwork data (2013).

Regardless, the majority of businesses operate informally (85 per cent), do not pay taxes (confirming the definition of informality in Rwanda), do not contribute to social security funds (76 per cent), and do not pay rent (79 per cent) (Figure 4). Not paying taxes and not contributing to the national social security fund might have spill-over effects. However, it should be remembered that informal food processing firms pay local tax (patente) at the sector level (administrative entity). Not paying rent is positively correlated to insufficient capital to start a business and to the most cited ways of starting business (alone and family business). Not paying rent, however, is the underlying cause of informality, meaning that business owners operate in the same premises they own, thus implying that many informal firms operate in their home settings or households.

Many firms are operating informally due to the factors cited above, and not because it is a means of running a good business. This, therefore, implies that the majority of employers in the informal sector (89 per cent) want to operate formally, even though there are some constraints and challenges, and 78 per cent think that the ongoing formalisation process in the country is fairly effective (Figure 5). The capacity-building to improve the quality of employment in the informal sector is very low when compared to the formal sector. The majority of employers in the informal sector (93 per cent) did not obtain formal on-the-job training in food processing. This situation is closely related to primary education level (a characteristic of employees working in the informal sector), insufficient working capital and difficulties in accessing capital due to lack of collateral.

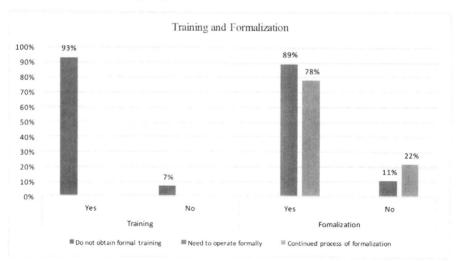

Figure 5. Employee Training and Formalisation Initiatives

SOURCE: Generated from fieldwork data (2013).

On the other hand, employers in informal registered businesses may not benefit from such training due to the fact that they are not members of the private sector federation. Training requires funds, hence insufficient capital is the big challenge for employers in organising training for themselves, even if they recognise that training could increase the quality of employment, productivity and profit in business. It is evident from Figure 5 that few individuals obtain formal on-the-job training in relation to what they really do. Employers are aware that training would add value to labour as a factor of production, which would increase output of the enterprise.

Informal firms agree with the aspect of formalising their operations (89 per cent), although they are reluctant to change their way of working for fear of paying taxes. They agree that formalisation would increase production, efficiency and increase competition but they are always afraid of change. They cite issues related to taxes and other payments such as insurance for employees. Some informal firms are already in the process of formalisation, with 78 per cent of the surveyed firms indicating that they have started the process. Operating formally would ensure high output for the business owners and more revenue collections for the government. Formalisation could also induce employment of skilled labour, thus enabling firms to increase productivity with efficient labour inputs.

4.2. Linear Probit Model

4.2.1. Informality and Productivity

The study first determined the significance of each covariate to explain the outcome. To examine the significance of each covariate, LPM was employed. Table 1 presents the significance of each covariate to explain the outcome. The significance of each covariate helps to verify the influence of each covariate on the outcome as discussed in the methodology section. The empirical results show that gender, experience before starting the business, tax on income, initiative for formalisation, sale prices, cost prices, and quality of product, are the covariates that significantly explain the outcome (informality) in the model.

Table 1. Probit Model results on informality and productivity

Informality	Coefficient	Sd Error	z	p>|z|
Gender	-0.822**	0.329	-2.500	0.012
Experience before starting business	-0.120***	0.036	-3.370	0.001
Age of firm	0.153*	0.194	0.790	0.430
Local tax	-1.437	0.782	-1.840	0.066
Initiative for formalisation	-1.187***	0.297	-4.000	0.000
Sale prices	0.691*	0.402	1.720	0.086
Cost prices	-1.029***	0.327	-3.150	0.002
Quality of product	0.628**	0.290	2.160	0.031
Log pseudo likelihood	-53.049			
Number of obs	117.000			
Wald chi^2 (12)	52.400			
Prob>chi^2	0.000			

*, **. *** represent 10%, 5%, and 1% levels of significance, respectively.

SOURCE: Fieldwork data (2013).

Following the restrictions made on covariate variables in the model, the results of the LPM verify the restrictions on gender (-), experience before starting a business (-), tax on income (-), government's initiatives for formalisation (-), cost prices (-), sale prices (+), and quality of product (+), as outlined in the methodology. A unit increase in sales and quality of product in an informal firm increases productivity by 0.69 and 0.62, respectively. Although many informal firms do not pay taxes, they pay fees to the district in which they operate. Results indicate that a unit increase on the tax on income reduces productivity by 1.43. Gender, experience before starting an informal firm and cost prices reduce productivity of the firm.

4.3. Marginal Effects

Marginal effects explain an explanatory variable's magnitude of influence with respect to productivity in the informal sector. In the analysis of results in Table 2, age of the firm, experience before starting a business, sale prices and cost prices are continuous variables. Their marginal effects can be interpreted as follows: a one year increase in age of a firm, increases the probability of productivity by 0.077, on average, holding other variables constant. Similarly, from the regression, a one unit increase on income tax will reduce productivity by 0.31, on average, holding other variables constant.

From the LPM, results indicate that the covariates — tax on income (*), sale prices (*), gender (**), quality of product (**), experience before starting a business (***), government's initiatives for formalisation (***), and cost prices (***) — are statistically significant at 10 per cent, 5 per cent, 1 per cent levels of significance, respectively, to explain the outcome, namely informality in the model. Therefore, the objective is to explain the effect of unit change of each statistically significant covariate on the probability P (informality = 1). This is addressed by computing marginal probability effects based on LPM estimates. Marginal probability effect allocates each variable's single number that expresses the effect of each covariate on probability (outcome = 1).

Table 2. Marginal effect results on informality and productivity

Informality	Coefficient	Marginal effects	z	p>|z|
Gender	-0.328	-0.131**	-2.500	0.012
Experience before starting business	-0.048	-0.014***	-3.380	0.001
Age of the firm	0.061	0.077	0.790	0.430
Local tax	-0.573	-0.313*	-1.830	0.067
Initiative for formalisation	-0.473	-0.118***	-4.000	0.000
Sale prices	0.276	0.160*	1.720	0.086
Cost prices	-0.410	-0.130***	-3.140	0.002
Quality of product	0.251	0.116**	2.160	0.031

*, **, *** represent 10%, 5%, and 1% levels of significance, respectively.
SOURCE: Fieldwork data (2013).

The empirical results show that if gender, tax on income, government's initiatives for formalisation, and cost prices change from zero to one, the probability for outcome informality taking value one decreases by 32.8 per cent, 57.3 per cent, 47.3 per cent, and 41 per cent, respectively, other variables held constant. If the categorical average of sale prices, quality of product, cost prices, and experience before starting a business goes up by an infinite amount, the probability of variable informality taking the value one rises by 27.6 per cent, 25.1 per cent, and decreases by 41 per cent and 4.8 per cent, respectively, other variables remaining constant.

One interpretation of the results is that informally established firms have low productivity, employ low skilled labour and have limited access to finances. A combination of all these factors affect productivity and growth of these informal firms. While further analysis on informality and productivity is called for, these results are suggestive.

5. Conclusion

Informality is a widespread phenomenon, with the informal sector constituting half of the economic activity in some developing countries. Informality has had an adverse effect on the growth of these economies, in terms of capacity to raise revenues. Recent studies have focused on determinants of informality. A particular focus of this study is the relationship between informality, productivity and employment. The results confirm a negative relationship between informality and productivity.

Furthermore, the results indicate that informal firms employ the larger proportion of the labour force, characterised by low levels of education, low skills and also pay lower wages. This chapter applies both exploratory data analysis and LPM to examine the relative importance of employment and productivity in explaining informality in Rwanda.

The LPM, using informality as the outcome, predicts that women employers predominate in Rwanda's informal sector. This chapter empirically demonstrates that if the experience before starting a business is increased, informality would decrease slightly. This indicates that many businesses opened by inexperienced individuals would be operating informally. The empirical results also show that both tax on income and the government's initiatives for formalisation have a negative effect on informality. This suggests that firms operating informally are not motivated to pay taxes and employers in the informal sector do not recognise the government's initiatives for formalisation. The model also predicts low sale prices, low quality of product and high cost prices in the informal sector. Even though the Government of Rwanda is discouraging informality, firms are willing to operate formally, with 89 per cent agreeing to change their operations from informal to formal. However, insufficient capital, as indicated by 82 per cent of the respondents remains the main challenge forcing firms to operate informally. The tax avoidance fraction (85 per cent) is huge and impacts on government revenue collections. Based on the empirical analysis, the chapter offers the following recommendations for informal workers:

a) Insufficient capital is a big challenge for firms, if they are to operate formally. As long as accessing funds continues to be difficult, firms are likely to continue operating in the informal sector. This should be addressed in the long-run by implementing strategies to avail funds to firms that demonstrate the potential for operating formally.

b) Education is the main variable for employment. The government should put more effort into promoting education for all. Policymakers should ensure that educated individuals acquire the quality jobs they deserve. Technological upgrading in the informal production units would improve job quality for educated individuals. Furthermore, technology would drive informal firms from being labour-intensive to capital-intensive means of production. Such a change is likely to improve productivity and output.

c) The informal sector is a last resort for the poor to make a living in a developing country such as Rwanda. Any discouragement of the production of these firms will generate high unemployment, poverty and income inequality. In addition, a large percentage of these firms are own-account enterprises, where the worker is the owner. Therefore, a government policy is required to promote social security coverage for informal sector employees

References

Abbott, P. 2010. *Fieldwork manual for household enterprise project*. Kigali: Institute of Policy Analysis and Research (IPAR)

Abbott, P. and Rwirahira, J. 2011. *Re-evaluating the role of the informal sector: The role of household enterprise in poverty reduction and employment creation in Rwanda*. Kigali: IPAR.

Amaral, P. S. and Quintin, E. 2006. A competitive model of the informal sector. *Journal of Monetary Economics*, 53 no. 7: 1541–1553.

Benjamin, N. C. and Mbaye, A. A. 2012. The informal sector, productivity, and enforcement in West Africa: A firm-level analysis. *Review of Development Economics*, 16 no. 4: 664–680.

Diego, F. and Kimie, T. 2012. Micro-determinants of informal employment in the Middle East and North Africa region. Social Protection Discussion Paper No. 1201. Washington, D.C.: World Bank.

Djankov, S., Lieberman, I., Mukherjee, J. and Nenova, T. 2003. Going informal: Benefits and costs. *In: The informal economy in the EU accession countries: Size, scope, trends and challenges to the process of EU enlargement,* edited by B. Belev, 63–80. Sofia, Bulgaria: CSD.

Fields, G. S. 1990. Labour market modelling and the urban informal sector: Theory and evidence. *In: The informal sector revisited*, edited by D. Thurnham, B. Salome and A. Schwarz, 49–69. Paris: OECD Development Centre.

Friedman, E., Johnson, S., Kaufmann, D. and Zoido-Lobaton, P. 2000. Dodging the grabbing hand: The determinants of unofficial activity in 69 countries. *Journal of Public Economics*, 76 no. 3: 459–493.

Gelb, A., Mengistae, T., Ramachandran, V. and Shah, M. K. 2009. To formalize or not to formalize? Comparisons of microenterprise data from Southern and East Africa. *Working Paper 175*. Center for Global Development. Washington, D.C.

Glaeser, E. L., La Porta, R., Lopez-de-Silanes, F. and Shleifer, A. 2004. Do institutions cause growth? *Journal of Economic Growth*, 9 no. 3: 271–303.

Hall, R. E. and Jones, C. I. 1999. Why do some countries produce so much more output per worker than others? *The Quarterly Journal of Economics*, 114 no. 1: 83–116.

Johnson, S., Kaufmann, D. and Zoido-Lobaton, P. 1998. Regulatory discretion and the unofficial economy. *American Economic Review*, 88 no. 2: 387–392.

Kucera, D. and Xenogiani, T. 2009. Persisting informal employment: What explains it? *In: Is informal normal?* edited by J. Jutting and J. R. de Laiglesa, 63–88. Paris: Organisation for Economic Cooperation and Development (OECD).

Langbein, L. and Knack, S., 2010. The worldwide governance indicators: Six, one, or none? *The Journal of Development Studies*, 46 no. 2: 350–370.

Loayza, N., Oviedo, A. M. and Serven, L. 2006. The impact of regulation on growth and informality: Cross-country evidence. *In: Linking the formal and informal economy: Concepts and policies*, edited by B. Guha-Khasnobis, R. Kanbur and E. Ostrom, 121–144. Oxford: Oxford University Press.

Loayza, N., Serven, L. and Sugawara, N. 2010. Informality in Latin America and the Caribbean. *In: Business regulation and economic performance: A Latin American perspective,* edited by N. Loayza and L. Serven, 157–196, Washington, D.C.: World Bank.

Martin, J. H., Martin, B. A. and Minnillo, P. R. 2009. Implementing a market orientation in small manufacturing firms: From cognitive model to action. *Journal of Small Business Management*, 47 no. 1: 92–115.

National Institute of Statistics Rwanda (NISR). 2013 Integrated household living conditions survey (EICV 3) report. Kigali: NISR.

—. 2014. Rwanda poverty profile report. Integrated household living conditions survey (EICV4). Kigali: NISR.

Perry, G., Maloney, W., Arias, O., Fajnzylber, P., Mason, A. and Saavedra, J., 2007. *Informality: Exit and exclusion. World Bank Latin America and Caribbean Studies.* Washington, D.C.: World Bank.

Schneider, F. and Enste, D. 2002. *The shadow economy: Theoretical approaches, empirical studies and political implications*. Cambridge, UK: Cambridge University Press.

Steel, W. F. and Snodgrass, D. 2008. World Bank region analysis on the informal economy. Raising productivity and reducing risk of household enterprises diagnostic methodology framework. For WEIGO Network and World Bank PREM Network. Draft Sept.

Taymaz, E. 2009. Informality and productivity: Productivity differentials between formal and informal firms in Turkey. METU Economic Research Center Working Papers 09/01. European Research Council, Ankara.

CHAPTER EIGHT

Vision 2020 Umurenge Programme (VUP) and Its Financial Direct Support Component to the Poor as a Strategy for Poverty Reduction in Rwanda: Challenges and Opportunities

Jean B. Ndikubwimana and *Marie P. Dusingize*

Abstract

This study analyses the challenges and opportunities of the social protection Vision Umurenge Programme Direct Support (VUP DS) to households living in extreme poverty, in Rusenge Sector, one of the poorest sectors in the Southern Province of Rwanda. The study employed the cross-sectional study design, dominated by the interpretative approach. Both primary and secondary data were used, through structured questionnaires, in-depth interviews and focus group discussions (FGD). Through purposive sampling, 61 respondents, beneficiaries of the VUP DS, were selected. Moreover, other senior managers of the VUP DS at central and local government were also included in the study. Data was analysed using the Statistical Package for Social Sciences (SPSS) for quantified data, and content analysis for qualitative data. The empirical findings confirmed the positive impact of the VUP DS programme on the social welfare promotion of households. Indeed, the beneficiaries who used to live in extreme poverty testified about the impact of the programme through the graduation from the status of extreme poverty to a level that enabled them to recover their human dignity. The study revealed that the programme has socialised the beneficiaries with a self-reliance philosophy through setting up income-generating activities, where local leaders and beneficiaries work in the framework of performance contract (imihigo), which brings about the culture of reciprocal accountability. In addition, it reduces irresponsibility in the achievement of the objectives of the programme. The study identified challenges related to bureaucratic pompous that led to delays in payment of the VUP DS and those related to the Ubudehe categorisation that resulted in cheating cases from the population and data falsification from local institutions' civil servants. The study recommends the alignment of the payment to the normal scheme of civil servants salary payment on a monthly basis and a system of tracking such malpractices that must be put in place.

Keywords: Poverty reduction strategy, VUP Direct Support, Rwanda.

1. Introduction

Hundreds of millions of people struggle with poverty around the world. Being poor is generally viewed in terms of deprivation of some of life's basic needs such as food, shelter, clothing, basic education, primary health care, and security (United Nations [UN] 2005). In Rwanda, from 2000 till 2014, growth rates have averaged 8.3 per cent per annum (National Institute of Statistics Rwanda [NISR] 2015), making Rwanda one of the top performers in Africa and an example of successful post-conflict reconstruction. This economic success has enabled significant progress in the fight against poverty, with poverty rates dropping from over 70 per cent at the end of the genocide against the Tutsi, to 56.9 per cent in 2006 and 44.9 per cent in 2010/2011 (NISR 2012; United Nations Development Programme [UNDP] 2007).

It must be argued that from 2000 to 2007, Rwanda's economic growth was undermined by the problem of inequality growing between social classes, geographic regions and gender. These disparities in all sectors could impinge negatively on Rwanda's progress towards the millennium development goals (MDGs) if nothing was done. The inequality phenomenon revealed the shortfall in policy redistribution, whereby one could observe an increase in the depth of poverty in several areas and a deterioration of living conditions at the bottom of income distribution (UNDP 2007). As a consequence of the inequality moving upwards, it was estimated that Rwanda would soon have exhausted its ability to reduce poverty rates through economic growth alone. Growing inequality is not only an obstacle to poverty reduction and sustainable economic growth, but it could also undermine social peace (Zorbas 2004; Cooke 2011; Hayman 2009). As a matter of fact, peace and justice entails equal treatment in everything that matters to people, and its absence leads to social problems. This is why inequality must be addressed in every society.

Progressively, in the light of the Rwandan government's response to these challenges of poverty and inequality, from 2007 to 2015, the long-term strategy, namely 'Vision 2020' and the midterm program known as Economic Development for Poverty Reduction Strategy (EDPRS) were underpinned by social protection intervention programmes such as 'One Cow per Poor Family', *Ubudehe*[2] Programme, and VUP. The VUP was a large-scale government-owned social protection programme. It was conceived during a high-level leadership retreat in February 2007, as a response to worrying poverty trends in the country. The VUP is a flagship programme of the EDPRS, 2008 to 2012. The VUP aimed to contribute to the national target to reduce extreme poverty from 36.9 per cent in 2005/2006 to 24.0 per cent in 2012. The purpose was to accelerate the reduction of extreme poverty in VUP target sectors (Goverment of Rwanda 2007). The programme had three main components: Direct Support (DS) – unconditional cash transfers to those who are impoverished and unable to work; Public Works (PW) – paid employment on productive community asset development projects; and Financial Services (FS) – increasing access to financial services for the poor [this includes microcredit, a matching-grant challenge fund and financial literacy] (Goverment of Rwanda [GoR] 2007). From 2010 to 2015, the results of the government's response to poverty reduction were very promising, to the extent that the MDGs were to be achieved (UNDP 2007). Hence, this study aims at investigating the contribution of VUP DS to poverty reduction in the achievement of human development. The study analysed the best practices of the programme and identified the challenges. The study also offers recommendations to policymakers and researchers. Due to limited time and resources, the study was restricted to Rusenge Sector and the VUP DS.

2. Literature Review and Theoretical Framework

This chapter discusses the VUP social support, how it works and why the GoR introduced it. It also undertakes a discussion of previous studies on VUP and its impact on the Rwandan community.

2.1. Vision 2020 Umurenge Programme (VUP)

VUP is a flagship program of the EDPRS, enshrined in Vision 2020. It is directed at poverty reduction in the poorest families across the country. Since 2000, GoR through the Ministry of Local Government (MINALOC) has embarked on different socioeconomic policies to eradicate poverty, especially in rural areas. The Vision 2020 Umurenge Programme (VUP) is one of these programmes (MINALOC 2008). Being both a support and cash transfer programme to accelerate social and economic development for the poor, VUP commenced in 2008 and comprised three components:

a) *Direct support*: This targets households in which no family member over the age of 18 years is either able to work or to participate in any employment opportunities within the framework of the programme. This includes disabled people, families headed by children and the elderly (Corry 2012). These are the extremely poor households without labour capacity. The financial support thus aimed at helping them to satisfy their basic needs such as food, and most importantly, to cover their health insurance.

b) *Public works*: This offers employment (public work) opportunities to different categories of poor people (extremely poor) who are able to take up the job opportunities. The condition is that these people must come from extremely poor households across districts.

c) *Credit packages*: This provides financial services (credit) to the extremely poor people through VUP-insured micro-loans (MINALOC 2009). Eligibility for any element of VUP was to be in one of the two participatory poverty categories under former six classifications. Currently, there is a process of classifying the Rwandan population in four categories. For the credit element, the loans were for investing in farming or non-farming income-generating activities.

The difference between these three components of VUP is that the public works and the credit packages are prescribed to the very poor households whose members fulfil the physical fitness to work, whereas the direct support package targets the poorest households whose people are not able to work. In other words, direct support is an entitlement whereby, if a household meets the criteria, it is entitled to the support, whereas in the case of the public works component, not every eligible household participated. The direct support consists of an unconditional money transfer that seeks to expand health and education coverage as well as to encourage the development of 'appropriate' skills handicraft or social service activities (MINALOC 2009). More importantly, when the beneficiaries of the direct support package receive new skills and the know-how to deal with their livelihoods, there is a possibility of graduating from the direct support scheme to the public works and the financial packages. The programme was piloted in the poorest *Umurenge* in each of the 30 districts of Rwanda, from 2008 to 2009. Subsequently, the programme was scaled up throughout the country, hence almost all sectors are now included.

2.1.1. The Organisational Framework of the VUP Direct Support Programme

The VUP Direct Support programme is coordinated by the Ministry of Local Government, and is implemented at district level. Districts play an important oversight and supervisory role, and manage the day-to-day activities of the programme in close liaison with districts and the *umudugudu*[3] communities (MINALOC 2009).

Table 1. The income transfer in the component of VUP Direct Support in line with the household size

Household size	Amount
Head of household	250 RwF i.e 0.35 USD
Second household member	150 RwF i.e 0.21 USD or 60% of the Head of household rate
Each other member of the household (maximum 3)	100 RwF i.e 0.12 USD or 40% of Head of household rate

SOURCE: Survey data (2015).

As Table 1 shows, if a family comprises three individuals, it will receive 500 Rwf per day, to make a total of 15,000 Rwf per month. Inversely, if the family comprises just one person, it will only receive 7,500 Rwf. It is obvious that as the size of the family becomes big, the amount to transfer decreases. It would be logical to give the reference amount of 250 Rwf to each member of the family. Two arguments can be formulated. One, it seems that GoR wants to discourage the dependence phenomenon and promote the culture of self-reliance. Two, the policy also did not omit the family planning targets because it is obvious that the family whose size is bigger will receive the smallest amount. One can argue that the amount is also small, but on the contrary, 'smaller' is better than nothing.

In this regard, the information of how people are categorised according to their level of poverty is very crucial because it helps decision-makers to know how to formulate policies targeting groups to alleviate poverty. In Rwanda, the implementation of VUP refers to the *Ubudehe* classification (Ministry of Finance and Economic Planning [MINECOFIN] 2002). That participatory poverty categorisation is an innovative way of classifying residents into poverty categories so that support can be given to the poorest and most vulnerable members of the community. It is participatory in the way that all citizens gather in the village (*umudugudu*) and place themselves into the category, following the set criteria and characteristics. It is innovative and enables Rwanda to provide support in VUP, scholarships in tertiary education and exemption for mutual health insurance payments. Hence, the category in which a person or a household falls within allows decision-makers to orient the social protection. For instance, people in the first and second category become beneficiaries of VUP in all its three components, namely public works, financial support and direct support (figure 1).

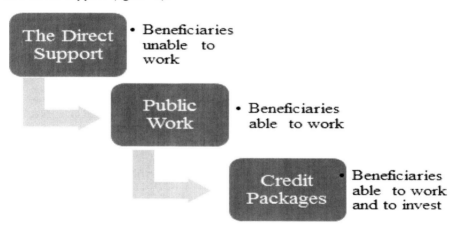

Figure 1. The Complementarity of the Three Components of VUP
SOURCE: Generated from fieldwork data, 2015.

2.1.2. VUP and Human Development in Rwanda

All social protection programmes in Rwanda are oriented towards the human development goal and ought to be analysed in a multidimensional approach, whereby VUP plays a big role. The multidimensionality of the social protection that aims at achieving the strategic vision 2020 is based on the premise that only one programme does not suffice to achieve human development. The latter must be achieved through EDPRS, VUP and other home-grown solutions such as the *Ubudehe* programme (mutual help programme) and One Cow per Poor Family. For instance, the One Cow per Poor Family programme is based on the premise that providing a dairy cow to poor households will not only improve their livelihood as a result of a more nutritious and balanced diet from milk, but will also produce agricultural output through better soil fertility as well as greater incomes by commercializing dairy products (GoR 2014). In the same perspective, the most successful antipoverty initiatives in the literature of development, to date, have taken a multi-dimensional approach, combining income support and job creation with expanded health care and educational opportunities, and other interventions for community development (United Nations Development Programme [UNDP] 2014). It is within this perspective that many nations embarked on human development through the multi-dimensional approach. This multi-dimensional approach had been successfully implemented in different countries. For instance, in the Republic of Korea and later in China, state ownership of the banking sector as well as macroeconomic, financial and industrial policies all increased the quality and quantity of jobs (UNDP 2014).

Therefore, if combined with other forms of social protection, VUP plays an important role in promoting human development. In other words, the financial support allows the beneficiaries to access health services, access education and initiate income-generating activities that enable households to become resilient to extreme poverty. In the Rwandan context, poverty is a state characterised by levels of capabilities that are, in the view of society, unacceptably low. The official definition of poverty refers to not having sufficient income to afford a minimum diet (2,300 calories a day) and buy some essential non-food items. Extreme poverty is not being able to afford the basic diet if all income is spent on food (NISR 2011). This definition is in line with the characteristics of the first class in *Ubudehe* categorisation, which is one of the targets of VUP. This class is known as *Umutindi Nyakujya* in Kinyarwanda, loosely translated as "those in abject poverty". These are people who need to beg to survive. They have no land or livestock and lack shelter, adequate clothing and food. They fall sick often and have no access to medical care. Their children are malnourished and they cannot afford to send them to school (MINECOFIN 2012).

When analysing the current achievements in the development sector in Rwanda, it can be concluded that the VUP helped some beneficiaries to graduate from vulnerability to better socioeconomic conditions as highlighted by UNDP reports.

Table 2. The trend of HDI from 1995 to 2013 among countries of the East African Community (EAC)

Countries	HDI in 1995	HDI in 2004	HDI in 2013
Rwanda	0,337	0,450	0,506
Kenya	0,525	0,491	0,535
Tanzania	0,423	0,430	0,488
Uganda	0,413	0,502	0,484
Burundi	0,325	0,384	0,384

SOURCE: Adopted from UNDP Report (2014).

From Table 2, it is clear that Rwanda made a tremendous improvement in HDI of 1.113, from 1995 to 2004, and a graduation of 0,056 from 2004 to 2013, with a total graduation of 1,169. In comparison with other EAC member states, Rwanda had a higher score than all countries, except Kenya which has a large economy within the EAC. The increase in HDI is proof of the improvement of the social welfare of the population, which was one of the targets of the social protection programs, VUP included. According to the Rwanda Human Development Report, tremendous improvements were made in food security, access to and quality of health care, and basic education; income per capita has doubled within one decade, whereas gross domestic product (GDP) has tripled since 2006 and the government has put in place measures to ensure that it is inclusive (GoR 2014).

2.2. Impact of VUP on the Rwandan Community

As was discussed in the previous pages, VUP social protection, which was initiated in 2008 by GoR, was directed at poverty reduction in the poorest families across the country. VUP is built on the assumption that households having the limited capacity to sustain themselves through livelihood shocks or cycles will be empowered in the short and long run. As a social protection programme, it comprises the system of regular and predicable cash transfers that provide income support to those living in poverty and those vulnerable to falling into poverty. As a means of ensuring access to other public services — such as health and education — it enables poor households to overcome financial barriers that they may face (Devereux 2001).

As indicated in Integrated Household Living Conditions Survey 3 (EICV 3), the extreme poverty declined from 40 per cent in 2000/2001 to 35.8 per cent in 2005/2006, and to 24.1 per cent in 2010/2011 (NISR 2011). Empirical findings presented during the 9th National Dialogue Council (December 15-16, 2011) also indicated that the achievements of the VUP scheme (2008-2011) include: 590,100 people who got a job; an estimated Rwf 15 billion generated; an estimated 81,693 people got direct cash assistance worth Rwf 4 billion; and 92,136 people received loans totalling to Rwf 8 billion (MINALOC 2011). The report of Berglund also revealed positive perceptions of the beneficiaries of VUP, in terms of cash transfer provision and its positive impact on meeting of the primary needs such as food, shelter and household materials (Berglund 2012). Not only did VUP contribute to the welfare of individual beneficiaries, but it was also taken as a social protection with disaster risk management, climate change adaptation and food security (Siegel *et al.* 2011). According to a recent study, VUP was taken as a model of graduation by offering low-interest loans to either individuals or borrower groups for micro-enterprises that diversify risks away from farming. The same study recognises the VUP impact on sustainable food security as it combines interventions that stabilise income or food production with those that raise income or food production, and are designed and delivered in ways that enhance social justice (Devereux 2012).

In fact, the core argument of VUP's role in social protection is that it builds resilience and provides the effectiveness and responses in case of shocks such as food insecurity resulting from climate conditions. According to UNDP (2014), strong social protection not only improves individual resilience, but it can also bolster the resilience of the economy as a whole; but more importantly is the role played by social protection in achieving human development. Social protection has a strong effect on human development as it promotes choices and capabilities (UNDP 2014). This capability approach was influenced by Sen in the 1980s and was based on the choices and empowerment enhancements inherent to human development (Davies 2009). In human development, choices and empowerment entail human resilience and vulnerable reduction. On the one hand, human resilience is about removing the barriers that hold people back in their freedom to act. It is also about enabling the disadvantaged and excluded groups to express their concerns, to be heard and to be active agents in shaping their destinies. On the other hand, people are vulnerable to poverty if they are below, or at risk of falling below a certain minimally acceptable threshold of critical choices across several dimensions such as health, education, material resources, and security (UNDP 2014). From this argument, it is clear that VUP targets in building resilience and improving socioeconomic conditions of the beneficiary households were taken by different reports as a way of realising human development improvement in Rwanda.

While from 2000 to 2009, many studies revealed that Rwanda's economy grew without paying attention to inequalities between social classes and geographic regions — a phenomenon that could impinge negatively on the MDGs achievements (Zorbas 2004; Hayman 2009) from 2010 to 2015 — the strong economic growth has translated into benefitting the entire population, with those in the lower wealth quintiles benefitting more than those in the higher quintiles. The Gini Coefficient fell from 52 per cent in 2005/2006 to 49 per cent in 2010/2011. Poverty fell significantly in all the provinces, as did inequalities, except in the Northern Province where it remained unchanged (Abbott and Rwirahira 2012). Furthermore, in comparison with other neighbouring countries, Rwanda's economy was growing at a healthy rate — 7.5 per cent in 2010, which was 2 per cent higher than the EAC and even more than Sub-Saharan Africa. This confirmed the country's macroeconomic framework stability. In 2014, Rwanda's economy grew by 7.1 per cent, 2.4 percentage points faster than in 2013, and registered faster GDP growth reflected by higher growth of the services sector, at 9.1 per cent, up from 5.4 per cent in 2013, when the economy suffered from the impact of the 2012 aid shortfall (World Bank 2015).

Though the VUP social protection policy ensures protective, preventive and promotive roles, studies also indicate some flaws associated with the policy. These flaws range from eligibility process to programme implementation. In the Second VUP annual review report, it was highlighted that the targeting system ran the risks of manipulation because the introduction of money led to falsifying of information by citizens, who hoped that if selected, they would become beneficiaries (Devereux 2012). Such manipulative practices could lead to ineffectiveness of the programme, if measures were not taken.

Moreover, other challenges were related to targeting accuracy among the poor and the non-poor, as targeting may be developed out of context and may not tackle the real problems experienced by the beneficiaries (Siegel *et al.* 2011). As a matter of fact, a programme such as VUP is likely to perform better in terms of targeting efficiency when it minimises the leaks to the non-poor, on the one hand, and in terms of targeting effectiveness when analysing cash transfers. Other challenges concern the question of sustainability of the programme. As questioned by some studies, VUP lacks the transformative function in the long run due to flaws of graduation model (Devereux 2013). Besides, VUP was questioned on how it ensures sustainability as it does not have a clear exit strategy as to how it will ensure continued access to financial support for poor households (Sukhwinder *et al.* 2012).

Hence, the sustainability of VUP DS should answer the question of how the programme can sustain itself in the long run, if the financial support is stopped due to external factors such as economic crisis or cut of financial aid to the government by donors due to political reasons. In other words, the sustainability of the programme implies the impact that makes the beneficiaries of the social protection policy resilient to any shock of poverty vulnerability. The intent here is the capacity-building of vulnerable people, enabling them to continuously build internal resources to carry on their developmental plans with a minimum of outside assistance, and to increase their access to the satisfaction of the primary needs, in other words, to lift them from marginality to a level that gives them dignity (Honadle 1980; Kay 2006).

Drawing from the points discussed in the literature review, the research answered the following questions: (1) From the perceptions of the beneficiaries of the VUP programme, specifically in Rusenge Sector of Nyaruguru District in the Southern Province in Rwanda, what are the opportunities and current challenges linked to the programme? (2) What are other possible policy factors that, if not addressed, may hinder the effectiveness and sustainability of the VUP? (3) What are possible solutions to these challenges? In responding to these questions, the study designed a methodology dominated by an interpretative approach due to the nature of the sample and the phenomenon under investigation.

3. Methodology

3.1 The Study Design
Given the nature of the study, the research used a cross-sectional study design. The cross-sectional study design is appropriate to studies that aim at finding out situations and attitudes, or issues as they stand at the time of the study (Kumar 2005). In fact, research went beyond a mere description of VUP DS and its beneficiaries, and sought to explain why things were in the way they were as well as identifying challenges and opportunities. The research began by elaborating of the introduction and literature review, then proceeded to the formulation of the research questions.

3.2 Population and Sampling
The study population included the beneficiaries of VUP DS in Rusenge Sector, a total of 61 beneficiaries. This number was fixed due to the fact that the study was conducted using a qualitative approach which collected the information from respondents through a structured questionnaire and interviews. In such qualitative research, a minimum of 30 respondents is required (Bailey 1994) and to minimise the margin error, the cases had to be doubled. The current study chose the qualitative approach in collecting primary data because the primary purpose for researchers was to find perceptions and personal experiences of beneficiaries toward the DS that can clarify and deepen understanding about the phenomenon being studied. According to Flick, quoted by Neuman (2011, 220), for qualitative researchers, "it is their relevance to the research topic rather than their representativeness which determines the way in which the people to be studied are selected".

Hence, the research used the purposive or judgmental sampling, whereby researchers selected only the key informants who satisfied the established criteria. In this case, the basic criteria were to be a beneficiary of DS and located in Rusenge Sector. Through purposive sampling the 61 respondents were broken down as follows: researchers administered household structured questionnaires to 61 households that were beneficiaries of VUP. Four focus group discussions were also conducted among the two cooperatives whose members were beneficiaries of VUP. Apart from those beneficiaries of the programme, an in-depth interview was held with five senior managers of VUP at national, district and sector levels, respectively.

3.3. Data Analysis Instruments

Data collection was based on the following instruments:

(a) Household Structured Questionnaires
Household structured questionnaires were used to collect data. The questionnaire was addressed to 61 beneficiaries of VUP DS, located in Rusenge Sector. It consisted of both open-ended and closed-ended questions. This type of questionnaire helped to obtain detailed information and allowed researchers to probe further into what beneficiaries of DS

think, beyond selected and fixed answers by researchers (Bailey 1994). The questionnaire was administered by the data collectors.

(b) In-depth Interviews

In-depth interviews were conducted to obtain information from programme managers of VUP at national, district and sector levels. Specifically, at national level, the in-depth interviews were addressed to senior staff at the Local Administrative Entities and Development Agency (LODA), whose role was to implement the local economic and community development policies and strategies, social protection and poverty reduction programmes, including VUP. At the district level, senior managers were contacted, whose daily role was to observe the implementation of the programme.

(c) Focus Group Discussions

Four focus group discussions were conducted with beneficiaries of direct financial support, each with five participants. Beneficiaries were invited to express their appreciation of support received as well as express the perceived opportunities and challenges associated with the programme. The objective of focus group discussions was to assess needs, develop interventions, test new ideas or programmes, and improve existing programmes (Trompo and Kombo 2011).

After developing an analysis protocol, quantitative data collected were analysed, using the SPSS software. The research not only summarised and explained the key findings, using a word processor, but also interpreted the findings.

3.4. Fieldwork and Quality Assurance Measures

Preliminary visits were conducted in the study area and institutions associated with VUP. The research instruments were pre-tested to assess their reliability by collecting information through blended techniques, namely direct observation, in-depth interviews, structured questionnaire, and focus group discussions. Data collected was entered and analysed using simple frequencies produced through SPSS software, while results from focus group discussions and in-depth interviews were analysed trough content analysis and explanation.

Six assistant enumerators whose role was to collect data using structured questionnaires were recruited. A supervisor (one of the researchers) was responsible for monitoring the exercise and checking the accuracy of data collected. Meanwhile, another researcher was responsible for focus group discussions among the beneficiaries of VUP. This exercise lasted one week, from the 11th of April 2015 to the 17th of April 2015. Individual interviews were conducted during the second week. This activity was conducted by the researchers themselves. It involved the key informants who participated in VUP management from the local to the central government. For data collected through structured questionnaires, the data quality was assured by the supervisor who held daily meetings at the beginning and end of the day to review progress and address any emerging issues that might have been encountered by data collectors. Furthermore, there was regular telephone communication between the field supervisor and the data collectors. From the 24th of April, researchers started processing the data in the SPSS, analysing data and compiling a final report.

4. Findings and Discussion

4.1 Study Area Description

The study was conducted in Rusenge Sector, one of the 14 Sectors of Nyaruguru District (Figure 2). The latter is one of the poorest districts in Rwanda, with 24.2 per cent (26.9 per cent male and 16.6 per cent female) living in extreme poverty (Nyaruguru 2013). Rusenge Sector was selected as the poorest sector to participate in the VUP in 2008 (Nyaruguru 2013).

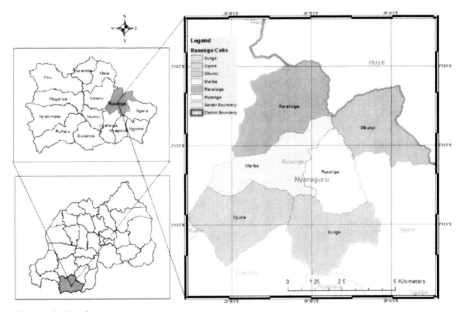

Figure 2. Study Area

SOURCE: Adopted from Centre for GIS and Remote Sensing (CGIS) (2015).

4.2. Presentation of the Findings

4.2.1. Description of Respondents

All respondents were located in Rusenge Sector in Nyaruguru District, and were from three cellules, namely Raranzige, Mariba and Cyuna, except the senior managers. The number of females (40) was more than the number of males (21). This is not surprising because the global trend is such that women are more likely to be poorer than men (Giddens 2009) due to social and cultural factors, especially in Africa, where women are given a status of second class citizens. In fact, when examining the district level, the whole number of women beneficiaries of VUP DS in the Sector of Rusenge is 197 while that of men is 74 (Nyaruguru 2013). This rate shows the female face of poverty as a consequence of gender inequality, which puts men in a favourable socioeconomic condition, while women find themselves in a subordinate position.

With regards to the age of the respondents, the research found out that the majority (80.3 per cent) of the beneficiaries of the DS were a category whose age was more than 65 years old. The category between 35 and 65 years old was considered as adult (18 per cent), while the youth accounted for 1.6 per cent (Table 3). This data indicates how the vulnerability of DS beneficiaries is linked to old age. In fact, generally speaking, apart from being a female, being old is another factor that contributes to poverty (Giddens 2009). In rural areas, farmers are mostly occupied by farming, which is largely subsistence in nature. Consequently, in old age they lack a meaningful income-generating activity. Thus, the social protection of VUP DS was established to assist them financially, since in most cases they do not receive financial support from relatives. The fact that the active population benefits from the VUP DS programme may be interpreted in two ways: Either they cannot work due to lack of physically fitness, or because they are students or non-accompanied minors heading households targeted by the programme.

Table 3. Respondents according to age group

Age group	Frequency	Per cent
Youth (18–35)	1	1.6
Adult (35–65)	11	18
Old (+65)	49	80.3
Total	61	100

SOURCE: Survey data (2015).

For the level of education, a big number of respondents consisted of people without any level of education (62.3 per cent); 23 per cent did not complete primary level education; and 14.8 per cent attained primary education (Table 4). This widespread low level of education that characterises the respondents is another indicator of their vulnerability. Indeed, education is a crucial factor that helps people to rise from low social status. This is because education allows people to develop skills which can be used to penetrate the labour market, hence acquire food and other basic necessities, both in rural and urban areas.

Table 4. Respondents according to the level of education

Education	Frequency	Per cent
None	38	62.3
Incomplete primary	14	23.0
Primary	9	14.8
Total	61	100.0

SOURCE: Survey data (2015).

Considering the marital status of respondents, the data presented in Table 5 indicate that a big number of respondents were widows and widowers, 54.1 per cent and 34.4 per cent, respectively; the divorced represented 9.8 per cent and the single represented 1 per cent. These characteristics indicate how poverty crosscuts all categories of people, even though it is experienced more by the most vulnerable, such as widows and widowers, and old people who are unable to work.

Table 5. Respondents according to marital status

Marital status	Frequency	Per cent
Single	1	1.6
Married	21	34.4
Divorce	6	9.8
Widow/widower	33	54.1
Total	61	100.0

SOURCE: Survey data (2015).

Regarding the profession of respondents, it was noted that a big number of respondents (92 per cent) were farmers (figure 3), meaning that beneficiaries of VUP DS are mainly farmers. The occupation of 'farmer' requires an interpretation.

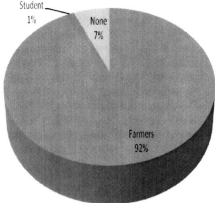

Figure 3. Professional Categories of Respondents
SOURCE: Generated from fieldwork data (2015).

In the Rwandan context, there is a general trend of referring to all people who do not have any occupation as farmers. The fact that a big number of respondents regard themselves as farmers attests to this because direct support is oriented to those households whose members are not able to work or who lack an occupation

4.2.2. Sources of Livelihood of Respondents before Joining VUP DS

The DS beneficiaries were asked who had supported them before VUP DS. The majority (47.5 per cent) stated that they did not receive support from someone before they joined the programme. Another segment of respondents were dependent on their families and neighbours. This explains the informal aspect of social protection in African societies, which is characterised by mutual assistance. It also indicates one of the characteristics of the African family that goes beyond the nuclear family to embrace other relatives. The beneficiaries were asked about the type of support they used to get before joining DS. Some (11.5 per cent) revealed that they used to live on *guca inshuro* (to work on others' land to earn an income). This means that they used to be physically fit and could work on others' land, but as time progressed, they lost the ability to work due to physical conditions, weakness from aging or chronic diseases. Others (11.5 per cent) stated that they received food from caregivers such as neighbours or relatives. The remaining respondents indicated that they did not receive any support from anybody and asserted that before joining the program they were self-reliant.

4.2.3. Beneficiaries of VUP DS since Its Inception in 2008

According to Table 6, VUP DS beneficiaries started to receive support in 2008. In fact, this is when the programme was introduced in the poorest sectors, hence many people were selected and others were added progressively. The big number of beneficiaries is noted in 2011/2012. This may be explained by two reasons: Either the government received enough funds from its partners or problems in the agricultural sector, such as poor weather conditions, led to an increase of citizens in need of social protection.

One may also note the fall in number in 2009-2010. Two reasons may be given for this. The rainy season was satisfactory, hence the number of beneficiaries reduced. Another reason is that the funds reduced because donors withheld aid. It must be remembered that in 2009, the Rwandan government crossed into diplomatic limbo in relation to the possibility of its backing the M23 rebellion in the Eastern Democratic Republic of Congo, which led to some donor countries cutting off financial aid.

Table 6. Beneficiaries of VUP DS from 2008 in the area of the study

Period since VUP inception Year	Number of beneficiaries per sex		Total No. of beneficiaries	Total amount in (Rwf) given	Summative amount and average			
	Female	Male			Average amount (Rwf)by a person/month	Average amount (Rwf)by a person/Per Day	Average rate exchange in US$	Average in US$
2008-2009	n/a	n/a	290	33,444,000	9,610	320	562	0.57
2009-2010	n/a	n/a	62	19,660,000	26,425	881	582.5	1.51
2010-2011	n/a	n/a	343	40,980,750	9,956	332	588.25	0.56
2011-2012	n/a	n/a	391	66,556,500	14,185	473	609	0.78
2012-2013	215	85	300	44,862,000	12,462	415	650	0.64
2013-2014	217	83	300	44,208,000	12,280	409	660	0.62

SOURCE: Official statistics from the office of the manager of VUP in Nyaruguru District (2015).

On the amount provided to each household beneficiary of the VUP DS, respondents declared that the starting amount was 7,500 Rwf for a household with one person. This is the basic amount which varies according to the household size. However, the additional amount progressively decreases. As mentioned earlier, the big size of the family leads to a decrease of the amount to transfer. If we take the reference of 7,500 Rwf for a household of one person per month, it would be logical to give the reference amount of 250 Rwf to each member of the family per day, which means that a household of six people may get 45,000 Rwf per month, but this is not the case. According to the Manager of VUP at district level, the formula is:

> 12,000 Rwf for a family of two members (of course, the head of the family receives 7,500 Rwf as a constant amount), 15,000 Rwf for three people in a family, 18,000 Rwf for four people in a family, 21,000 Rwf for five and above.

Two arguments can be made regarding this formula. Firstly, it seems that the government wants to discourage the dependence phenomenon. Secondly, the policy also did not omit family planning targets because it is obvious that the family whose size is bigger will receive the smallest amount. Following the description of the respondents and the functions of the programme, the following sections analyse the impact of the VUP DS.

4.2.4. The Impact of VUP DS in Rusenge Sector

Figure 4 highlights the impact of VUP DS in Rusenge Sector. Respondents indicated two important elements with a high percentage (24.6 per cent) — poverty alleviation and recovery of dignity — as notable outcomes of VUP DS. In VUP, the concept of recovery of dignity is very important, given the social characteristics of the beneficiaries of the programme. In fact, the programme targets the very poor households whose members live in abject poverty. These are people who lack social status and are isolated from the community due to extreme poverty. Therefore, when respondents link VUP and recovery of dignity, they really indicate the impact of the programme on their livelihood situations.

The recovery of dignity aspect also emerged from the results of focus group discussions, whereby beneficiaries reported on material benefits as well as immaterial benefits gained from the programme. Respondent 'A' in the focus group discussions had this to say:

> With that support we regain our dignity, we don't have enough land, we don't have energy to work, we don't have any other type of support. DS reintegrates us within our community. We regain a certain level self-reliance through the performance contract, because once we get money we must sign a contract with chiefs of our villages about what we intend to achieve (Respondent 'A', Nyaruguru, April 28, 2015).

One senior manager of VUP revealed the following:

> The beneficiaries of VUP had almost lost hope in life. Imagine someone who lives begging without knowing the source of that support; he only waits for death. Then after joining the programme, he is taken care of, he finds daily revenue, at least to cover one year (Senior Manager, Nyaruguru, April 29, 2015).

Furthermore, the respondents revealed that the programme helped them to deal with food insecurity. Apparently, the VUP DS builds resilience and puts beneficiaries in a situation of preparedness for dealing with food insecurity. For instance, the respondents stated that the money from VUP DS is used to buy food and seeds for crops. Respondent 'B' in the focus group discussions stated:

> We used to live in uncertainty, where we could not foresee what to eat the following day. But now the money we get from VUP DS helps us to determine our destiny as we use it to purchase households items of immediate necessity, food being the priority. We also find means to pay health insurance and to pay fees for our children (Respondent 'B', Nyaruguru, April 28, 2015).

Figure 4 indicates that 9.8 per cent of the respondents stated that the VUP DS kept them from begging. As a matter of fact, living in abject poverty means experiencing indigent conditions, in which a person may resort to begging. You beg when you do not have any other alternative way of surviving. The respondents affirmed that VUP DS prevented them from begging. Respondent 'C' in the focus group discussions stated:

> I had already lost hope for the future as I was begging for food from house to house. Now through VUP DS, I am assured that the basic needs are met, and consequently, I no longer beg! (Respondent 'C', Nyaruguru, April 28, 2015).

The respondents (11.5 per cent) also hailed the programme on the grounds that they were able to hire daily workers. The phenomenon of hiring a daily worker consists of providing a daily salary to someone who digs or weeds the land or the house surroundings of the VUP DS beneficiaries. It must be remembered that the majority of VUP DS beneficiaries are old or unable to work, even though they may own land. Therefore, as they lack the physical fitness to farm or maintain their property, collect firewood or fetch water, they hire those who are able to perform these services. When beneficiaries of VUP DS were asked to provide the daily cost in case of hiring workers, they stated that it varies according to the type of work, but for land cultivation, it ranges from 500 to 600 Rwf.

Another important element associated with the impact of VUP DS is savings (8.2 per cent). As it is known, one of the goals of VUP is to empower beneficiaries with the capacity that prevents them from falling into poverty. In development, saving is a source of wealth because it is an enabling factor of entrepreneurship and the latter brings about income, which in turn promotes wellbeing. The respondents mentioned two types of savings. The first type is a part of the pension kept at Umurenge Savings and Credit Cooperative (SACCO) which becomes an initial share in the cooperative. The second type of savings is household savings which is encouraged as a way of avoiding extravagant expenditure. It is from this household savings that beneficiaries would be able to hire workers to fetch water for them or to perform other duties in the home. To supplement the above arguments, respondent 'D' revealed this in the focus group discussion:

> When we get the pension, we are told to use it prudently. Therefore, we try our best to use it carefully, even though it is not easy as needs are more than the amount given (Respondent 'D', Nyaruguru, April 28, 2015).

In the in-depth interview, one senior manager of VUP stated that the savings allowed the beneficiaries to set up a business premises in Raranzige Cell. He was asked how the old people who were not able to work could undertake business, and he explained that they had their next of kin (*abishingizi*) who represented them in the management of the business.

Based on what is reported, it can be concluded that the DS protects beneficiaries against social marginalisation/social exclusion, resulting from extreme poverty. The VUP DS enables the disadvantaged and excluded to realise their rights, express their concerns openly, be heard and to become active agents in shaping their destiny. The VUP DS allows beneficiaries to regain the freedom to live a life that one values and to manage one's affairs efficiently (see Figure 4).

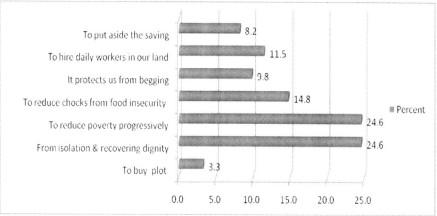

Figure 4. The Impact of VUP DS in Rusenge Sector
SOURCE: Generated from fieldwork data (2015).

4.2.5. Level of Appreciation of the VUP DS by Respondents

The majority of the beneficiaries (77 per cent) of DS maintained that the pension is adequate for living on; 9.8 per cent asserted that the pension was more than adequate for living on, while 13.1 per cent considered it as inadequate. As it stands, the majority of respondents (Figure 5) appreciated the contribution of the programme because it enabled them to meet their basic needs.

Where the DS is seen as more than adequate for livelihood, this is due to the fact that some of the beneficiaries used to live in extreme poverty and could not meet their basic needs, but thereafter, VUP DS presented a socioeconomic panacea. For those who consider it as inadequate, one can argue that although the amount is small, smaller is better than nothing, especially in the context of people who are unable to work and who do not have any other means of livelihood, but with VUP DS, they at least receive a monthly pension.

Respondent 'E' in the focus group discussions expressed the following:

> We cannot say that the DS is inadequate to meet our social needs because it is a gift from our government. It would be ungrateful to term it as inadequate since it is given to us freely without anything else in exchange; and the government considers us and knows what is important for us, hence plans for us accordingly (Respondent 'E', Nyaruguru, April 28, 2015).

The fact that there are beneficiaries of DS who consider the support as inadequate in meeting their social needs can be explained by the fact that the support is shared among many members of a household, and the amount decreases when the family is big.

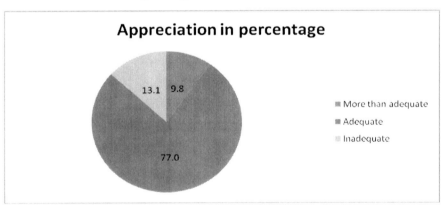

Figure 5. Appreciation of the VUP DS
SOURCE: Generated from fieldwork data (2015).

4.2.6 Impact of DS on Poverty Reduction in Rusenge Sector

The respondents also appreciated the extent to which the programme helped them to shift from extreme poverty, whereby the majority (52.5 per cent) were in very strong agreement, 31.1 per cent strongly agreed, 14.8 per cent just agreed, and 1.6 per cent disagreed (Figure 6). When respondents were requested to provide tangible facts in relation to poverty alleviation, they explained that VUP DS helped them to climb out of poverty through meeting material needs such as household items, clothes, soap, and utensils. More importantly, they hailed the programme as it enabled them to become self-reliant, even with just a few resources that enabled them to join others in cooperatives or associations.

The above responses were supported by the findings from focus group discussions, of which respondent 'F' expressed the following:

> Without this financial support, I would have been overwhelmed by the isolation and vulnerability. So far, I have bought a plot on which I have built my own house in the village. The support does not suppress poverty, but it reduces it progressively. It also helps to restore dignity because at this age I am not able to work for other, but at least the support prevents me from begging or dying from hunger. Without the support, I would not exist (Respondent 'F', Nyaruguru, April 28, 2015).

The few respondents who disagreed explained that there was mismanagement of DS, for instance, the beneficiaries who are represented by next of kin in the programme had engaged in some malpractices, involving mismanagement of bank accounts. This problem of dishonesty was also raised in the interview with the senior manager of the VUP at district level, who indicated that representatives of unaccompanied people could attempt to use some money for their own interests.

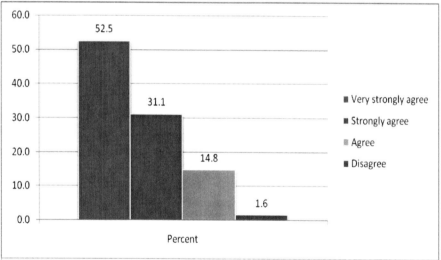

Figure 6. Impact of DS on Poverty Reduction

SOURCE: Generated from fieldwork data (2015).

4.3. Challenges of VUP DS

The research also explored the factors that could hinder the effectiveness of the programmer, as discussed in the following section.

4.3.1. Delays in Pension Delivery

According to Figure 7, the main challenge mentioned by 91.8 per cent of respondents is the delay in receiving funds, which is a managerial problem. Respondents indicated that there was a time schedule for delivering the pension, but it was not respected, hence disrupted their plans for the application of the support. This challenge was also mentioned by one senior manager of VUP in the in-depth interview. He revealed that the support was earmarked as a transfer from the Ministry of Economic Planning (MINECOFIN). However, in most cases, it took about three months for the support to arrive in the district account. When the researchers inquired about the reason for such delays and the possible implication, the senior manager explained that it was due to bureaucratic procedures which had a negative repercussion on the effectiveness of the programme. The manager explained that the managerial issue was not only found on the side of public institutions, but also on the side of the beneficiaries who could spend the pension extravagantly. According to him, a pension scheduled for one month could be consumed before the end of the month, hence leaving a household in an insecure position. When asked about solutions to this problem, the manager revealed that they had introduced a system of performance contracts (*imihigo*),[1] which required a beneficiary to clearly indicate the goals to be achieved from use of the pension.

Another issue related to management involved the death of the head of household, leaving minors behind. Such a scenario was expresed by respondent 'G' in the focus group discussions:

> When the head of a household dies, leaving behind minors, the payment to the orphans may take a long period due to bureaucratic issues and implication of modifying the names of the new bank account holder (Respondent 'G', Nyaruguru, April 28, 2015).

The DS beneficiaries were invited to offer some suggestions regarding these challenges, and many suggested that providing the funds on time would allow them to plan effectively. Preferably, beneficiaries recommended a monthly delivery as this would be more helpful. Others suggested a weekly delivery. On the issue of bureaucratic delays during pension transfer, the manager of the VUP at the district level suggested that all social protection transfers ought to be paid in the same manner as salary payments to civil servants.

4.3.2.Leakage and Misallocation of Support

In an interview with one of the senior manager of the the VUP DS, it was revealed that sometimes the pension went to the people who did not deserve it. Cases of cheating sometimes emerged when analysing the files of beneficiaries. The manager was asked to provide the possible causes of misallocation of support, and he stated that in spite of the *Ubudehe* classification exercise, which was carried out publicly in community meetings, misallocation of funds could be due to citizens providing false information in the hope that if placed in the poorest category, they would receive free social protection benefits.

The research also investigated if there were other factors that could hinder the effectiveness of the programme. The purpose was to find out their involvement and the ownership they have in the programme design. The majority of respondents (Figure 7) expressed that VUP DS was designed by the government to provide regular pension to the households that were classified by *Ubudehe* in the category of extreme poverty.

Even though the respondents expressed their satisfaction as to how the exercise of *Ubudehe* was conducted in public meetings involving the entire community, they criticised malpractices by some leaders who modified the results from the community decision on *Ubudehe* categorisation. Respondent 'H' testified:

> Sometimes households are categorised in a given category they belong to by the community meeting at the village level. Surprisingly, when a list is published, some people find that their categories were modified (Respondent 'H', Nyaruguru, April 28, 2015).

In line with this challenge, the researchers sought to investigate factors that could be behind the practice. The respondents revealed that some local leaders attempted to create data for inclusion in *Ubudehe* classification as a way of achieving high targets of performance contracts, a traditional approach known as *imihigo*. Though respondents revealed that data had been created by some local leaders in the *Ubudehe* classification, one of the managers of VUP said that in case of dissatisfaction over *Ubudehe* classification, the programme provided an avenue for appeal. He also revealed that citizens attempted to falsify information because they knew that *Ubudehe* classification was the landmark of social protection provision. For instance, apart from the VUP package, fees in tertiary education and health insurance are provided to people originating from households whose *Ubudehe* categories were the first or the second.

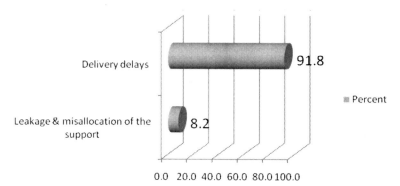

Figure 7. Challenges of VUP DS

SOURCE: Generated from fieldwork data (2015).

4.4. Discussion of Findings

4.4.1. Lessons Drawn and Best Practices of VUP DS

The direct support to vulnerable people is one of the components of VUP, a social protection programme that aims at alleviating poverty among the vulnerable people. From the findings, the strengths of the programme are three-fold, namely unconditional cash transfer to the households living in extreme poverty, the capacity-building component and its impact on the mindset change of the beneficiaries.

On the one hand, though the cash transferred is small, it goes hand in hand with the promotion of household economy of beneficiaries living in extreme poverty. This is evidenced by the beneficiaries who praise the programme as it helps them to graduate from the status of extreme poverty to a level that allows them to recover their human dignity. This aspect indicates the extent to which the VUP DS helps marginalised people to be socially and economically reintegrated.

The second dimension is capacity-building. In fact, the programme has been socialising the beneficiaries with the self-reliance philosophy, through setting-up income-generating activities. As highlighted in the findings, the local leaders and beneficiaries work within the framework of performance contracts (*imihigo*). The leaders must deliver public service in line with the goal to achieve and the beneficiaries of the VUP DS, in turn, use the pension according to the performance contracts they sign with local leaders. It is a reciprocal accountability in which each side is responsible for meeting the terms of the contract. This reciprocal accountability is one of the strengths of the VUP DS programme as it keeps both sides working towards the same orientation of achieving the goal of poverty alleviation. In other words, this culture of reciprocal accountability is identified as a best practice of the VUP DS as it avoids irresponsibility and administrative inertia.

The last dimension, though not the least, is the change of mindset. As has been discussed, the VUP in general, and specifically the direct support component, was based on the philosophy of bringing about ownership and responsibility. The strategy of cash transfer per se, which reduces the amount of money as the family size increases, contains a philosophy of encouraging family planning and the promotion of self-reliance. This is because Rwanda's demographic pressure ($406/km^2$ — see GoR 2014) may constitute a threat to sustainable development if measures are not taken. From this perspective, in today's Rwandan government philosophy, the culture of aid dependence does not hold. Thus, capacity-building and the self-reliance philosophy that are practised progressively along with the VUP DS are expected to bring about sustainable development. If the beneficiaries of the programme are empowered progressively, in the long run, to reach a phase whereby they become more resilient, sustainable development will be achieved. This can be realised through capacity-building which enables the beneficiaries of the VUP to continuously build internal resources to carry on their developmental plans with a minimum of outside assistance, and to lift them from marginality to a level that gives them dignity.

4.4.2. Challenges

From the findings, the challenges relate to managerial issues and problems related to *Ubudehe* functioning. As seen earlier, the VUP DS is associated with *Ubudehe* classification, which is the cornerstone of the social pension distribution system in Rwanda. Cases of cheating by the citizens arise from the fact that other forms of social protection such as education fees and health insurance schemes are distributed in accordance with this classification. Besides, there are also problems linked to bureaucracy which are explained by delays in pension transfers to the beneficiaries or misallocation due to administrative errors. Therefore, for the VUP DS programme to become more efficient and effective, remedial measures are necessary.

Moreover, the linkage between the *Ubudehe* categorisation and VUP is oriented in the perspective of performance contracts *(imihigo)* and the whole process could be discussed in a paradox of divergent views between local leaders and the local citizens. In the framework of *Ubudehe* categorisation, the findings indicated that local leaders sometimes falsify data as they are anxious about the achievement of performance contracts *(imihigo)*. The latter is underlain by the cultural philosophy of personal commitment, whereby a public pledge is simply considered as a 'public duty" and/or even a 'public debt' and it is instigated by the new public management philosophy that aims at improving effectiveness, efficiency and accountability in public administration. The *imihigo*, inspired by the new public management philosophy (Kaboolian 1998), has intrinsic values of keeping on track of the pledges made, but also has the negative impact of keeping citizens in a weak position as they are excluded from the political arena. In fact, this dichotomy of *Ubudehe* categorisation and VUP inspired by new public management could hinder any substantive full participation by which citizens can meaningfully affect policy and administration (Box *et al.* 2001; Terry 1998).

5. Conclusion and Recommendations

The study conducted on the VUP DS found some strengths and weaknesses associated with the programme. Some of the strengths identified were, for instance, the unconditional cash transfer to households living in extreme poverty, the capacity-building component and its impact on the change of mindset of the beneficiaries. Though the cash transferred is small, it promotes the household economy of beneficiaries living in extreme poverty. This is evidenced by the beneficiaries who praise the programme as it helps them to graduate from the status of extreme poverty to a level that enables them to recover their human dignity. This aspect indicates the extent to which VUP DS helps marginalised people to become socially and economically reintegrated. The VUP DS also has a positive impact on the mindset of the beneficiaries. In fact, the programme has promoted a self-reliance philosophy through setting up income-generating activities. As was highlighted in the findings, the local leaders and beneficiaries work within the framework of performance contracts *(imihigo)*, a reciprocal accountability in which each side must be responsible for meeting the terms of the contract. In this vein, leaders are expected to deliver public service in line with the targeted goals, while the beneficiaries of the VUP DS, in turn, use the pension in line with the performance contracts concluded with local leaders. The contract emphasises the purchase of new household commodities and establishing of income-generating activities. The final positive impact of the direct support component was the ownership and responsibility, and promotion of self-reliance philosophy resulting from the programme.

The study also identified challenges and problems. There was a problem of delay of cash transfers from the central government to the local governments. If such delays take up to three months, as testified by respondents, it is likely to have a negative impact on the performance of the programme. The study also identified challenges related to the *Ubudehe* categorisation, which involves cheating by the local population and falsification of data by civil servants in local institutions. Thus, the study offers the following recommendations:

a) There should be programme reform aimed at institutional performance, whereby the payments should align to the normal scheme of paying the salary of civil servants on a monthly basis. A regular delivery strategy would not only solve the problem of delays, but would also allow the beneficiaries to use the pension efficiently because their action plan will not be disturbed.

b) A system should be established to check the practice of cheating. This may involve regular crosschecking of the community meetings.

c) The existing system of appeals, involving all stakeholders, must be enhanced to avoid the malpractices revealed by respondents.

d) Administrative disciplinary measures should be reinforced for civil servant implicated in maladministration practices.

e) For public trust reasons, *imihigo*, which guides all public policies in public administration in Rwanda, should be planned, implemented and evaluated through involving local citizens, to avoid data exaggeration and to increase accountability from local civil servants.

Notes

[1.] *Imihigo* is as old as pre-colonial Rwanda. *Imihigo* is a cultural practice in the ancient tradition of Rwanda whereby an individual would set himself/herself targets to be achieved within a specific period of time, and involves following specific principles and having the determination to overcome possible challenges. In modern-day Rwanda, the *imihigo* practice was adopted as a means of planning to accelerate the progress towards economic development and poverty reduction. *Imihigo* has a strong focus on results, which makes it an invaluable tool in planning, accountability, monitoring, and evaluation processes (MINALOC 2012).

[2] *Ubudehe*: It must be remembered that the exercise of *Ubudehe* categorisation is done every year, to update data. Since 2015, the number of categories has been reduced from six to four, with the first and second categories comprising the very poor people. The data is still being treated at the district level.

[3] *Umudugudu:* This is the lowest administrative entity in the structure of public administration in Rwanda.

References

Abbott, P. and Rwirahira, J. 2012. Against the odds: Achieving the MDGs in Rwanda. Rwanda Public Observatory Report Number 3. Kigali, Rwanda: Institute of Policy Analysis and Research.

Bailey, K. D. 1994. *Methods of social research.* NY: Simon and Schuster.

Berglund, A. 2012. *A local perspective of the Vision 2020 Umurenge Programme and the land tenure regularization programme.* Kigali: Swedish International Development Agency (SIDA).

Box, R. C., Marshall, G. S., Reed, B. J. and Reed, C. M. 2001. New public management and substantive democracy. *Public Administration Review,* 61 no. 5: 608–619.

Corry, B. 2012. *Policy framework for social cohesion.* Kigali: Institute of Policy Analysis and Research (IPAR).

Cooke, J. G. 2011. *Rwanda: Assessing risks to stability.* Washington, D.C.: Center for Strategic and International Studies.

Davies, M. 2009. Climate change adaptation, disaster risk reduction and social protection: Complementary roles in agriculture and rural growth. *IDS Working Paper* 320. London, UK.

Devereux, M. G. 2001. Livelihood insecurity and social protection: A re-emerging issue in rural development. *Development Policy Review,* 19 no. 4: 507–519.

———. 2012. *3rd annual review of DFID support to the Vision 2020 Umurenge Programme (VUP), Rwanda.* London: Centre for Social Protection Institute of Development Studies.

———. 2013. *Informal and formal social protection systems in Sub-Saharan Africa.* Addis Ababa: Organisation for Social Science Research in Eastern Africa (OSSREA).

Giddens, A. 2009. *Sociology.* Cambridge: Polity Press.

Goverment of Rwanda (GoR). 2007. *Vision 2020 Umurenge: An integrated local development programme to accelerate poverty eradication, rural growth and*

social protection. Kigali: Ministry of Finance and Economic Planning
(MINECOFIN).

————. 2014. *Rwanda 2014 national human development report:
Decentralization and human development—accelerating socioeconomic
transformation and sustaining accountable governance.* Kigali:
MINECOFIN.

Hayman, R. 2009. Going in the 'right' direction? Promotion of democracy in
Rwanda since 1990. *Taiwan Journal of Democracy,* 5 no. 1: 51–75.

Honadle, B. W. 1980. A capacity-building framework: A search for concept and
purpose. *Public Administration Review,* 41 no. 5: 575–580.

Kaboolian, L. 1998. The new public management: Challenging the boundaries of
the management vs. administration debate. *Public Administration Review,* 58
no. 3: 189–193.

Kay, C. 2006. Survey article on rural poverty and development strategies in Latin
America. *Journal of Agrarian Change,* 6 no. 4: 455–508.

Kumar, R. 2005. *Research methodology: A step by step guide for beginners.*
London: Sage Publications Ltd.

Ministry of Local Government (MINALOC). 2008. *Vision 2020 Umurenge
Programme (VUP): Baseline survey - final report.* Kigali: MINALOC.

————. 2009. *Vision 2020 Umurenge Programme (VUP): Direct support
operational framework and procedure manual.* Kigali: MINALOC.

————. 2011. *Office of the Prime Minister. Homegrown initiatives.* Kigali:
MINALOC.

————. 2012. *Economic development poverty reduction strategy II.* Kigali:
MINALOC.

Ministry of Finance and Economic Planning (MINECOFIN). 2002. *Population
and human settlement census.* Kigali: MINECOFIN.

————. 2012. *Ubudehe classification.* Kigali: MINECOFIN.

National Institute of Statistics Rwanda (NISR) 2011. *EICV3 thematic report:
Social protection.* Kigali.

————. 2012. *The evolution of poverty in Rwanda from 2000 to 2011: Results
from the household surveys (EICV).* Kigali: MINECOFIN.

————. 2015. *Gross domestic product 2014.* Kigali: MINECOFIN.

Neuman, L. 2011. *Social research methods: Qualitative approach.* NY: Pearson
Education.

Nyaruguru, 2013. *District development plan.* Nyaruguru: MINALOC.

Siegel, P. B., Gatsinzi, J. and Kettlewell, A. 2011. Adaptive social protection in
Rwanda: 'Climate-proofing' the Vision 2020 Umurenge Programme. *Social
Protection for Social Justice,* 42 no. 6: 71–78.

Sukhwinder, A., Hansford, F., Attah, R. and Williams, R. 2012. *Assessment of the
Ubudehe credit scheme, Rwanda.* Kigali: Oxford Policy Management.

Terry, L. D. 1998. Administrative leadership, neo-managerialism and the public management movement. *Public Administration Review,* 58 no. 3: 194–200.

Tromp, D. L. A. and Kombo, D. K. 2011. *Proposal and thesis writing: An introduction.* Nairobi: Paulines Publications Africa.

United Nations (UN). 2005. *Handbook on poverty statistics: Concepts, methods and policy use.* NY: UN.

United Nations Development Programme (UNDP). 2007. *Turning vision 2020 into reality: From recovery to sustainable human development. National human development report Rwanda.* NY: UNDP.

———. 2014. *Sustaining human progress: Reducing vulnerabilities and building resilience.* NY: UNDP.

World Bank. 2015. *Rwanda economic update: Managing uncertainty for growth and poverty.* Washington, D.C.: World Bank.

Zorbas, E. 2004. Reconciliation in post-genocide Rwanda. *African Journal of Legal Studies,* 1 no. 1: 30–52.

CONCLUSION

Herman Musahara

In concluding this collection, a look at the approach and motivation of the book will provide an idea on how far the gaps have been filled. Firstly, the method used was that of a knowledge harvesting exercise. The chapters were premised on the existence of data and information in ongoing and completed research on inclusive growth and development which have not been professionally processed to be used for sharing and policy dialogue. It can be concluded that this approach has been successful but with some caveats. That there is knowledge on the issue was supported by a response from researchers of all levels and ranks. Editorial work had to select among those that are appearing in this volume. Research was from various countries and regions and no one can truly get a general idea of evidence of challenges and opportunities for inclusive growth and development in the region.

Nonetheless, some gaps can still be seen and need to be covered by research. Inclusive growth and development is a 'forest' and only a 'few trees' have been spotlighted. On looking at the chapters, it is clear that several other aspects of inclusive growth and development need new or further evidence. In this regard, it is correct to say that there has been considerable attention to the study on inclusive growth and development; and yet, a correct conclusion one can get from assembling the collection is that there are still needs for fresh collection of research in several aspects of the overall theme. We shall outline some before the end of this conclusion.

Thirdly, one can conclude that not all countries face the same challenges of promoting inclusive growth and development. While some face this challenge because they have experienced rapid growth but have still problems of inequality and poverty, others have in fact to face the challenges of meeting even the basic needs. They still have to grapple with policies that will stimulate decent levels of living. Countries in Eastern and Southern Africa do not see the challenges homogenously and thus will seize opportunities of policy reform from different contexts and political economies. That said, however, the evidence given is far from exhaustive. Save some chapters that have taken a regional focus, only a limited number of countries have been covered. And indeed, their selection was based more on the criteria of peer reviewers that included the need for a wider geographical coverage.

Another issue that looks simple is that there is still interchangeability of concepts of inclusive growth and inclusive development as if they are the same. Of course, an aspect of this arises from the lenses one uses in looking at them which are influenced by the disciplines. Through the chapters one can see the influences of economics, sociology and politics as instances of the type of evidence and interpretations given. One can conclude that the end of producing this collection is a beginning of nurturing multidisciplinary approaches to analysis that can influence future policy pathway in Africa. The collection should give a lesson that policy should not be shaped by one discipline. The notion of inclusion, for example, goes beyond economic definition of inequality reduction and redistribution to non-quantifiable definition of exclusion by gender, age, religion and disempowerment. Related to this problem, which can be seen from the collections, is that scopes of looking at inclusive growth and development differ and can depend on how the original research source had been designed.

Finally, there was a need to look at which methodologies could best be used in studying and looking for evidence on inclusive growth and development. Closely related to disciplines and the requirements of those who commissioned the original research, each chapter sheds light on challenges and opportunities of methodologies.

The introduction is based on the chapters that have been included in the book. It provides a generic conclusion that the book covers, one way or another, Eastern and Southern Africa. The book has provided evidence from different countries and different aspects of inclusive growth and development. But, it also notes the possibility of broader and diversified research into the theme.

Chapter 1 has also regional coverage as a scope looking at 9 of the countries in the region. It shows the evolution over time of the concept of inclusive growth and development. These have been borne in the womb of the development discourse from the 1950s to the age of Millennium Goals and now the Sustainable Development Goals. The latter has led to a broader notion of inclusion that embraces economic growth and poverty reduction, social inclusion, environment and climate change sensitivity and good governance. These concepts, it is concluded, have relevance in the new dialogue of emergence of Africa and what is required to make the emerging economies more inclusive. This chapter serves to clear the question of mixing up concepts such as pro-poor growth and inclusive growth and truncating exclusion to economic inequality alone or sociological discrimination as another instance. The conclusion that social science research needs to play a role in providing further evidence for the SDGs and Agenda 2063 points to the possible use of the book.

Chapter 2 takes a closer look at one country – Mauritius – and one sector of trade. It concludes that employment level in the country has a positive effect on economic growth. With trade openness, and using as an example the success of the EPZ sector, it shows that more jobs including female labour were created and a higher standard of living attained. It establishes, although this has to be carefully assessed under different contexts, a uni-directional causality between openness and economic and social welfare. The extent to which the conclusions on the Mauritius trade experiences are applicable to each country and the region provides another challenge for further regional evidence. But, in the same vein, the chapter pinpoints conclusions that are generally useful. These are, for example, the complex interactions between employment, inflation, real government expenditure on social aid and welfare and human development as drivers of economic growth. It rightly concludes that trade policies need to be taken together with development strategies. The conclusion on the need for diversification and reducing reliance on limited economic sectors is clearly general to all countries. The challenges related to human resources, infrastructure and further policy reform coming from a study on a relatively developed economy like Mauritius are evidently useful to other places in the region, as well.

Chapter 3 draws conclusions from a specific country and specific aspects of the theme. The country is Ethiopia and the issues are how inclusive growth and development or lack of it is influenced by the rural-urban divide. The chapter provides another case for having concepts clarified and common understanding established. The chapter used Ethiopia to address the challenge of rapid economic growth with evident presence of poverty and inequalities in the country. The study then concludes that divide in the sectors poses serious policy challenges to inclusive growth and development but admitting that the borders between the divides are sometimes blurred in concept and practice and in some cases confusingly contradicting, especially pro-poor growth and inclusive growth, which was mentioned as an issue addressed in the book.

The chapter narrows down the challenges to conclude that the most notable pillars that underpin inclusive development along the rural-urban continuum in Ethiopia include wider and equal access to basic infrastructure, access to social services such as education and health beyond the primary levels, greater access to financial services and employment opportunities, reduced poverty, inequality and exclusion. What the author points out as the notable usefulness of the analysis is that understanding the nature and challenges of rural-urban divide, poverty, and inequality in the country could help to scientifically investigate the reasons why these development anomalies remain long-lasting while the country has registered double-digit growth rates.

The chapter also concludes that in a country where pro-poor policies have been implemented for more than a decade, the prevalence of widespread rural poverty calls for policy makers' evaluation of the inclusive development efforts especially why the poorest of the poor are not benefiting from the double-digit growth. Indeed, these conclusions are at the heart of the collection. The rest of the conclusion of the chapters suggests some answers to a likely question of 'so what next?'. The most important lesson that can be taken up by policy makers from the chapter is improving access to quality education and health services with broad participation of all members of society. There is also using improvement in physical infrastructure, raising productivity of labour and land, capital transfer and enhancing production and consumption linkages.

Also Chapter 4 is on Ethiopia but from a rigorous and economic analysis using household survey data for 2495 households. It focuses on poverty and vulnerability in the rural areas only. As in the last chapter, it concludes that both depth and severity of poverty has been reduced in Ethiopia. So also were levels of vulnerability. But the chapter concludes that these reductions varied from one region to another and from one period to another. For vulnerability, the changes were sluggish and characterised by shocks. The chapter concludes further that there has to be an intraregional look at poverty reduction with both short-run and long-run perspectives. A take home lesson from the case is that economic growth has reduced poverty differently on a regional basis. The chapter is a case of using economic analysis in analysing aspects of inclusive growth, particularly poverty reduction and vulnerability, and should be read along with other dimensions of analyses.

Chapter 5 is on South Africa, a relatively well off economy but with ample lessons on inclusive development. It concludes that there is a disjuncture between economic growth, poverty reduction and social inclusion in South Africa. It states that these have historical and structural accounts and have sub components. Poverty has been reduced since 1994 but not to the expected levels. Grants used as social protection have not reduced inequality, especially among black South Africans. Growth, poverty and inequality have been entwined in a complex way with unemployment and the education system, making it imperative to have a more integrated and multi-pronged approach to addressing the challenges. Inequalities based on race and gender are noted as being major challenges in the economy. The chapter provides an answer for long-run economic growth that addresses the needs of the poorer social groups. Having come from a legacy of apartheid, South Africa presents a good case of a challenge of large economies with notable social and economic development but with multidimensional forms of social exclusion, including political systems that have to be addressed.

Chapter 6 is a case of Uganda on Universal Health Coverage, using Thailand as a model economy. It reaches a conclusion that Thailand has reached universal coverage and Uganda has not. It concludes that both countries are using multiple models such as Bismarck, Beveridge, NHI and OOP in different combinations in order to deliver social health-care protection to their citizens. The public and private sectors are used in varying proportions in the provision of health-care services. The author states that both countries are excluding some portions of their populations, especially the poor, women, children or foreigners in the case of Thailand and this is more pronounced in Uganda. Political will, as in the case of Thailand, is identified as an important driver of SHP, which in turn influences budgetary commitments. Another important factor is creating viable institutions, such as Ministries of Public Health and National Health organs that the chapter shows have made Thailand a model of SHP. On the one hand, the chapter shows the existence of best practices but also notes some challenges that still need to be addressed even in the successful models. These challenges include equity, quality and efficacy. That the multiple weaknesses analysed in relation to Uganda can be fixed by first securing political will and creating institutions as in Thailand is relevant to many other economies in the region that have not put in place universal health coverage schemes. As for methodology, the chapter has shown that desk-based facts and documentations can also be used in knowledge harvesting. By using Thailand as a model, the chapter shows comparative analytical methods can be used as a tool in looking for policy solutions.

Chapter 7 uses Rwanda to study informality in the economy. The chapter is in the realm of economic analysis. That a lot of jobs are created in the informal sector to address poverty makes it relevant to inclusive growth inquiries. A particular focus of this study is the relationship between informality, productivity and employment. The conclusions are that there is a negative relationship between informality and productivity. Furthermore, results indicate that informal firms employ the majority of the labour force characterised by low education levels, low skills, lower wages, and women. A more inclusive growth, it can be construed from the chapter, needs to address problems of informality. These are mentioned in the conclusion of the chapter as access to finance. Education for all is another inclusive measure that would address informality. Informality, as pointed out, is the last resort for the poor and addressing its problems is addressing challenges the poor face.

Chapter 8 is also on Rwanda but more directly on the role of social protection. Unlike several studies we encounter looking at social protection at macroeconomic and national level the chapter uses data from the smallest administrative unit in poor community in Southern Rwanda. With both quantitative and qualitative information, a conclusion is definitely that direct cash transfers are good for poverty reduction but face a lot of challenges that have to be addressed. Inclusive and sustainable development is important but the process towards its attainment has a cost and problems to solve.

A final remark in the conclusion is on the overall value of the collection. Besides providing a publication record to authors and editors, the collection serves to provide evidence for policy interventions in the respective countries and in the region. After the publication of a peer-reviewed book, all sorts of knowledge platforms can be created to get ideas for policy action based on the evidence. The book has also shown where gaps need to be filled by way of further inquiry. In the age of SDGs and Agenda 2063, the book should serve as a starting point for further energising the role of social science research in the post-2015 period.